Major Trade-Offs

Corey Moss-Pech

MAJOR TRADE-OFFS

The Surprising Truths
about College Majors and
Entry-Level Jobs

The University of Chicago Press · Chicago and London

The University of Chicago Press, Chicago 60637
The University of Chicago Press, Ltd., London
Published 2025
Printed in the United States of America

34 33 32 31 30 29 28 27 26 25   1 2 3 4 5

ISBN-13: 978-0-226-84020-8 (cloth)
ISBN-13: 978-0-226-84022-2 (paper)
ISBN-13: 978-0-226-84021-5 (e-book)
DOI: https://doi.org/10.7208/chicago/9780226840215.001.0001

Library of Congress Cataloging-in-Publication Data

Names: Moss-Pech, Corey, author.
Title: Major trade-offs : the surprising truths about college majors
    and entry-level jobs / Corey Moss-Pech.
Description: Chicago : The University of Chicago Press, 2025. |
    Includes bibliographical references and index.
Identifiers: LCCN 2024044558 | ISBN 9780226840208 (cloth) |
    ISBN 9780226840222 (paperback) | ISBN 9780226840215 (ebook)
Subjects: LCSH: College graduates—Employment—United States. |
    Internship programs—United States. | Wages—College
    graduates. | Education, Humanistic—United States.
Classification: LCC HD6278.U5 M67 2025 |
    DDC 331.11/4—dc23/eng/20241119
LC record available at https://lccn.loc.gov/2024044558

♾ This paper meets the requirements of ANSI/NISO
Z39.48-1992 (Permanence of Paper).

To Sara, Eleanor, Daniel, and Lucy

CONTENTS

FIGURES AND TABLES

Figures

Tables

1: INTRODUCTION

Fields of Study and the College-to-Work Transition

Mort, an undergraduate English major at Capital State University (CSU),[1] seemed anxious when he explained why he chose to major in English. "I tried to not major in English," he said. "I didn't want to major in English because people always say, 'What are you going to do with an English degree?' and they make jokes about English major[s] being unemployed. . . . But I liked my English classes so much that I finally submitted."

Mort "submitted." In that original interview in April 2016, he told me he was worried about the employability of an English degree. He said, "I think even as a freshman there was this deep fear that I would get a degree and then have nothing to do after college." Mort's perspective is not unique and, in fact, reflects a student population and a national press who express concern about the practical utility of English and other liberal arts degrees.

I interviewed Mort again in April 2017, almost a year after he graduated from CSU, a large Midwestern public research university. By then, Mort was in graduate school, training to become a high school English teacher, and had quite a different perspective about the value of his English degree. Mort told me that, as a student teacher, he frequently used the skills he learned in college to the direct benefit of his students. Specifically, Mort brought writing skills he developed through his English classes into his student teaching assignment. "My students get fantastic and explicit and well-structured writing instruction and lots of time to revise and collaborate and prove that they're implementing the feedback that they received," he said. The techniques he brought to the classroom were based on writing skills he developed across three classes with one of his undergraduate English professors and he was now directly translating skills from his major into his chosen profession. Mort also reported enjoying his work and that, after graduate school, he hoped to find employment as an English teacher. However, for English majors, it is difficult to find a "good job" (by traditional employment indicators) immediately after college. Mort had to attend graduate school and student-teach for a year before seeking stable employment in his field.

In contrast, students majoring in more "practical" disciplines rarely reported the same kind of uncertainty Mort felt about choosing a major. Courtney, for example, a business major at CSU whom I interviewed in January 2016, told me that majoring in business had been on her mind "forever," and was especially relevant when she "thought about considering a career." Because CSU students cannot declare a general business major, Courtney chose to study logistics, hoping it would lead to a stable corporate career; its practicality was obvious to her.

After graduation, Courtney immediately started working as a retail inventory analyst at a greeting card company called National Paper where she had previously interned. She knew National Paper hired many entry-level workers from their internship pool, so she reported little stress about entering the labor market after college and, indeed, she had a job with a 401(k) paying $50,000 lined up before graduation.

From these facts alone, one might assume National Paper hires former interns and business majors like Courtney so the company will benefit from recent graduates' knowledge and skills, but this is not the case. When we spoke again in 2017, Courtney told me, "I have on a really good day two hours' worth of work to do." Of the work itself, Courtney said, "I don't enjoy it at all." She told me, "The majority of my job, like 90 percent of my job [is] I get emails and phone calls from salespeople in the field, and they tell me they have issues." Courtney's overall impression of her job was negative. "There's nothing [to do] . . . ," she said. "I'm so bored." In fact, she reported that on a typical day she spent a lot of her time walking around a large outdoor mall with her coworker. One day they went out for lunch "for two and a half hours . . . we came back, and we still didn't have a single email, our bosses didn't even notice we were gone." So, upon closer inspection, we learn that Courtney got a secure job right out of college that paid a relatively high salary for a recent graduate, but her education was underutilized, and the tasks required little of her skill set and time.

Mort and Courtney graduated from the same university in the same year, but their experiences in college and their labor market trajectories diverged significantly. Mort spent an extra year in graduate school in an attempt to secure the type of work he wanted. Courtney, meanwhile, transitioned quickly into stable employment, but spent her first job unhappily completing mundane clerical work that did not require any of the skills she learned in college.

Mort and Courtney are two of the ninety-one college seniors across the four majors of business, engineering, communications, and English whom I interviewed for this book. All students completed internships, representing undergraduates who are at least somewhat career-oriented. I interviewed almost all these students again one year later in order to illuminate college graduates' experiences entering the labor market from various fields of study. I wanted to know: how do students from the same college but with different types of majors enter the labor market? Who actually uses skills from academic coursework in entry-level jobs? And what is the relationship between skill usage and getting a stable job with a good salary? In other words, I was interested in *the process*—how students enter the labor market—and their *outcomes*—whether they got jobs, their salary levels, and whether the jobs required the graduates to use the skills they learned at school.

Internships proved to be an important component in answering these questions. They played a large role in connecting recent graduates to the labor market, as Courtney's experience shows. What came as a surprise, and what this book will fully unveil, is the way the content of students' college majors applied to their entry-level work. This is a blind spot for the public and media, so their concerns about practicality and the "value" of a college degree are not wholly informed. The issue is much more complex than it appears from popular debate and understanding it can lead to better informed opinions about what college degrees are worth and how students use them.

The specific stories Courtney and Mort told me are broadly representative of the experiences of the men and women I interviewed from their respective majors.[2] The kinds of employment opportunities available to graduates of CSU differed based on their fields of study. In some ways (e.g., salary), these divergent outcomes are not surprising and match media narratives about college majors. However, in other ways (e.g., on-the-job use of degree skills), Mort and Courtney's experiences depart considerably from popular commentary on how fields of study differentially prepare students for the workforce and why so-called practical majors provide graduates with advantages in the labor market. As I show in this book and in contrast to common public narratives, these graduates' divergent trajectories by major do not align with which students have more "in-demand skills" to employers. In fact, liberal arts majors in my study, like Mort, were *more likely* to use their degree skills in entry-level work than graduates of practical disciplines, like Courtney.

Popular Narratives about College Majors

The popular press is saturated with articles questioning the value of higher education and whether college degrees pay off for graduates. A 2015 article in the *Atlantic* proclaimed, "The era of the overeducated barista is here to stay."[3] In fact, the imagery of the recent college graduate working as a barista is backed by some evidence. For example, an article from *Inside Higher Ed* from February 2020 notes that the unemployment rate for young college graduates is higher than for the general population and that over 40 percent of recent college graduates are underemployed.[4] Another report released in February 2024 put the underemployment rate for college graduates closer to 50 percent and found that over 70 percent of graduates who start out underemployed remain underemployed ten years after completing college.[5] This means there are millions of Americans who spent the time, energy, and resources necessary to earn a college degree who are working in jobs for which that degree is not required.[6] By extension, a bachelor's degree no longer guarantees a middle-class job or lifestyle. Nonetheless, people with college degrees who are employed still, on average, earn higher salaries than people without them and many college graduates do obtain stable, middle-class jobs.[7]

In their attempts to safeguard against college graduates' underemployment, the popular press, policymakers, and higher education administrators emphasize the importance of "practical majors" as an avenue to professional success for students. Commentators and researchers often assume practical or vocational degrees provide students with the specific knowledge or skills needed for the occupations matched to those degrees in a way that liberal arts degrees do not.[8] Encouraging students to focus on practical, skill-building disciplines is framed as higher education adapting to students' job-related interests and the changing economy. In this view, a shift to the so-called practical arts (fields matched to specific occupations such as engineering or nursing)[9] allows "higher education to contribute more effectively than it once did to the economic life of the country."[10] Discussing practical arts in terms of concrete skills makes it easy for the public to imagine translating higher education degrees into occupational success. Even the title—"practical arts"—connotes utilitarian outcomes. A recent article in the *Seattle Post-Intelligencer* discusses the pros and cons of "majoring in something you love versus something practical," framing this as a dichotomous choice[11] and portraying English majors as readers of Shakespeare who follow their passions and remain largely unconcerned with eventual employment. Meanwhile, engineering graduates are thought to be designing algorithms or making robots to meet the needs of twenty-first-century employers in cutting-edge industries.

Not surprisingly, this framing of "practical" majors versus "passion" majors has entered the public consciousness. Job market analytics company Burning Glass Technologies released a widely publicized report in 2018 on the relationship between college majors and labor market outcomes. They reported on public perceptions, stating, "The public perceives STEM fields as practical, even necessary, in a fast-changing world. . . . Study engineering, the thinking goes, and you will get a good job."[12] On the other hand, they write, for the public "the liberal arts have become a favorite target of criticism . . . a degree in philosophy prepares you to ponder the deeper meaning of working as a barista."[13] Although the report also dispels some myths about college majors, it presents a public view that is critical of the liberal arts and exalts the utility of more applied majors.

To be sure, graduates' employment outcomes often do diverge by major. The 2018 Burning Glass Technologies report and a more recent update in 2024 found large differences in how college graduates fared in the labor market based on their fields of study. Engineering majors secure the lowest rate of underemployment.[14] Findings like this tend to be widely reported in the media. A 2016 article in the *Atlantic* with the subheading "Is there really a Millennial underemployment crisis? Yes, but only among liberal arts majors"[15] reports, "A large chasm has opened between the fates of young liberal arts majors and their peers in STEM (science, technology, engineering, and math) fields."[16] The article goes on to say, "The former are struggling to find work that pays . . . the latter are mostly finding lucrative work."[17] A *Washington Post* article published in 2022 on the "most-regretted college majors," reports younger millennials are leaving the liberal arts ostensibly because they are "increasingly fixated on majors with better job prospects."[18] The article's headline also suggests humanities and social sciences degrees are *simultaneously* the "most-regretted" and the "lowest-paying."[19] Even the *New Yorker* published a widely read article in February 2023 titled "The End of the English Major."[20] In sum, according to the popular press, practical arts degrees pay off more than liberal arts degrees and students are (wisely) flocking to practical fields of study.

Policymakers and media narratives alike assume that the shift of students into practical disciplines and the employment advantages received by graduates of these majors arise because these fields of study provide in-demand skills to students. But this way of thinking is more than fifteen years old; in 2008 the US launched its "decade of STEM," which garnered much media attention and provided significant funding to STEM education based on this assumption.[21] At the national level, the Obama administration aimed to create more STEM education with the rationale that STEM gives students skills that create jobs and enhances America's national competitiveness.[22] At the state level, in 2012, then-Governor Rick Scott of Florida assembled a task force that proposed higher tuition for students studying history and other humanities disciplines at state universities,[23] reasoning that tuition rates should be lower for those in "specific, high-skill, high demand degree programs."[24] Media narratives continue to bolster these kinds of arguments. For example, two recent articles from national outlets state, "Since new technical skills are always in high demand, young college graduates who have them earn a short-run salary premium,"[25] and that students are leaving the humanities for "skills-focused STEM majors."[26] In sum, political and popular arguments in favor of increased investment in the practical arts assume these fields pay off specifically because they impart in-demand skills.

There are, however, those in the popular press who argue for the employability of liberal arts graduates. For example, articles from the *Atlantic* spanning from 2013 to 2018 assert "Students Are Abandoning Humanities Majors, Turning to Degrees They Think Yield Far Better Job Prospects. But They're Wrong,"[27] "First-Generation Students Are Finding Personal and Professional Fulfillment in the Humanities and Social Sciences,"[28] and "Graduating with a Liberal Arts Degree Won't Ruin Your Job Hopes."[29] These articles focus on the mixed evidence of the long-term employment deficits facing liberal arts majors,[30] presenting data that many liberal arts graduates attend graduate school or move into management positions.[31] An essay from the *New York Times* connecting the liberal arts to these professional moves is worth quoting at length: "Why do the earnings of liberal arts majors catch up? It's not because poetry suddenly pays the bills. Midcareer salaries are highest in management and business occupations, as well as professions requiring advanced degrees such as law. Liberal arts majors are more likely than STEM graduates to enter those fields."[32] This passage makes several claims of note. First, studying poetry will not provide skills that will pay off. Second, midcareer salaries in management and business are high and likely to be occupations where liberal arts graduates are well represented. Third, liberal arts graduates are more likely to get advanced degrees, like a law degree, which offer long-term earnings potential. Why do liberal arts graduates end up in management positions or with advanced degrees? The same *Times* article suggests this is because liberal arts disciplines give students "soft skills," like "problem-solving, critical thinking, and adaptability."[33] Other definitions of soft skills include individuals' innate abilities to connect with others, which liberal arts graduates may also be presumed to have.[34] In general, articles on liberal arts graduates' employability emphasize these "soft skills" and how they enable liberal arts graduates to somewhat close the earnings gap with practical arts graduates over time.[35]

While policymakers and the popular press get some things right about how degree type differences relate to employment, they perpetuate certain myths I dispel in this book. I begin here by assessing the accuracy of three popular claims from common public narratives that I investigated in my study.

Separating Myth from Reality in the Popular Narratives

Popular claim #1: Degrees in practical disciplines lead to better initial labor market success.

This claim reflects reality. The popular press and extant research get it right when they say that—in the short term—practical arts degrees pay off at higher rates than liberal arts degrees. Unemployment rates are lower for graduates with practical arts degrees, who tend to attain jobs more quickly after graduation, enjoy higher salaries (initially and in the long term), and more often find work that matches their academic disciplines than liberal arts graduates.[36] However, the reason for this success is largely misunderstood.

In this book, I show *how* practical arts graduates enter the labor market more successfully than liberal arts majors. More specifically, I demonstrate that practical arts graduates often have access to internships that lead directly to postgraduation employment, while liberal arts majors are rarely afforded such opportunities. Practical arts majors often have jobs lined up right after college that pay a middle-class wage. Their liberal arts peers, on the other hand, often spend three to six months after graduation looking for work and often must settle for either low-paid temporary jobs or jobs that do not match their aspirations.

Popular claim #2: Practical arts degrees provide in-demand skills needed for entry-level work.

This is a myth. Popular media narratives describe practical arts degrees as providing skills that employers seek. But this was not the case for Courtney, nor for the large majority of practical arts graduates in my study whose entry-level jobs drew little, if at all, on skills or knowledge attained through their college coursework. Most engineering graduates, for example, did not get jobs actually doing engineering work and most business majors specializing in logistics did not get jobs actually doing business logistics. Instead, these graduates were far more likely to find work involving mundane clerical tasks or sales. These jobs may pay well and come with benefits, but there is a real disconnect between the skills learned in school and the work most practical arts graduates are doing after college—and many graduates I spoke with found this disconnect distressing.

Popular claim #3: Liberal arts fields only provide "soft" skills.

This, too, is largely a myth. In fact, the liberal arts graduates I interviewed were much *more* likely to actually use skills they learned at school in their work than were practical arts graduates. Liberal arts majors' "soft skills" were relevant, but also graduates' major-specific skills were very much in demand among employers. My book provides examples and illustrations of such skills. For example, some English majors described learning to write in different voices and then deploying their skills as writers or editors for different kinds of businesses. Here I uncovered a paradox whereby employers pay practical arts majors *more* for *less* demanding work for which specialized schooling was not necessary. By contrast, the problem liberal arts graduates face is that, while employers *require* college-learned skills, they do not *pay* much for those essential skills.

The Real Trade-Off between Majors

In seeking to understand how choice of major affects the college-to-work transition, I uncovered a trade-off college students face when choosing a major, but it is not the commonly framed trade-off of acquiring job-relevant skills or pursuing a passion. Instead, many of today's students may—at least initially—have to decide between *highly paid clerical work* and *low-paid skilled work*. This trade-off is presented in two ways. First, there are differences, by discipline, in *how* graduates from each type of major enter the labor market. The different processes show that the trade-off begins to unfold while students are still in school. Second, there are differences, by discipline, in two key initial employment *outcomes* of interest: the likelihood of quickly and seamlessly obtaining a good entry-level middle-class job soon after college ends[37] and the extent of meaningful, on-the-job use of skills acquired through coursework.

The ways college graduates navigate the job market and enter the workforce vary considerably for the practical arts (business and engineering) versus liberal arts (English and communications) majors in my study. More specifically, as I referenced above and describe at length in the remainder of this book, there are two kinds of internships typically available to college students. The first, which I term *career conveyor-belt internships*, are specifically designed to move students into career-starter jobs after graduation. Students are recruited on campus by firms that provide direct pathways into employment. The second kind of internship I call *dead-end internships*. Instead of being able to leverage existing connections between the university and employers, students with dead-end internships typically use personal connections to identify internship opportunities—often without pay and even more rarely with the possibility of moving into a permanent position. Students who take dead-end internships have a more difficult time entering the labor market. These two kinds of internships map fairly well onto the majors in this study. Most engineering and business students accessed career conveyor-belt internships and most English and communications majors ended up with dead-end internships. These internship differences did not cause labor market disparities between majors but were central to the trade-off in outcomes because they were an important part of the process moving students into jobs or underemployment.[38]

The real trade-off between types of major manifests in the postgraduation outcomes. The quality of graduates' entry-level jobs along two dimensions (traditional employment indicators and skill use at work), comprise the heart of the trade-off between majors. Practical arts graduates often move more seamlessly into entry-level jobs but rarely use any technical course content at work. Their jobs often come with high pay, full benefits, and opportunities for advancement. Liberal arts majors, in contrast, often struggle to find jobs, accept work with relatively low pay, and may not find opportunities for advancement. Yet these graduates often use the skills they learned in college. Ultimately, there is no positive relationship between graduates' employment conditions and skill use at work.

By exposing the "real trade-off" between major types, I undercut some misconceptions and assumptions that perpetuate the popular myths. This clarification corrects a real problem: liberal arts skills are applicable—and essential—in the labor market, but commentators, researchers, students, policymakers, higher education administrators, and employers often do not recognize this fact.[39]

In sum, this book enhances and advances popular understanding of the college-to-work transition. I show that graduates with practical arts diplomas do not benefit primarily from skill acquisition, but these types of degrees are expeditious tools for moving on to stable work. I also show how, even in the short run, liberal arts graduates often enjoy much better employment outcomes than are reported because many actually use their academic skills at work. In other words: there are ways other than wages and benefits to measure job quality. If we include measures of fulfillment—like use of skills mastered in college—then many liberal arts majors fare quite well. My study is also a step forward in scholarly research; I assess and advance prevailing academic explanations for differential early employment outcomes and I add to sociological understandings of internships and the degradation of white-collar work in the contemporary economy. In all, I aim to contribute to a new way of thinking about the college-to-work transition with regard to practical and liberal arts degrees and labor market entry.

How representative are the phenomena I uncover in this book? From the practical arts, I focus on business and engineering majors. Business is the most common undergraduate major; one in five US college graduates earns a business degree.[40] Engineering is the most *exalted* major, considered high status by those who study it and those who do not.[41] Graduates of these two fields comprise a large white-collar workforce seeking entry-level corporate jobs. By examining these two majors, I can speak to the experiences of many similar practical arts graduates who attain entry-level office jobs. From the liberal arts, I examine English and communications majors. The media focus primarily on English as representative of the decline of the liberal arts and humanities.[42] Communications is a liberal arts discipline that hews closely to professional fields. As such, they make good cases and students' experiences in these majors likely apply to many other graduates of similar liberal arts disciplines.[43]

The Stakes of Dispelling Myths about College Majors

The stakes are high for understanding the real trade-off between fields of study. Students, administrators, and policymakers continue to question the value of the liberal arts and therefore the employability or contributions of those who study them. Surveys of undergraduates show that students consider engineering and business fields more prestigious than disciplines in the humanities or social sciences[44] and students are enrolling in the liberal arts in ever smaller numbers. Since the 1970s, despite the huge growth in college attendance, there has been an *absolute decline* in liberal arts majors.[45] This means the entire expansion of American higher education over the past fifty years has been growth in practical arts majors. Just since the year 2000, the number of bachelor's degrees conferred in engineering has almost doubled; business degrees are up 80 percent; and enrollment in health fields nearly tripled to comprise approximately 10 percent of all undergraduate degrees.[46] The rise of practical arts disciplines is mirrored by a decline in the liberal arts. Degrees granted in the humanities have been in decline since 1967, with the current downward trend continuing, especially in English and foreign languages.[47] The social sciences have held steady since the 1990s, but that is mostly due to an increase in economics majors. Finally, STEM disciplines account for the greatest growth over the last thirty years, leaving many non-STEM fields struggling for enrollment.[48] These trends were further accelerated by the Great Recession of 2007–2009, with many humanities fields shrinking enrollment by more than 10 percent just since then.[49] Even at elite institutions, once considered the primary vestige of the liberal arts, erosion occurs. For example, an article in the *Daily Princetonian* based on the university's enrollment data showed that the number of undergraduates majoring in social sciences dropped 3 percentage points over the first decade of the 2000s, and in the two years from 2018 to 2020 humanities majors fell from 25 percent to 14 percent of students.[50]

Even with declining numbers of students majoring in the liberal arts, general education requirements could conceivably sustain these fields' enrollments. Typically, undergraduate curricula, even those that emphasize practical arts, require students to take a minimum number of courses in the arts and sciences.[51] One could argue that the holistic approach to education, requiring a core of liberal arts courses for students of all disciplines, keeps the liberal arts alive and well. But this approach has not sustained the liberal arts, whose budgets are shrinking precipitously.

Small and large universities alike need to make tough fiscal choices and the biggest budget cuts hit liberal arts programs; a trend that, although accelerated by COVID, is not new.[52] Indeed, a slew of higher education reporting during the COVID-19 pandemic shows that drastic budget cuts in higher education disproportionately affect liberal arts disciplines.

One reason is because commentators and higher education administrators believe social science and humanities programs are less likely to be funded by corporations, foundations, and the federal government.[53] Universities also often make these decisions partly because they *wrongly* assume liberal arts programs are less profitable for the university;[54] however, contrary to common ideas about which disciplines provide higher profits for schools, liberal arts departments can, in fact, pay off more because they do not require expensive labs or equipment and can teach large numbers of students in basic classrooms.[55]

The story at our representative institution, CSU, follows these national trends. Publicly-available reports show that total enrollment in the arts and sciences is holding steady at around 40 percent and has remained relatively stable over the last twenty years.[56] However, the university stopped breaking down these public reports into subsections (e.g., arts, humanities, biological sciences) after 2010. University undergraduate enrollment grew by roughly 4,000 students between 2005 and 2010, yet humanities enrollment in spring 2010 was *three students fewer* than in 2005, suggesting the distribution of students within arts and sciences likely tracks with national data. Since budgets are linked to enrollments, this reshuffling of students into practical disciplines has led to cuts in budgets and personnel for many liberal arts departments. At CSU, general education requirements also pit liberal arts departments against one another. For example, engineering majors must take an ethics course as part of their degree requirements, and the philosophy department, sociology department, and others, competitively vie for these students (and therefore their tuition dollars).

Dispelling myths about college majors will help break down the sharp dichotomy between supposed "passion" and "practical" fields of study. One of my aims is to add nuance to our understanding of how exactly these fields (and their students) are similar and how they diverge. Despite public discourse pitting types of majors against each other, at a place like CSU there are many similarities across fields of study. Liberal arts disciplines and practical arts disciplines both teach a range of liberal arts and occupation-specific skills (a topic I cover in chapter 2). In contrast to popular myth, students majoring in English or philosophy at CSU are not spending their entire college careers reading Chaucer or Plato. Instead, they are learning how to write blog posts or solve logic problems. Moreover, liberal arts students are learning skills that employers claim to seek and value, like critical thinking, writing a persuasive argument, or working on a team. Job ads often ask for skills such as critical thinking and good verbal/written communications, yet they rarely list liberal arts majors as desirable for those positions.[57] And yet, as sociologists Richard Arum and Josipa Roksa show in their book *Academically Adrift*, students in social science, humanities, natural science, and mathematics, on average, score much higher on assessments of these liberal arts competencies than those studying business, engineering, or computer science.[58]

Further, at schools like CSU, race and class are also salient. CSU is a predominately White institution and both women and students from lower social classes are underrepresented in competitive-admit majors like business and engineering that hoard their career services with exclusive access to internships and jobs.[59] This creates an environment where the highly prized, competitive-admit majors are disproportionately comprised of middle-class White men. Ultimately, media narratives mistakenly purport that liberal arts students do not learn anything useful to contribute to the economy early in their careers and are therefore "passion" majors rather than "useful" majors, and many of these disciplines are dominated by women or teach culturally feminized skills, which has implications for gender inequality in the labor market.[60]

In the US, approximately two-thirds of English and communications majors are women. Men are overrepresented in business and engineering,[61] the two most prevalent majors among men in college.[62] The skills associated with men tend to have a higher value in economy and society (i.e., math and science skills),[63] and the fields/skills associated with women are devalued in the labor market (i.e., writing and communication skills).[64] The devaluation of the liberal arts and the skills associated with them, therefore, also devalues the kinds of students who are more likely to major in them (i.e., women and men from disadvantaged backgrounds).[65] Though of course the reverse logic is also possible—women and racial minorities are devalued in society and therefore things associated with women and people of color are devalued including the liberal arts and skills associated with them. In either case, the intersection of inequality between the liberal arts and skills associated with women doubly disadvantage women.

In sum, dispelling certain myths about how degree fields relate to the labor market could conceivably change public perception about college majors and help reverse the decades-long decline of the liberal arts, employers' devaluation of the skills taught in liberal arts majors, and the low labor market value of the people who study liberal arts disciplines. It could also help us see the advantages of the practical arts with more clarity. People who choose to study a practical arts discipline thinking they will learn skills that are immediately in demand risk disillusionment upon entry into the labor market. They may even change professions before ever having the opportunity to use the technical skills they learned in school. Even those who do stick with their field may opt to move into managerial roles or auxiliary functions without ever drawing on the technical training they received in college.

This is not to say we should view practical arts degrees negatively. Rather, we should understand that, early in graduates' careers, these majors' primary offer is the opportunity for stable, well-paid employment, not opportunities to immediately use technical skills. Meanwhile, liberal arts majors may be advised to contend with longer initial job searches and lower salaries—relative to practical arts graduates—which often result in finding more meaningful, skills-based work early in their careers.

Skills and Culture in the College-to-Work Transition

My study challenges some of the assumptions and conclusions of prevailing academic explanations for labor market disparities by college major. The most common explanation for why practical arts graduates enjoy employment advantages over liberal arts graduates reflects something called *human capital theory*.

Human capital theory, pioneered by economist Gary Becker, suggests that some fields better prepare students for the workforce than others and that these better-prepared graduates enter the labor market more easily and with higher pay.[66] The theory assumes that students learn skills in school and deploy them in the workforce; these learned skills are graduates' human capital.[67] For example, as the economy requires more complex engineering, the number of engineering majors will increase and, due to the demand for the learned skills they deploy, their economic rewards also increase.[68]

Although human capital theory applies to many social science questions and has nuanced assumptions and methodological approaches, when it comes to differences between disciplines and graduates' economic success after college, scholars have assessed if human capital theory explains students' college-to-work transitions primarily through occupation-to-degree matching.[69] For example, if a computer science major gets a job in a technology firm or a job with a technology-related job title, then that graduate is considered to have a job matched to the degree obtained. If, on the other hand, an English major attained that technology position, this is considered evidence of a different theory of the college-to-work transition, one that relies on innate skills or general competency rather than specific training.[70] Occupations more frequently match with degrees among practical arts graduates than liberal arts graduates.[71]

Importantly, using occupation-to-degree matching as a proxy for human capital theory relies on an untested assumption about skill usage. If—as was common in my study—a business graduate with a business job title is doing clerical work all day, that person is still coded as having an occupation-to-degree match. In reality, however, the underlying mechanism of human capital theory does not explain this labor market outcome. The student may be talented, motivated, and career-oriented, but still not use degree-specific skills at work. In this example, unobserved traits or skills, characteristics of the employer, demographic information, or a selection effect may be driving the graduate's college-to-work transition, but technical human capital—those learned skills—is not deployed.

Given this flaw in applying human capital theory, we need an alternative framework, perhaps one that considers cultural prestige independent of skills learned in school. In other words, perhaps business and engineering degrees pay off, even if graduates never use the technical skills they learned, because of the social status these majors have. This framework must account for culture, but in a way focused enough to be useful. One such alternative originates from the work of sociologist John Meyer: *institutional theory* of the college-to-work transition posits that colleges create and legitimate social positions in society (e.g., "college graduate" or "engineer") that have value independent of the content of a student's education.[72]

Recent scholarship in institutional theory builds heavily on the work of Pierre Bourdieu to show how individuals come to embody these social positions, a process that privileged students complete more successfully than their less privileged peers.[73] To obtain their desired social positions, students need to accrue specialized knowledge. However, specialized knowledge in this line of research means cultural capital, defined as the correct cultural knowledge and self-presentation to succeed in a given setting.[74] Researchers have often examined how students at prestigious schools build the necessary cultural capital to be successful in elite labor markets.[75] Current trends in institutional theory make clear that the unequal distribution of cultural capital across students at different universities results in the unequal sorting of graduates into jobs.

Understanding this sorting gives us important insight into the college-to-work transition. For example, graduates of the nation's top twenty *public* universities often work in firms and have job titles different from those who graduate from America's top twenty *private* colleges.[76] Prestigious degrees pay off for graduates of the nation's most elite colleges *regardless of major* because the cultural value of the institutions bestows unique access to certain employers in fields like law, banking, technology, or consulting.[77] Likewise, research outside elite settings shows the important role cultural capital (i.e., culture rather than skills) plays in social mobility or class reproduction among students at the same non-elite institution.[78] I build off the work of Bourdieu and institutionalists by identifying, within a single institution, *college majors as unique sites of cultural capital* that students accrue, independent of the human capital they also gain from their fields of study.

While institutional theory has merit, it does not fully explain differential employment outcomes because no previous research focuses explicitly on differences within a single university by major. More specifically, institutional theory does not discuss how specialized knowledge in prestigious majors explain graduates' differential employment outcomes relative to graduates from less prestigious fields at the same school.

On average, US students rate business and engineering as more prestigious than communications and humanities fields and majoring in prestigious fields *does* yield greater economic returns than majoring in less prestigious fields on average.[79] However, we do not know to what extent prestige pays off financially if the graduate never uses major-specific skills at work. As the late sociologist David Bills wrote in 2003, "neither Meyer nor other institutionalists have been preoccupied with developing a theory of individual-level job assignment."[80] This is because institutional theorists are more concerned with the legitimacy of credentials in wider society than with the content of education. They simply argue that some social positions come with more status and material rewards than others, and this drives differences in labor market outcomes. Specifically, practical arts degrees have a higher cultural value while liberal arts degrees are devalued in the economy and society (except when they are associated with elite institutions). Institutionalists tend to look at aggregate trends rather than individual attainment.[81] But I focus on individuals and what recent graduates do at work, so we can see if prestigious fields of study ultimately pay off regardless of whether graduates deploy their degree-specific skills (human capital).[82]

In sum, by examining the relationship between the two outcomes of interest—(1) graduates' employment conditions and (2) their entry-level job tasks—I challenge assumptions of human capital theory and add to our understanding of institutional theories. I show that the primary way scholars assess human capital theory does not, when applied, fully explain the employment advantages practical arts graduates enjoy. Specifically, a graduate might land a job that is quite good in terms of pay and stability, it may match the degree name, and, yet it may require very little of the graduate's skill set (human capital)—as was the case for Courtney. Further, institutional theorists have long assumed, but never evaluated that, in such cases, prestigious disciplines do pay off, even for graduates who never use their degree-specific skills, an assumption confirmed by the prevalence of cases like Courtney's, whereby business or engineering majors attain "good" jobs but do not draw on their technical skills. In other words, degree fields as unique sites of cultural capital pay off for students regardless of whether they acquire or use major-specific human capital. Meanwhile, the fact that English and communications majors earn relatively low salaries while using their skills further undermines human capital theory and supports institutional theories. This is because, despite skill use, employers do not pay much for graduates with a liberal arts education from a school like CSU. When we better understand these theories, we can better counter media narratives by showing that practical arts disciplines do not inherently better prepare students for the labor market than liberal arts fields.

The Role of Internships in the College-to-Work Transition

With intense competition for entry-level jobs, many employers routinely require a college degree *and* relevant work experience.[83] For students, this means finding internships while in college to increase their marketability to employers and subsequent labor market outcomes.[84] Thus, internships have become nearly ubiquitous in recent years. This is a new development; internships existed almost exclusively in the medical and governmental sectors as recently at the early 1990s, then grew exponentially by the year 2000. By 2008 over 50 percent of college graduates reported interning while in college, meaning at any given time there are millions of interns in the economy.[85] Of course, participation varies considerably, as low-income, first-generation, public school students and those at less selective schools report lower levels of internship participation than students from more privileged backgrounds.[86] A survey of the CSU 2016 graduating class found that approximately 75 percent of students participated in an internship.[87]

With the rise in the number of internships came increased awareness that internships can profoundly affect early professional opportunities for new college graduates. It is thus imperative to better understand just how internships influence employment outcomes. Indeed, variation in internship quality is not well understood, though research shows that students with paid internships fare much better in the labor market than students with unpaid internships.[88] And while studies often include internships as a control variable in hiring research or even manipulate internships as an explanatory variable,[89] this type of research does not explain the processes or mechanisms by which internships shape and influence the experiences of recent college graduates in seeking, securing, and performing in entry-level jobs. This was a central purpose of my study: to examine just how internships shape the college-to-work transition for a group of recent college graduates from a large, public university. More specifically, my findings advance sociological understandings of internships by first probing *how* these internships operate and then tracking the students' experiences in their internships and on their paths to employment. I demonstrate that those participating in career conveyor-belt internships can move easily into entry-level work, while those with dead-end internships struggle to attain their first job.

The two kinds of internships I discuss in this book reflect how important institutional connections are in hiring. Higher education institutions serve as hubs connecting students to other sectors in society, specifically the labor market.[90] Firms and universities may even form corporate partnerships funneling students toward certain employers.[91] My research reveals it is the presence or absence of institutional connections between colleges and employers that distinguishes which students access career conveyor-belt internships and which are directed toward dead-end internships.[92] While it has long been established that people often use network connections to find jobs,[93] in this study I highlight the unique and powerful role played by established network connections between schools and employers for structuring differences between majors at the internship stage of the college-to-work transition.

I further establish that these institutional network connections disproportionately benefit practical arts majors at CSU (and likely other similar large public universities).[94] As a result, we see clearly that the commonly observed superior early labor market outcomes enjoyed by practical arts graduates are, in fact, obtained through an infrastructure that leads from internships to stable, remunerative jobs. Moreover, by examining the specific work experiences of these graduates, I show that stable jobs and better pay are more closely related to the internship experience than any college-acquired skills. Based on the information I uncovered, we may help shift popular discussion to explore the applicable value of college degrees in the practical arts as they are currently designed. These fields match students with entry-level jobs primarily through career conveyor-belt internships, and in the book's conclusion I discuss the implications of this for the wider ecology of higher education.

Variations in Entry-Level Jobs by College Major

When it comes to areas of study, past research does not fully explain the independent effects of college major on early employment outcomes or what entry-level jobs for different majors commonly entail. Research has shown that practical arts graduates have better initial outcomes by traditional employment indicators than liberal arts graduates,[95] but in the long run liberal arts graduates make up ground and see faster rates of growth in occupational status over time.[96] The important takeaway is that liberal arts graduates experience the largest employment deficits at the beginning of their careers; however, researchers often compare college experiences and employment outcomes between majors across schools (i.e., liberal arts majors at an elite private school versus practical arts majors at a regional public college) or they examine the average effects of disciplines on career outcomes across large data sets of college graduates.[97] One important finding from this type of comparative research is that liberal arts graduates of elite colleges can access elite labor markets,[98] which is not the case for liberal arts majors from less elite schools.[99] By comparing students from the same non-elite university, I can better isolate how students from different majors enter the labor market. Of course, an important caveat is that college majors can be quite different, depending on the type of institution.

In my study, I distill the differences in *job type* and *job content* for students from the same university with different majors. In terms of job type by traditional employment indicators, I show that liberal arts graduates earn less money in their entry-level jobs than practical arts graduates and that their jobs are also *qualitatively* different. More specifically, many practical arts graduates end up with "new organizational careers." Named by management scholar Marilyn Clarke, new organizational careers are comanaged by employers and employees in a way that fosters commitment but differs from the traditional organizational careers of the mid-twentieth century when firms provided lifetime employment and a series of well-defined promotion opportunities.[100] Employers providing new organizational careers still offer workers opportunities to spend their whole career (or at least long stretches of employment) with one organization, but employees do not progress linearly up a well-defined career ladder.[101] Established, large firms in key industrial areas, such as durable manufacturing, remain the most likely to offer new organizational careers. Moreover, these employers still dominate many regional labor markets, including in the American Midwest.[102] For recent graduates of non-elite colleges, like CSU, new organizational careers represent the most successful type of entry-level job by traditional middle-class employment standards.

In my study and more broadly, liberal arts graduates who fail to secure a new organizational career are likely to end up with "precarious employment" after graduation. Sociologists Arne Kalleberg and Steven Vallas define precarious work as "uncertain, unstable, and insecure and in which employees bear the risks of work (as opposed to businesses or the government) and receive limited social benefits and statutory protections."[103] To some commentators, all individuals who cannot find stable employment are technically precarious workers. No matter how one defines precarious work, its rise disproportionately affects younger workers and is associated with a host of other negative effects for life after college, such as social isolation.[104] I found that many liberal arts graduates spent months looking for permanent work after college and during that time they might wait tables or work in retail. Even when they do find full-time positions these might be low-paid or offer little room for advancement. Thus, precarious work was common among liberal arts majors new to the labor market.

With regard to the *content* of entry-level jobs, I found some early employment advantages for liberal arts majors. Research shows that, even when people have stable, high-paying jobs, if they do not find purpose or meaning in their jobs, they experience dissatisfaction.[105] Practical arts majors like Courtney disproportionately reported finding their jobs boring and unfulfilling as they mostly completed clerical work. By contrast, liberal arts graduates like Mort, despite precarious employment (for example, being a student teacher while in graduate school), found the substance of their work satisfying because they regularly used their degree skills. In this situation, people were less likely to question their major choice and felt fulfilled by work that they could not do without that academic preparation.

In sum, my empirical findings reveal several important contributions to the sociology of work and economic sociology through examining how entry-level jobs systematically vary by major. By decoupling new organizational careers from the content of entry-level work, I challenge popular thinking about how skills are rewarded in the labor market and add nuance to research on the degradation of white-collar work, which often shows pay and complexity of work tasks declining in tandem.[106] I also show what kinds of entry-level jobs are accessible to graduates from different majors, how they get the jobs, and what the jobs entail. This is a process we know surprisingly little about, despite the importance of first jobs for employees' long-term economic trajectories.[107] These contributions should help us understand with more nuance the real trade-off in labor market outcomes between graduates with different majors and challenge the myths perpetuated by media narratives about the value of a college degree.

Defending the Liberal Arts

It is important to note that, in contrast to mainstream media narratives, many articles in the popular press (including some already cited), defend the liberal arts. In fact, a simple Google search of "defense of the liberal arts" yields more than nineteen *million* results. A Google Scholar search of the same term yields almost 500,000 results. Some argue for the long-term economic payoff of a liberal arts education while others emphasize the importance of fostering broad intellectual skills and more engaged citizenship.[108] Commentators view investment in the liberal arts as a public good and criticize universities for yielding to narrow-market thinking for themselves and their students.[109] For high-status students at elite institutions, the prestige of the liberal arts may even derive from their distance from the labor market. For students at more typical colleges or universities, liberal arts may be seen as impractical or idealistic.

The noneconomic defense of the liberal arts is perhaps best encapsulated by a series of reports written in 2019 with funding from the Mellon Foundation.[110] Although one of the reports focuses on the economic costs and benefits of a liberal arts education, it acknowledges that defenders of the liberal arts "often stress the nonpecuniary benefits of such an education."[111] Another Mellon Foundation report states, "The guiding justification for why those domains are needed is that they contribute uniquely to well-being, and possibly health, across the adult life course."[112] Defenders of the liberal arts often advocate for specific ways the humanities help students learn or grow and present vague (at best) ways they engender labor market success. Yet, as Professor of Creative Writing Rachel Toor has argued, focusing on the many nonpecuniary benefits of a liberal arts degree rarely convinces skeptics.[113]

Ultimately, this book provides a new way of defending the liberal arts. What is often seen as a weakness of liberal arts disciplines—lack of practical utility—is actually a strength, based on the real trade-off young people make when selecting a college major and career path.[114] Students can declare a practical arts major, move smoothly into a new organizational career, and likely engage in clerical work. Or they can major in the liberal arts, struggle to enter the labor market, possibly end up underemployed or with precarious work, and yet realize greater opportunities for using their learned skills.

This is not what I set out to find. I thought my study might document more precisely just how practical arts majors navigate early employment decisions when their degrees and skills are in such high demand. Yet, I found that, even when the economic disparities between students of different majors are the widest (early in their careers),[115] liberal arts graduates use their degree skills while practical arts graduates rarely do. Therefore, even if we focus solely on entry-level jobs, liberal arts degrees prepare students well for working. Yes, the trade-off with the practical arts is real, but it is more nuanced than we thought. Students starting from relatively similar places do end up on quite different trajectories, but what those trajectories look like in practice decidedly upends popular narratives.

How I Studied the College-to-Work Transition

At present, we know little about how students from a variety of majors at large, public universities navigate internships and labor market entry. We also know very little about how students' networks or university-employer networks operate throughout the transition from college to work, although research has established that graduates of large, public universities tend to find work in different firms and with different job titles than those who attended elite, private institutions.[116]

As a large midwestern public research university, CSU was an ideal site for my research. Over 70 percent of US college students attend a public institution and over 10 percent of all undergraduates attend public research universities like CSU,[117] a typical state flagship university ranked among the top one hundred national universities but not the top fifty, according to *U.S. News and World Report.* CSU is a state flagship school and accepts most applicants who apply. For the class of 2020, over 60 percent of first-year applicants received offers of admission. This led to an incoming class of roughly 8,600 students, over 70 percent of whom came from in-state.[118]

Demographically, the CSU student profile is generally typical of American higher education.[119] Matching national trends, women make up the majority of students at CSU. Meanwhile, over 75 percent of CSU undergraduates are White, compared to 55 percent across the US.[120] Of the nearly 25 percent of the student body who are not White, 7 percent are Black and 5 percent are Hispanic.[121] Nationwide, Black and Latinx students represent 10 percent and 20 percent of undergraduates, respectively.[122] Although CSU's numbers may seem skewed compared to national figures, Black and Hispanic students are typically underrepresented at four-year colleges.[123] This is especially true in the Midwest, where state campuses often have less diverse student populations than more elite schools that can recruit for diversity.[124]

Choosing CSU as a research site has many advantages beyond its demographic similarity to comparable public universities. Large state universities provide comprehensive liberal arts and preprofessional education, whereas elite schools mostly offer exclusively liberal arts majors, and colleges serving primarily low-income or first general students offer mostly practical arts degrees.[125] For schools at both extremes of the educational hierarchy (the sites of most sociological case studies), we would expect less variation in employment outcomes by majors than at a school like CSU. Due to cultural value, the brand of elite institutions is enough for students to achieve labor market success while students who study at schools at the bottom of the academic hierarchy have trouble entering the labor market regardless of field.[126] But when we look at a school like CSU, that internal division in student outcomes becomes apparent.

For my study, I interviewed ninety-one CSU students from four carefully chosen majors (business, engineering, English, and communications) during their senior year[127] and again after labor market entry.[128] Students were eligible to participate if, for the first round of interviews, they were seniors, declared in one of the four majors, and completed at least one internship or were currently interning.

I included only students who undertook internships for three reasons. First, as mentioned above, most US students now complete internships. Second, since popular narratives often argue that liberal arts students are less career-oriented than practical arts majors, by only interviewing those with internship experience, I ensured that the liberal arts students who participated in my study do, in fact, seek to enhance their employability. Third, variation in internship quality is not well understood beyond distinguishing paid versus unpaid. Studies often include internships as a control variable or as an explanatory variable;[129] however, researchers have yet to examine precisely how internships help students enter the labor market. This is partially because case studies of internships usually focus on the nonprofit or aesthetic fields,[130] except the (rare) scholars who study one industry in-depth (e.g., marketing students and marketing internships).[131] What is left, and what I was seeking to understand, are the processes through which internships differentially contribute to labor market entry.

I conducted two waves of in-depth interviews: wave one with ninety-one participants while they were college seniors and wave two with eighty-five of the original group roughly one year later when they were recent graduates.[132] First wave interviews took place over the 2015–2016 academic year and second-wave interviews were conducted between November 2016 and December 2017. I interviewed three of the eighty-five second-wave respondents twice because our initial postgraduation session took place after they had accepted job offers but before their employment began. Since these respondents sat for an additional wave two interview, the study comprises data from 179 unique interviews.

I took an *interinstitutional* approach, so this is one of few books that substantively examines *both* higher education and labor market institutions.[133] This approach allowed me to disentangle cultural from human capital mechanisms connecting students to work and I am therefore positioned to challenge both popular and scholarly accounts of how degree fields differentially prepare students for the labor market. I traced what students learned in school, what their internships and entry-level jobs were like, and can thus determine when skills covered in academic coursework were used in either internships or entry-level jobs.

Structure of the Book

This book follows students' journeys from college to the labor market chronologically, but also conceptually. I present empirical evidence to dispel the myths and discuss the reality of the practical and liberal arts in two parts. Part 1 examines how the trade-off between types of majors starts during college. This section of the book shows that, despite similarities in students' learning, ambitions, and skill use during their internships, access to the kinds of internships that lead to entry-level jobs vary by major. Chapter 2 opens with discussion of what students learn in school and their aspirations during senior year and shows how students of different majors and their fields of study were more similar than one might expect. Chapter 3 shows how career conveyor-belt internships operate and demonstrates that student access to them varies by major. Finally, chapter 4 focuses on skill use in internships to show that access to career conveyor-belt internships and subsequent job opportunities are not related to students displaying technical competencies.

Part 2 focuses on students' job searches and early employment after graduation. Chapter 5 traces the process of how students look for work, shows how difficult that process can be for many liberal arts majors, and describes where students ultimately end up. Chapter 6 examines what students do at work, showing that liberal arts graduates are more likely to have work with substantive tasks than practical arts graduates. Chapter 7 investigates which graduates use degree skills at work. I carefully mapped the curriculum from each major onto students' entry-level work tasks and asked graduates how their degrees related to their jobs. Findings reveal that many liberal arts graduates applied specific tools and concepts from their major to their entry-level jobs. Practical arts graduates rarely used their specific degree skills in entry-level work and, instead, often discussed the relevance of their general liberal arts competencies as the most salient part of their undergraduate education.[134]

In the conclusion, I advance a new framework for understanding the college-to-work transition. Through my interinstitutional approach, I offer a corrective to media narratives and I expose the cultural and organizational infrastructure that links college majors with employers to offer a new vision for higher education and the labor market. This vision values the education all students receive and advocates for jobs that provide decent pay and benefits but also give new employees opportunities to undertake tasks that draw on their wide array of degree skills. The evidence from my study suggests less negativity is warranted in how we discuss the liberal arts with regard to employability, and that we should be clearer about the precise advantages practical arts graduates enjoy early in their careers. This new understanding of the college-to-work transition may level the playing field among majors in their capacity to secure entry-level work and thus revitalize the liberal arts. Ultimately, my findings could then lead to students receiving a well-rounded education that piques their interests *and also* prepares them for the contemporary workforce.

PART 1: STUDENTS' COLLEGE AND INTERNSHIP EXPERIENCES

2: THE STUDENTS AND THEIR MAJORS

Popular media labels majors as either "passion" or "practical," yet this is not how students think about their chosen fields of study. Sociologist Erin Cech shows that students from liberal arts and preprofessional majors are equally likely to prioritize passion-related considerations in choosing their majors and careers.[1] In my study, students from all four fields viewed their majors as practical and had modest career aspirations. Most students I interviewed wanted to work in jobs related to their degrees. They believed their courses of study would prepare them for professional success by providing skills they would use at work. In fact, almost every student in this study wanted a stable middle-class job and thought their specific choice of major would help them achieve that goal. No one wanted to write the next great American novel or become CEO of a *Fortune* 500 company. In this regard, CSU and likely other, similar schools are fundamentally different from more elite colleges, where students may aspire to prestigious jobs and choose courses of study that they likewise perceive as high status.[2]

All the students in my study sample, regardless of major, learned some "practical" job-related skills and also developed some general liberal arts competencies through their courses, which indicates that the curricula are all similarly oriented toward the labor market. It is not true that liberal arts majors learn only general "soft skills" nor that business and engineering majors learn solely technical engineering or logistics concepts. Importantly, across all four majors, students learn skills well aligned with what employers claim to seek, suggesting the higher education ecosystem works well.

Despite these important similarities across my study respondents, the practical arts graduates I interviewed did end up, on average, with superior labor market rewards, at least by traditional employment indicators. This chapter gives an overview of the students who participated in this study and provides evidence that debunk two common explanations for differential employment outcomes. I found that students in both types of majors are "realistically" career-oriented and that both types of majors teach skills that employers claim to want or need.

One important way that the four majors *are* different at CSU is in demographic composition, especially gender. Nationally, approximately two-thirds of English and communications majors are women, while business and engineering are both disciplines with a majority of men.[3] Inequality scholars have known for generations that feminized majors and occupations have inferior economic outcomes.[4] In general, women are more likely than men to choose "risky majors," defined as those that come with heightened risk for low income or unemployment immediately following college.[5] These majors tend to cluster in the arts and sciences and include communications and English.[6] Further, the men who enter majors dominated by women and associated occupations tend to be disadvantaged in intersectional ways, such as having a disability or belonging to a racial or ethnic minority group.[7] Among the students I interviewed (and at CSU in general), business and engineering majors were much more likely to be White middle-class men, and English and communications majors were more likely to be White middle-class women or men from less advantaged backgrounds.[8] Therefore, the differences in opportunities available to students fell along gendered and other demographic lines, making the labor market differences between the practical and liberal arts even more consequential for social stratification outcomes.

Chloe, a communications major, provides an example typical of the CSU undergraduates I interviewed. Chloe is an in-state student from an upper-middle-class family in the state's eighth largest city with a population under 100,000. She originally went out of state for college but transferred to CSU because "it's closer to home." She started as an English major but switched to communications because she wanted more business skills. She said, "[I] realized I wanted to get some business applicable skills, so I transferred into strategic communication, and I have a professional writing minor." The professional writing program at CSU is housed in the English department and many English majors take courses in this program as well. Chloe, like many communications majors in this study, aspired to work in public relations (PR), but not at a glamorous New York City agency. Rather, when we spoke during her senior year, she was applying for jobs around the state hoping to work at a firm that focuses on travel or tourism.

Communications at CSU provides a liberal arts education that is also practical. Chloe told me, "It's very rhetorical based. You look at a lot of different elements of persuasion and how that translates to your actual work career." She thought this would be useful for her career and said of her classes, "We look at case studies, and we listen to these podcasts of how people are relating to each other in the world. And it's actually fun; we take different communication theories and then apply them to the case study, and I really like the work we're going over right now." Chloe chose communications because it matched her practical ambitions of working in PR, for which she thought the coursework would prepare her well.

In the remainder of the chapter, I demonstrate how the students who participated in this study are similar and how they vary by major. To do this, I first provide an overview of the students, then discuss their ambitions and the skills learned in each major. Finally, I review how these skills match what the university says students will learn and what employers claim to seek in new employees.

The Students in This Study

All ninety-one enrolled seniors at CSU I interviewed were either participating in or had recently completed an internship. Each had declared a major in one of four fields: business with a specialization in operations and logistics,[9] engineering with a concentration in industrial and systems engineering (ISE), communications, or English. While the majors I include are not generalizable to all the practical and liberal arts, they provide a firm basis for examining the different experiences students have by major type at large state schools. The four selected disciplines cover a professional field, a STEM discipline, the social sciences, and a humanities discipline.

While some consider communications a practical arts discipline, researchers often include it in the arts and sciences.[10] At CSU, communications is housed in the social and behavioral sciences unit of the College of Arts and Sciences. Still, communications could be regarded as a hybrid of the social sciences and the practical arts; however, I found many opportunities available to engineering and business majors that are not offered to English and communications graduates, which reinforced my decision to consider communications together with English as liberal arts and business and engineering as practical arts. Most notably, I stress an important distinction between the practical arts and liberal arts beyond course content and relation to an occupation: access to career resources not open to the arts and sciences population of a university. At CSU, communications majors have access only to the arts and sciences general career services, websites, and fairs. In general, we can think of the four selected majors as a spectrum from "most" to "least" technical in terms of occupational specificity: engineering, business (which in other colleges can be a more general degree, but is not at CSU), communications, and English.

The business operations and logistics track and engineering ISE track both focus similarly on issues of supply chain management and manufacturing processes. ISE is comparable to other engineering areas as it combines traditional manufacturing engineering with computer science and data analytics. And of course, all students in business and engineering at CSU follow the core business and engineering curricula. English and communications majors are likewise similar; most courses and matched industries are writing and communications focused.

Of course, there are women-dominated practical arts majors (e.g., nursing)[11] and men-dominated liberal arts fields (e.g., economics). My choice of majors does not allow me to disentangle the effects of practical arts versus liberal arts from men- versus women-dominated majors; however, that is not the point of this type of analysis. Following an intersectional feminist approach to social science,[12] I aim to show social processes that affect typical students who on average share a suite of characteristics. In other words, while English is a liberal arts field dominated by women, I am not interested in the marginal effect of "liberal arts" or "women-dominated," but in how women-dominated, liberal arts majors fare in the labor market.

The four majors were selected because of their combined characteristics. Engineering is the most exalted major in media narratives and in surveys of college students.[13] Business is the most common major in the US. Thus these two fields are exemplars of the turn toward "practical" majors in higher education. It is not a research design flaw that these are characteristics of the two majors *and* men are overrepresented in these fields. In fact, the overrepresentation of men has likely influenced the shaping of these characteristics of the two disciplines. At the other end of the spectrum, English is the biggest media target of the crisis in the humanities.[14] Again, the overrepresentation of women in this major is an important implication of that media narrative.

The sample of students in my study reflects the overall demographics at CSU. Most respondents were women, White, and middle class. In fact, the 25 percent of non-White students in my study closely match the college's overall rate.[15] In all four disciplines, most students identified as middle class. Most communications and English majors I interviewed were women.[16] Most non-White students were concentrated among the communications majors. In fact, most of the Black students who participated in this project studied communications. This is somewhat of an anomaly as surveys show over 80 percent of communications majors nationally are White.[17] Almost all the non-White students I interviewed in ISE and business were Asian or South Asian. Hispanic and Black students, who are underrepresented at four-year colleges and especially in the Midwest,[18] were more likely to be communications or English majors in this study. The modal practical arts student in this study is a White middle-class man while the modal liberal arts graduate is a White middle-class woman. All students I interviewed identified as either a

TABLE 2.1 Sample Demographics by Major

	ISE	Business	Communications	English	Total
n	24	23	26	18	91
Gender (%)					
Men	50	74	23	22	42
Women	50	26	77	78	58
Race (%)					
White	71	57	58	89	75
Non-White	29	13	42	11	25
GPA (median)	3.35	3.54	3.50	3.69	3.50
Self-identified class (%)					
Upper / upper-mid	33	36	19	28	29
Middle	50	41	62	39	50
Working/lower	17	23	19	33	21
Geographic origins (%)					
In-state	87	74	73	89	81
Out-of-state	9	22	27	11	16
International	4	4	0	0	3

cisman or ciswoman, though this was not an intentional sampling decision. Surprisingly, the ISE students had the lowest median GPA; however, GPAs are not comparable since engineering and business students occupy separate colleges from the liberal arts majors. Full study sample demographics are presented in table 2.1.

Over 80 percent of the students I interviewed came from the state in which CSU is located. Of the out of state students, only six came from a state that does not share a border with the state CSU is located in. Three international students participated, two from China and one from India.

As with Chloe, most students attended CSU because it is close to home or the cheapest option. Other students enrolled because their parents or other family members were alumni. For example, Steve's (ISE) family moved to the city CSU is in ten years ago. He told me, "I was in the marching band in high school, and I fell in love with CSU's marching band, that's why I chose CSU." Though Steve is not in CSU's marching band, he went on to say of the school, "It's twenty minutes from home and I still help my family out a lot." When asked if he was considering other schools, Steve told me, "The

TABLE 2.2 Student Aspirations Senior Year of College by Major

	ISE	Business	Communications	English	Total
n	24	23	26	18	91
Related to major (%)					
Yes	17 (71)	20 (87)	19 (73)	15 (83)	71 (78)
No	3 (13)	1 (4)	5 (19)	3 (17)	12 (13)
Undecided	4 (17)	2 (9)	2 (8)	0 (0)	8 (9)
Modal aspiration	Engineer at manufacturer	Manager at corporation	PR	Publishing	N/A

day my CSU acceptance came I was in the middle of filling out a new [college] application and as soon as I saw the acceptance, I delayed everything [else] and went with [CSU]." This culture of sticking close to home and prioritizing the state flagship was common among the students in this study.

The "Practical Passions" of CSU Students

With this overall picture of who the students are, we turn to what they wanted to achieve professionally. Most students I interviewed tended to have realistic ambitions, which I refer to as "practical passions." This is because the aspirational jobs they had in mind fit their interests *and* seemed attainable. While some students chose their majors to reach specific professional goals and others came to their goals only after selecting a field of study, by senior year the majority had career aspirations related to their majors. In the study sample, only eight students were undecided or had no idea what they wanted to do in the future. Of course, all students in this study had internships, so students without internships may have different experiences and outlooks. A summary of respondents' ambitions appears in table 2.2.

Most engineering and business majors I interviewed wanted to be engineers, managers or supervisors at manufacturing facilities, or work in supply chain management. Steve, a student from a lower-middle-class background, chose CSU for reasons unrelated to his major, but his aspirations matched his field of study. He fell in love with airplanes as a kid but thought aerospace engineering would be too narrow. Since he liked the TV show "How It's Made," which traces product manufacturing processes, he knew he wanted to stay in engineering. And although engineering is popularly viewed as a practical major, for Steve it matched his passion. He picked industrial engineering as a specialty during his tour of the CSU Engineering Department and he aspired to be a plant manager at a manufacturing facility. When I asked Steve where he sees himself in five years, he said, "I'm hoping to be some sort of production manager. I know I can't be a plant manager in five years but moving my way up into something like that." This response was typical among business and engineering majors; the majority wanted to work in manufacturing as an engineer or manager, some wanted to go into consulting, some had educational aspirations such as an MBA, and a few had entrepreneurial aspirations. Of those who wanted to own a business, all thought in terms of, for example, eventually opening a gas station after establishing themselves in a traditional corporate career; no one wanted to start the next Facebook.

Steve wanted to be a plant manager but knew it was unlikely to happen in the next five, or even ten years. His ambitions were on a realistic timetable, and they were motivated by what he had seen at home over the years. When I asked why he wanted to be a plant manager, he spoke of the importance of having a good boss. He told me, "One reason I want to be a plant manager, with my dad over the years, I've seen bad management. With my mom, she's got a terrible boss. And I want to be that change in the industrial environment, make people's lives better, because I see what happens when people get home, and it's awful." While being a plant manager likely comes with a middle-class salary and a certain amount of respect, CSU students rarely mentioned prestige, money, or status as incentives for their career choices. Instead, each was aiming for a realistic position related to their field of study.

In this respect, students at large public universities differ from those who attend elite private colleges. At elite schools, majors are less salient, as students from disciplines as diverse as engineering and English seek prestigious jobs in finance, consulting, or tech.[19] This reinforces the idea that majors at highly rejective colleges may be qualitatively different from those at a more representative school (like CSU) and that fields of study are important for understanding typical student experiences at typical colleges.

Although the choice between practical or liberal arts is often framed as a choice between majoring in something utilitarian versus something students are passionate about,[20] respectively, the students at CSU from all majors had practical passions. And although telling students to follow their passions can lead those from underprivileged backgrounds astray,[21] in this study the "passions" expressed by students seemed pragmatic and realistic regardless of class background.[22] Because Steve loved a TV show about manufacturing processes and his parents had suffered working under bad bosses, he aspired to become a plant manager. Chloe wanted to work in PR but aimed her ambitions at local tourism or travel companies.

Greta, an English major from an upper-middle-class family, was typical of those who wanted to work in publishing or editing. For Greta, this meant working for a publisher near her Midwestern hometown—mostly textbook companies or e-learning firms. Greta told me about her postgraduation plans: "My goal is to stay in [city CSU is in], at least for a year. I really love it here, and I have a lot of fantastic friends and I'm not ready to leave yet, so I've been looking for jobs. I've been looking in the publishing and e-learning industry, but I've also made some great connections through my internship in the nonprofit sector and I'm hoping that goes somewhere." Greta, like Chloe and Steve, wanted to stay close to home. She had applied to six jobs at the time of our interview, including to a large textbook company that also makes e-learning tools. That company told her they did not have an opening in her area and asked if she would be willing to move to Chicago, a city in the same region as CSU. Even this was too far. She told me, "At this point of my life I'm not sure I'm ready to just up and move for an entry-level job that I may or may not want to stay with long term." Greta's aspirations were bounded by what she saw as attainable and by what fit within her comfort zone. Still, she sought employment that would match her interest in publishing, making her case a good illustration of practical passions.

Finally, Burt, a business major from a working-class family, also aspired to be a plant manager or to run his own business. Burt told me about his occupational goals, starting with his background working at a sign manufacturer, then relating it to his operations major: "Having a background in manufacturing, the operations side of manufacturing was always the part that I was more interested in. I don't necessarily want to be a floor manager, but at some point, being a plant manager. My stepmom actually works for a manufacturing company in Tree City, where she is a plant manager. I have a good friend of mine also who worked for Midwest Motors and then kind of struck out on his own as a lean consultant and does lean consulting now for hospitals." The influence of Burt's good friend and stepmom shaped his ambitions. He hoped to get a job right out of college and stay there for five years before moving up or on to consulting. Similar to Chloe, Burt's own business ambitions were somewhat moderate. When he talked about starting his own business in the future, he specified he would like to consult for "smaller companies to help them improve their processes and their efficiency." He was not hoping to be the founder of the next McKinsey.

While many students aimed to work in specific industries or mid-level management positions, some respondents had less crystallized ambitions. These students, regardless of major, thought their fields of study would provide flexible career opportunities. For example, Roberta, an ISE student from a middle-class family living in the same city as CSU, declared her major after attending a Society of Women Engineers (SWE) event hosted at her high school. Perhaps surprisingly, part of the reason she chose ISE as a subfield was its versatility. Roberta said, "I didn't know specifically what I wanted to do, and it sounded like ISE had a lot of different things you could go into. I felt like it was pretty open, and it was engineering but it was also business, so it wasn't like straight out sitting at a computer the whole day and typing in code. So that definitely appealed to me because I didn't know what else I wanted to do, and I'm happy with the choice." During our first interview, Roberta was still not sure exactly what she wanted to do after graduation but hoped to stay in engineering. Broadly, she wanted to work at one of the large automotive firms that have offices and factories in the region.

Likewise, several English majors mentioned the occupational versatility of their degree, showing a commonality between the least technical and most-technical degrees in this study. Katie, an English major from a middle-class family that lives in-state, aspired to work that included professional writing. At first, she thought she would be an English teacher, but she quickly soured on that plan. She told me, "I wasn't sure what I wanted to do beyond that," but she didn't mind that because "I figured English was very versatile." Chris, one of the few men among the English majors I interviewed, had a wide range of interests. He is from the state's largest metropolitan area, comes from a working-class background, and was recruited to CSU through a diversity scholarship program. Chris was one of only two Black men in the sample; both studied English. He aspired to work in editing, but his true passion was video game design and development. Chris said his major aligned with all of his interests—design, journalism, music, poetry. He said, "English is kind of multipurpose," adding it would "probably give me a more widespread amount of fields, just in case, because you never know where you will be." Note Chris had a modest ambition (editing) and a more passionate aspiration (video game design and development), and he thought his English major could help him achieve either path, although he knew the former was more attainable. Ultimately, the students come from a range of backgrounds that spanned working class to upper-middle class, yet for many their aspirations were "practical passions" related to their majors. This finding matches prior research that shows students and career aspirants weigh passion-considerations similarly, regardless of background, identity, or major.[23]

The Range of Skills Taught across Disciplines

At a school like CSU, all majors teach a range of occupationally specific and general liberal arts competencies. Establishing this fact is an important first

TABLE 2.3 Skills Business and Engineering Majors Cover in Their Classes

Business—operations and/or logistics	ISE
Logistics/data analytics	Probability and statistics/data analysis
Workflow process optimization	Simulating and organizing workflow processes
Lean manufacturing principles	Lean manufacturing principles
Forecasting and production scheduling	Manufacturing design and production processes

TABLE 2.4 Skills Communications and English Majors Cover in Their Classes

Communications	English
Organizational communications	Writing mechanics
Persuasive communications	Professional writing
Create media campaigns	Literature analysis
Writing and editing other content specific to communications (e.g., press releases)	Writing and editing other content

step to dispelling that key myth that liberal arts students do not learn specific skills they will use at work. It also lays the foundation for investigating the match between degree content and entry-level job tasks.

During the first wave of interviews, I asked students to describe what they were learning in their classes. I then aggregated this information to show the curriculum for each major. Practical arts majors learned a combination of pragmatic occupational skills and more general skills. Business majors specializing in operations and logistics learned some general skills, such as data analysis and probably and statistics. Specific to their field, their courses covered logistics analytics, workplace process optimization, lean manufacturing principles, and how to conduct forecasting and production scheduling. ISE students likewise learned general skills like probability and statistics, but also more specific skills like how to simulate and organize workflow processes, principles of lean manufacturing, and manufacturing design and production. Practical arts skills are presented in table 2.3.

Liberal arts majors similarly covered a mix of general and field-specific skills. Communications majors learned organizational and persuasive communications. They also learned to create media campaigns and were trained in various forms of writing and content development (e.g., blogs, press releases). English students learned the mechanics of writing, professional writing, literature analysis, and other kinds of writing, editing, and content creation. Liberal arts skills are laid out in table 2.4.

All participating students expected to use major-related skills in their eventual work. Business major Shawn had typical responses for how he thought his degree would relate to his career. He focused on logistics because he liked combining office work with field experience. While Shawn did not have a specific career aspiration, he said, "I see myself working within logistics for the rest of my life." When I asked Shawn about the courses he was taking, he told me about his transportation class: "It really includes both analytics and decision-making because you're really learning about the details within each mode of transportation, whether it be rail, air, truck. . . . You're learning [about] making the decision on which one to use and then applying the analytics and statistics side of which one is going to be more effective for the type of product that you're trying to transport." The topics Shawn outlined are classified in table 2.3 as "logistics analytics." When I interviewed Shawn during his senior year, he had a job lined up for after graduation. I asked him if the skills he learned in his classes would benefit him in his future job:

SHAWN: I'm going to say probably 80 percent of the material that I've learned in those classes will be applicable.
CMP: So, like your transportation class, when you're learning about deciding between trucks, boats, whatever, you're going to use those skills?
SHAWN: Yeah, I'll use those. . . . What I'll be doing [is] setting up contracts with suppliers and carriers to figure out what's going to be the most profitable for us and effective, so yeah, I will use those skills.

Shawn believed that his education in business logistics gave him the skills needed for his entry-level job.

Steve also thought that his engineering degree would be useful in his first job. Specifically, he discussed aspects of "Manufacturing Design and Production Processes" and "probability and statistics" that he would use if or when he works in a plant. For the former, he told me about his "machines course, it's a hands-on manufacturing one." Each week, his class works in the basement of the engineering building where the school has "a huge machine shop in there, mills, drill presses, water jet cutting, plastic injection [tools]." He was also taking a course called "Design of Experiments (DOE)." He explained, "It's the application of statistics, and the process of doing designed experiments to actually get good, scientific information and make decisions on a process." The two courses covered a lot of the areas featured in the engineering section of table 2.3. Steve said:

The machine class, I think, is very nice because we have a theoretical textbook that goes into the formulas of everything, and then we have a, we use a machinery handbook. And when I go to the plant I'm working at now and I go to the production supervisor, he's got three different machinery handbooks, so that means it's used in industry. The DOE, the professor for it is actually from the business school, his master's is in statistics, he spent years in the air force [doing] research. And he worked for a glass company, and he talks about all the times that he's used it.

Steve's and Shawn's responses were representative of the practical arts students I interviewed. They outlined the specific skills they learned in their disciplines and often speculated that these exact tools, concepts, or skills would be valuable in their eventual work. Some skills were occupation or industry specific (e.g., work in the machine shop) and others were general liberal arts competencies (e.g., how to design experiments and make scientifically valid conclusions).

Liberal arts majors similarly viewed their studies as providing practical and general skills they would use in future work. Communications major Chloe thought she would use persuasive communications skills professionally. Greta, the English major aspiring to work in publishing, also reported that her degree provided professionally useful skills. Greta's course of study is indicative of typical modern-day English classes: rather than "just" learning Shakespeare or conducting literary analysis, English majors perform a range of professional writing exercises and undertake professional development. Greta said that in one of her classes, "We treat literature as a sort of business case study and then come up with alternative endings for the book that try to maximize a certain character's outcome. It's really interesting." In another one of her classes, she had to do "research on jobs" she might be interested in. Greta enjoyed this assignment, saying she appreciated "the built-in career search time that class is providing for me." Other students mentioned writing blog posts and other kinds of professional writing or career development as part of the curriculum, a key difference between the English curriculum at places like CSU and more elite colleges.[24]

Some English majors were self-conscious about people questioning the value of their degree. Several students mentioned that they practiced responding to questions about the skills their major provides. Greta said, "As an English major you sometimes have to defend your reason for studying things." This language, like Mort's in chapter 1, showed an awareness of media narratives denigrating the employability of an English graduate. It also suggested these narratives were not confined to the media but were more popular narratives that extend to how students talked about their fields of study while in college. As such, Greta was prepared to answer my question even before I asked it. She said her degree gives her the skills to "engage with a really complex piece of text. And then sort of condense it and then, like, tailor information to specific audiences, so I think all those skills are needed in a workplace." She added that English degrees also provide other skills, not necessarily useful for the workplace, but still good to have; she thought learning literature from a variety of cultures or perspectives makes one "a better human being." Overall, liberal arts majors understood their degrees to provide practical skills they would use at work. Again, like their practical arts peers, some skills were occupationally specific (e.g., blog posts) and others were more general (e.g., engaging and condensing complex text).

In all four majors, the skills students learned also have gendered connotations in wider society and economy. For example, communications skills are gendered as typically feminine and technological skills tend to be seen as masculine.[25] Research has long shown that skills and occupations associated with men tend to be valued more highly in the labor market than those associated with women.[26] So, while all students expected to use their learned skills, even if they were successful, they entered a system with gendered disparities in employment quality (which I explore in later chapters). Of course, individual women in technical fields like business and engineering could benefit from the cultural value of the "masculine" skills they acquired, but the gendering of the skills themselves relate to graduates' different occupational outcomes.

What Colleges Sell and What Employers Say They Are Buying

Finally, students' ambitions and the reported curricula match what colleges emphasize as the labor market utility of their programs. Students' conceptions of what they would gain from their majors matched the language CSU departments use on their websites to describe degrees. For example, the English department's page lists information about Shakespeare and Jane Austen, but they also advertise career preparedness. The website mentions students writing blog posts, producing YouTube videos, writing technical reports, and social media campaigns. They have a career preparation course, a career preparation website, and multiple links to articles dispelling the myth that English majors are unemployable. They even link to the National Association for Colleges and Employers' "eight competencies linked to career readiness," with a list of how English courses provide students with these competencies.[27] The communications department's website is also oriented around professional skills. Although there is less content on career preparation, they stress that CSU teaches students how to be successful communicators and provides students with "practical and analytical skills and knowledge."

The ISE website at CSU also highlights skill learning and job preparedness. They have sections on their home page on career opportunities, career satisfaction, and employment rates. They advertise providing students with "technical, management, and human-centered design skills" and list many of the specific skills.

Surprisingly, the business school's home page and the logistics or operations department pages do not emphasize skill acquisition. Instead, these programs promote their rankings and career prospects. Still, although these pages do not indicate what is taught in the classroom, they show that all graduates become work-ready, and this matches students' perceptions.

On the employers' end, businesses claim to want the skills students reported they learned in school. Data from job ads supports this claim. Indeed.com, the highest-trafficked job website in the US, lists the top eleven qualities and skills employers seek, regardless of specific position, as: communications, leadership, teamwork, interpersonal, learning and adaptability, self-management, organization, computer, problem-solving, open-mindedness, and a strong work ethic.[28] These are skills most college students should acquire, regardless of major. Analyses of job ads show that the most common competencies required for engineering jobs are actually soft skills as well as previous experience with engineering, and technical knowledge.[29] For operations jobs, the most common skills are communication, statistics and modeling competencies, and general analytic skills.[30] Communications jobs see people with general writing skills, web content skills, and the ability to make promotional materials and social media posts.[31] Given the match between classroom learning and job ads, in the specific fields and overall, it appears graduates from all four majors should be desirable to potential employers.

Similar Students, Divergent Trajectories

Overall, I noted in this chapter two key ways students from all four majors at CSU were similar. First, students' ambitions were surprisingly aligned. Of course, the content of students' aspirations varied by major, but most students in all majors wanted practical middle-class jobs that related to their degrees. I did not find that the practical arts majors had more realistic ambitions or were more career-oriented than liberal arts majors, as media narratives often suggest. The liberal arts students I interviewed were just as career-oriented, indeed: some of the most motivated students in the sample studied communications or English and completed multiple internships during college, a process I discuss in the next two chapters. And these students did not hope to work in high fashion or write for famous outlets. Rather, many hoped to stay close to home and work for organizations that were familiar to them.

Second, all curricula taught a mix of practical and general skills that students believed would serve them well professionally. CSU English majors are equipped with skills like technical writing and engineering majors learn general liberal arts competencies as well. These skills are highlighted by the departments and align with what employers claim to want in new hires. Ultimately, the liberal arts students in this study, and the university departments, projected a keen understanding of the specific skills that would be applicable in the labor market. The details about each fields' curriculum will come up again in later chapters where I discuss whether skills covered by the academic curricula matched graduates' entry-level work tasks, as many students expected.

The one way the students in my study differed by type of major was by demographic background, which is representative of the situation across the country. The implication of these differences is that these students' labor market trajectories will reproduce inequality that already exists in American society. In other words, middle-class White men will enter stable, high-paying employment and the others will have a more difficult time. The rest of this book covers these divergent trajectories. The trade-off between majors starts during college with differences in internship types, which is the subject of the next chapter.

3: CAREER CONVEYOR-BELT AND DEAD-END INTERNSHIPS

The road to new organizational careers starts early, at the internship stage of the college-to-work transition. Many practical arts students obtained "career conveyor-belt internships" that led directly to secure jobs. In striking contrast, liberal arts students were more likely to have "dead-end internships" that did not lead to employment. When we examine the concepts of career conveyor-belt and dead-end internships, we uncover important differences by major in how students access employers and labor markets while still in school.

Chloe, the communications major, did not have access to a career conveyor-belt internship, despite completing three different internships in her time at CSU, and she struggled with labor market entry. She did eventually find a job in PR, the field she was targeting, but it required a lot of hard work that practical arts majors rarely put in to find their desired entry-level jobs. Importantly, Chloe's summer internship before senior year did not offer a direct pathway to permanent employment and was therefore a dead-end internship. Chloe spent that summer in London where she interned at a PR firm called Ravine Communications. Chloe found her internship through *a study abroad program organized outside of the university*, which she learned about from a friend who had done the same program. Chloe had previous work experience and was involved in communications-related extracurricular activities on campus. With her background, Chloe was confident she picked the right internship and hoped to have a great experience in England—a capstone event in her final summer of college. However, this was not the case.

Overall, Chloe did not have a good experience at Ravine Communications. She said, "I felt like I couldn't ask anyone any questions ever. 'Cause everyone was just really stressed out, and they're not necessarily the nicest there." Chloe was "off in the corner by myself . . . my second day they placed me in the corner." She was not assigned to a team in an organization that divided the full-time employees into work teams. When I asked if she felt bad about that, her response was "of course I did." In the end, Ravine Communications had no process in place to turn Chloe into a full-time employee, even if she had been interested. At the end of the summer and her studies, she had no immediate job prospects.

In clear contrast, Arthur was an industrial and systems engineering (ISE) major *recruited on campus* for a career conveyor-belt internship that automatically turned into entry-level work. Arthur interned with Downstate Oil and Gas, a division of a *Fortune* 100 company, during his junior and senior years and it was his first industry experience. He said, "They are kind of ready to start bringing in juniors and seniors and hire them full time too in the future." To find the internship, Arthur applied for every opportunity he found through engineering career services (ECS). He thought he was applying for summer internships yet ended up with a fall co-op.[1] They "do their fall recruiting for the summer and their spring recruiting for fall co-ops and I didn't realize that [because] I was just applying for everything and then when I got the offer it said for the fall." He said, "I had to miss a good amount of [football] games, but it was 100 percent worth it." For Arthur in the ISE program, opportunities abounded.

Arthur enjoyed his internship. Unlike Chloe who reported feeling excluded and said her colleagues were not nice to her, Arthur said he liked "meeting new people and learning more about the company that I'm now going to work for, learning the process, the products they offer, how this stuff is being used." Arthur reported feeling included in the organization. At the conclusion of his internship, he interviewed for a full-time position at Downstate. He said, "They do [interview] Downstate interns first and fill [open positions] with other outside interns." Arthur had secured his position with Downstate before our first interview and was still employed there during our second interview.

Chloe and Arthur's cases illustrate how the trade-off students make when choosing a major starts early, at the internship stage of the college-to-work transition. Although both students interned in industries closely linked to their majors, only Arthur was recruited at CSU through career services and had a pipeline into permanent employment that qualifies as a new organizational career. Chloe, despite being proactive about finding an internship, did not have these kinds of opportunities. While Chloe ultimately found a job that matched her interest shortly after graduation, this was not generally true of the liberal arts majors in my study.

Here, I first discuss the relationship between internships and employability. I show which students I interviewed received which type of internship. I then go into the specifics of both types and demonstrate that career conveyor-belt internships are often made available to business and engineering majors through campus recruiting, which is much less common for English and communications majors. Next, I show how career conveyor-belt internships are the only kind that lead directly to entry-level jobs, although students from both internship types want postgraduation employment. Finally, I consider some of the reasons why career conveyor-belt internships may be more available to practical arts majors than liberal arts students as a prelude to a fuller discussion of these disparities later in the book.

Taken together, the evidence presented in this chapter shows how practical arts majors usually enter the labor market more easily than liberal arts majors. Additionally, while the different internship types do not cause labor market inequality, they demonstrate how the sorting of students into disparate job types after graduation begins to unfold while they are still at college, which reinforces media narratives about the unequal "employability" of different majors.

Internship Recruitment Disparities by Major

As noted in chapter 1, we cannot ascertain how internships improve students' employability from existing research. Case studies of internships find they typically involve routine clerical work, seemingly ruling out the possibility that internships increase students' human capital and thus lead to greater employability.[2] Alternatively, using an internship as a variable in an audit study or experiment is potentially useful for thinking about the signals internships send to employers, but these studies cannot get at real-world examples of how individual internships help students move into the labor market.[3]

In reality, connections between firms and schools play an outsized role in which students find internships that lead directly to stable postgraduation employment and which students do not. Research finds that students at elite institutions are often recruited into internships that lead to jobs with prestigious employers, regardless of field of study.[4] By contrast, career services offices at non-elite universities often work as gatekeepers to limit opportunities to certain subsets of preferred students.[5] Prior research shows that this gatekeeping function tends to weed out students based on ascriptive characteristics, such as race, class, or gender.[6] At CSU, internship gatekeeping was also based on fields of study, which, as already shown, can serve as a rough proxy for student characteristics such as race, class, and gender.

The distinction between career conveyor-belt and dead-end internships began with differential access to university-affiliated recruitment. Practical arts students were recruited on campus for *career conveyor-belt internships*, meaning the employers had a process in place for the intern to interview and

■ Career Conveyor-Belt Internship   ■ Dead-End Internship

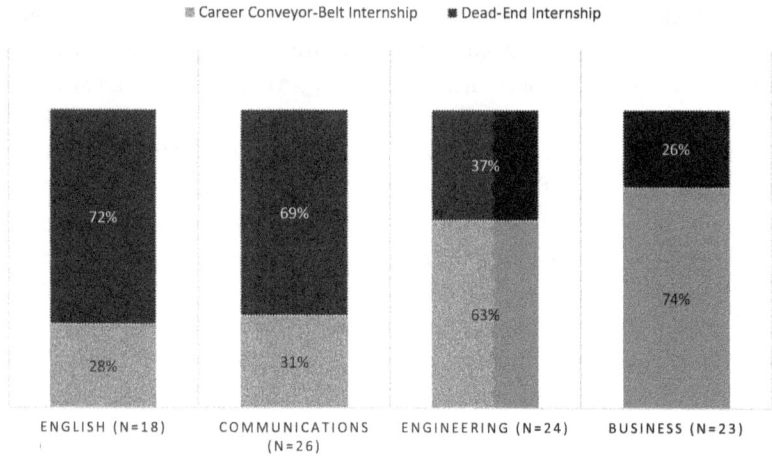

FIGURE 3.1 Internship Type by Major
Note: Full sample, *n* = 91.

perhaps be offered a permanent position. Students were usually aware of this process. Theoretically, this type of internship could be accessible to students in all fields of study, but in practice they were disproportionately available for business and engineering majors.

Of the ninety-one student respondents in my study, thirty-two ISE and business students had career conveyor-belt internships and only thirteen communications and English students had similar opportunities. The proportions reversed when I looked at students with *dead-end* internships: fifteen for ISE and business respondents and thirty-one for communications and English majors. Figure 3.1 shows the distribution of majors in internship types.

Recruitment through University-Employer Connections

Employers commonly hired students for career conveyor-belt internships by recruiting them directly from the university. Sixty-eight percent of internships that resulted in an employment opportunity were found through university connections. The most common site for recruitment was the career fair, although firms also posted openings on career services websites. Firms recruiting on campus were clustered in industries such as manufacturing, health care, or finance. They were usually large and well-established, the kinds of businesses where you would expect to find organizational careers.[7] At CSU, the career services offered to engineering and business students were closed to all other students and many employers only hired from specific majors deemed relevant to the company. As such, most career conveyor-belt internships were obtained by ISE and business students because more opportunities were directly and exclusively presented to them.

Jackie, an ISE major, had a summer internship at Syringa, one of the largest automotive companies in the world. Heavily involved in the CSU branch of the Society of Women in Engineering (SWE), Jackie was charged with setting up an SWE networking event the night before the career fair. This required inviting several of the companies participating in the fair, including Syringa. She reported, "I was just talking to the HR guy and then he just seemed to really like me. . . . The opportunity just presented itself." She even said she "never had an engineering co-op," so was surprised when they offered her the internship. Jackie was nervous to show the human resources (HR) representative her résumé because she "had a 2.9 GPA, and a lot of engineering companies like you to have a 3.0, so I was really scared to show it to him." Jackie's example is illustrative of the advantages of university-affiliated recruiting. She likely did not have the human capital best suited for the job, with a sub-3.0 GPA and no engineering work experience, yet, since Syringa attended the event she helped coordinate, she was offered an internship with an employment opportunity, and she is still working with Syringa at the time of this writing.

Operations and logistics students had similar recruitment opportunities. Like Arthur, business major Shawn ended up with a fall co-op rather than a traditional summer internship. Shawn told me about meeting representatives from a large energy company at the career fair: "I had the opportunity to speak with them at the career fair and I definitely wanted to take advantage, so I went up and they offered me an interview after speaking with one of their individuals for about twenty minutes, did a next-day interview, [. . .] did well, got a call about a week later about an opportunity to take a semester off and do [a co-op]." This example again shows how advantageous physical presence during the internship selection process is and how quickly after the career fair students might receive internship offers.

While English and communications majors in my study had fewer opportunities to access career conveyor-belt internships, some attained them by actively leveraging university-firm connections. Mort, an English major, applied for every internship on the career services website that mentioned English majors. While he noted that "It did not take me a long time because I can tell you now, there's not that many, just a handful every semester," he did secure an internship at a marketing company that offered a career conveyor-belt internship. Notably, Mort chose to forgo the opportunity for a post-internship job, opting instead to attend graduate school to become an English teacher.

Alan, a communications major, was unsure what he wanted to do professionally and attended the arts and sciences career fair. He was skeptical of unpaid internships, so he said, "[I] basically went to all of the insurance companies and banks, I figured they were big enough to have a paid internship program." The entire process was "pretty quick. Like I talked to them at the career fair, scheduled an interview for the next day and within, I want to say it was like two weeks maybe, I had gotten an offer." Alan ended up interning with Diamond Bank, a major financial institution. Thus, by going to the career fair and interning in the banking industry, Alan became one of the few liberal arts majors in this study who obtained a well-paid internship that led to permanent employment.

Students majoring in communications or English needed to decide early if they were more interested in a paid internship at a large corporation or if they wanted to wait for an internship with an employer more traditionally related to their major. Jade, a communications student, had a career conveyor-belt internship at Bluebird Health, one of the biggest health care organizations in the state. She explained, "They start the application [early]; it's due in November." When I asked if she applied to other internship sites as well, she said, "No, they want you to accept pretty early too so by the time a lot of those comm[unications] internships opened up like they were finalizing." The structure of industry labor markets and her unwillingness to wait on the possibility of a communications industry internship led Jade to accept a position with Bluebird Health. As I show in chapter 5, a similar process unfolded when communications and English students were deciding whether to accept postgraduation jobs with large corporations or hold out for something more aligned with their aspirations.

Not all students found their career conveyor-belt internships through on-campus recruitment; however, the network presented significant advantages for business and engineering students. These students were often sought after at their career fairs and could find multiple opportunities on the career services websites. As Mort demonstrated, fewer opportunities were open to English majors, even on CSU's online internship bank. Industries that recruited through the university and were open to English or communications students were more likely to be in large established sectors, like finance or health care. They hired interns early, forcing students to choose between accepting quickly or waiting to find something in a potentially more desirable, or major-related, industry. These students found internships that were technically open to many majors, perhaps making them more competitive to obtain, while business and engineering students often obtained internships restricted to their major. And while the main outcome of interest was which students attained new organizational careers, practical arts graduates also enjoyed higher rates of degree-occupation matches through the recruitment opportunities available to them.

Finding Internships through Informal Networking Activities

Most English and communications students drew on personal connections to get their internships and ended up with dead-end internships. To be sure, students found internships in other ways (i.e., online searches), but this was much less common. While companies were willing to take on an intern and sometimes rotated through interns every summer or semester, it was up to students to find and secure these positions. Students used connections including friends, family, and professors to find these opportunities. For my study, I considered professors as part of personal networks because relationships between professors and employers were not mediated through university career services nor did firms actively recruit students. Ultimately, establishing personal connections rarely helped students obtain internships with job opportunities.

Allison, a communications major, found her media internship after learning about the company from a friend's uncle, who was on the executive board at a similar organization. While this company was not actively recruiting interns from CSU, the personal connection may have helped Allison get the internship. She had tried websites like Internmatch.com and Internships.com without success and also created profiles on LinkedIn and other websites. Hardly any students in this study found internships through these kinds of websites.

Vicky, also a communications major, was not even attempting to find a summer internship. However, while attending a non-university-sponsored networking event, she was offered an opportunity to intern at a local start-up. She said, "It was kind of informal 'cause I went to one of their parties, like a winter party or a Christmas party, and it was all fun and they were like, 'you know, you are so cool, why don't you just, you should intern for us,' and I was like, 'all right.'" Vicky's case, like Allison's, demonstrates how liberal arts majors who did not use university-sponsored career services found internships through personal networking.

Practical arts students could also end up with dead-end internships when they networked outside the university. Mickey, a business major, hoped to find an internship in Fort Collins, Colorado, because he liked that city. He found a position there with Beaver Industries, a manufacturer. He said, "I applied everywhere in Fort Collins, and I ended up networking with one of the marketing directors at a logistics conference and I ended up talking with him and he helped me get my foot in the door." This independent networking event at a professional conference was not a university-affiliated career connection and led to a dead-end internship.

Marly, an engineering major, found her internship at a manufacturing company because, she said, "My mom actually works there." She returned for a second summer, saying, "Then last summer I applied to a bunch of places, but a lot of companies were really slow in getting back to me. So, I was kind of worried that I wouldn't hear back from somebody in time. So, I contacted them, and just kind of asked if I could come back and they said 'yeah.'" Eventually, Marly heard from other companies but had already committed to going back to her mother's firm. Marly's and Mickey's examples show that the networking *methods* were also important for determining internship type.

It was likely that using personal connections to find an internship led to working in firms that had either no permanent position available, no funds to pay for an additional employee, or no interest in hiring the student full time. Marly found her internship because she reached out to the company where her mother works rather than through the career fair, which is more common for engineering majors. The following year, she inquired about coming back for a second summer and they accepted her again. Yet when Marly asked about staying on as a permanent hire, she was told "they didn't have a place for" her. Marly's experience perfectly encapsulates the shortcomings of finding internships through personal connections. The firm was happy to have her intern for multiple summers and even pay her for a full-time role, but they were not prepared to offer her permanent employment.

Several students found their dead-end internships through their professors. This group is comprised mostly of English students, some communications students, and one engineering student. Some of these respondents took classes specifically designed to help students secure internships through connections professors had established with organizations. For example, Lana was an English major who interned at a publishing company magazine after taking such a class. She walked me through this process: "You meet with the coordinator of the program, and you submit application materials, and you review your application materials with her until they're perfect, and then you discuss sites and placements for your internship. You can come up with your own as long as the coordinator approves it, or she has the list of previous partners. So, I picked from the publishing section." On the positive side, the gatekeeping function of the professor usually required internship sites to give students interesting work tasks related to their major.[8] However, these students were unlikely to find career conveyor-belt internships since they were approaching organizations where employment opportunities were not necessarily built into the internship experience.

Previous studies have pointed to the success of midcareer professionals in using personal networks when looking to change jobs.[9] However, extending the concept to internships muddles the different ways network ties are used in recruitment for entry-level jobs and within or between similar labor markets. Engineering and business students without career conveyor-belt internships were more likely to find internships via personal networks. The few English and communications majors who were recruited on campus were much more likely to obtain career conveyor-belt internships. This finding indicates that internship procurement via university-firm recruitment and personal networks, respectively, contribute to inequality in accessing internships that offer employment opportunities both between—and within— the four fields of study.

Disparities in Employment Offers from Internship Sites by Major

There is an intention and a process through which internships may become employment opportunities. I begin with examples of career conveyor-belt internships. Business and engineering students expected their internships to lead directly to entry-level jobs for good reasons. Practical arts students in career conveyor-belt internships were quite aware of the firm's process for turning interns into employees, which usually meant all the interns applied for positions. Although it is possible that employers used internships for what sociologists James Rosenbaum and Amy Binder call "on-the-job screening,"[10] most students in career conveyor-belt internships knew this was happening and most received job offers. Also, because of precedent and institutional knowledge within programs, students, professors, and career services workers in the colleges of business and engineering knew which firms came to campus and recruited students for internships that lead to jobs.

Many students who obtained dead-end internships also wanted their internships to become jobs. These students, mostly communications and English majors, were disappointed: Their companies did not have a process set up for this and rarely offered employment opportunities.

How Internships Become Employment Opportunities

Arne studied logistics and had a career conveyor-belt internship with a snack company. When his internship ended, he was offered and accepted an entry-level job with the firm. Arne was assigned a few large projects, and at the end of the summer he gave a final presentation on the work he completed. According to Arne, these intern presentations formed the basis of any job offers that would be forthcoming (although, of course, interns may be continually evaluated during the internship). Arne told me, "We had the last presentation for thirty interns for the supply chain. . . . Most of the decisions are transparent; they ranked each of us. I believe everyone got an offer. Once I went through, a week later, HR called us, and we got the offer and we got the email. And we have about two weeks to accept the offer." This was a common process: there was an evaluation, then HR contacted interns to set up formal interviews or present job offers, which students accepted or declined.

Jackie, the ISE student mentioned earlier, got her offer in the middle of her internship. She said, "They made me an offer in June, but they didn't really finalize the paperwork until August." Jackie told me one of her friends "actually went up to Syringa at the career fair, and [Syringa] said that they hire like 80 percent of [their new hires from] their interns." Clearly, internships are an important point in the stratification process that begins at college even within majors that leverage career conveyor-belt internships.

The career conveyor-belt metaphor is particularly apt because, for many business and engineering majors, the process from studies to internship to employment seems automatic. Jackie received an employment opportunity after just a few weeks at her internship, and Arne told me, "I believe everyone got an offer." Arne framed this widespread hiring of interns as a negative, saying, "I want to be more special." Stephen, another engineering major, also received a job offer from his internship. When I asked him about the other interns he said, "The ones I kept in contact with, all of them except the international students [got offers]. So, I'd say about 90 percent of them." With these high rates, these internships clearly offered conveyor belts directly into employment. This shows that labor market factors sorted these students in ways that may or may not be related to sufficient human capital (skill) acquisition in college.

The few communications and English majors with career conveyor-belt internships had similar experiences in terms of process. Alan, the communications major who interned at Diamond Bank, one of the largest financial institutions in the world, acquired his internship through a university connection—the career fair. At the end of his summer internship, the bank hired him for a full-time position that started the following May, an offer he also had to accept quite quickly. Interestingly, his job offer was not for a certain department or position. He said, "They're not going to tell me anything until closer to the actual start date. And, yeah, so it's, they keep things very close, they keep their cards close to their chest." Alan's experience points to an important phenomenon we see across career conveyor-belt internships. Since large organizations hire many interns for full-time work after graduation, they often extend vague offers and then place graduates into positions or departments closer to the start of their employment. Hired interns could end up in a different department doing very different work from what their internship entailed. This was the case even for some engineering students and is further evidence that degree-specific human capital likely did not have a key role in the hiring process.

The main difference for communications and English majors who found employment through career conveyor-belt internships: The work rarely matched their degrees. Communications student Jade, who interned at Bluebird Health, demonstrates how sometimes career conveyor-belt internships offered to liberal arts students did not match their professional aspirations. She said, "I'm going back to Bluebird but I'm not going into communications; I'm going into pharmaceutical sales and that's not like something I was like, 'I want to grow up and do pharmacy sales.'" She explained, "A lot of PR jobs don't even open until February so you know by that [time] the opportunity would have completely passed, and it was one of those [things] I did struggle with." Like engineering and business majors, liberal arts students wanted stable employment opportunities, but opportunities were unusual in their preferred sectors and occupations, forcing some interns into tough decisions.

For some English majors with career conveyor-belt internships, the subsequent employment consists of contract work, not a permanent position. There was no equivalent experience among the business and engineering interns. Genna, an English major, interned at a small media firm, which she found through a personal connection. Despite its small size, the firm tried to replicate the conveyor belt–style internship-to-job process of larger organizations. Genna said of her employer, "They were so impressed with the work that I've been doing during my internship they were like . . . we can offer you a three-month contract where you would be getting paid. So, I decided to take the contract." Other English majors with career conveyor-belt internships also found themselves doing contract work immediately after the internship and before a permanent job offer arose. During her wave two interview, Genna said, "[the firm] ended up keeping me on after my contractor position was up." She continued to work full time for the media company but in a permanent position. This shows that, while communications and English majors sometimes gained entry to the career conveyor-belt process, it was not as seamless, and the possibility of permanent employment was less assured than for engineering and business graduates.

Genna's example highlights just one of the three ways communications and English majors with career conveyor-belt internships were still disadvantaged compared to their practical arts peers. The two other ways include: (1) liberal arts-accessible internships clustered in sectors outside of their fields of study, and (2) liberal arts students nearly always compete with a broader pool of applicants for internships, which were commonly open to students from all disciplines.

It is important to note that some students with career conveyor-belt internships decided to eschew the employment opportunities presented by the firms. From among the respondents in my study, four turned down job offers. Roberta, an ISE student who counted discarded shampoo bottles at her manufacturing internship, said she struggled over doing such menial work, so she turned down the job offered to her. She told me, "I don't want to go into a job where I have a feeling of dread when I accept it and I'm not excited to accept it." Overall, she said of the internship, "I don't really look back with too fond memories." Although Roberta did not like her internship and even failed to get along well with her boss, she nevertheless received a job offer. In the next chapter, I discuss in greater depth how the tasks assigned to interns could affect whether they decided to accept a job offer but did not seem related to whether the internship had processes in place for turning interns into employees.

The organization at which business student Thomas interned also offered a pathway for employment through their program, but, like Roberta, Thomas decided he did not want to pursue the opportunity. He said, "I realized I didn't want to work for the company, right off the bat, and they offered a track where if you did really good, they might offer you [a position,] but then [by] week three or four, I realized I did not want to work for this company. And so that kind of just like killed my attitude of like 'Let's be the best employee we can be.'" Thomas had an unrewarding experience and chose not to pursue a potential job opportunity although he was aware that path was open to him.

In sum, firms with career conveyor-belt internships often actively recruited students at the career fair or on the career services websites at CSU. And though these firms ostensibly evaluated students based on their performances, they often extended employment offers to interns en masse—without apparent regard to any individual's human capital.

Career conveyor-belt internships tend to be clustered in the manufacturing, health care, and financial sectors and these industries are more likely to hire business and engineering interns than liberal arts graduates. As a result, the labor markets to which liberal arts students gain entry via career conveyor-belt internships are unlikely to match their degrees. The conveyor-belt internship open to communications major Jade was in pharmaceutical sales, whereas the conveyor-belt internships open to Arne, Stephen, and Jackie matched their practical arts majors. When career conveyor-belt internships did match liberal arts degrees, as was the case for Genna, they could lead to precarious contract work. This shows that career conveyor-belt internships were an essential component in the process through which practical arts majors ended up in new organizational careers often matched to their majors at higher rates than liberal arts majors.

Internships as Short-Term "Employment"

Sociologist Alexandre Frenette calls interns "provisional labor," crediting their short-term nature for their negative outcomes.[11] However, as we have seen above, in many industries and organizations, internships were not short-term employment, but rather a strategy for recruiting future employees. Many of the students I spoke to who had dead-end internships wanted to stay with their internship firm after graduation but could not.

Mickey, the business student who interned for a manufacturing firm he found through networking unrelated to the university's career services, struggled with this situation. The firm did not provide a career conveyor belt, yet Mickey "thought it would really help me get a job." It did not. Mickey's case further confirmed that the seamless college-to-work transitions typically associated with the labor market trajectories of professional students starts with the established relationships and pathways to employment through university connections to which practical arts students had unique access.

The majority of students with dead-end internships studied English or communications. These students were often at least as career-oriented as their practical arts counterparts. Gloria, a dual English and communications major, interned at a marketing company. Although this position was unpaid, Gloria built up the courage to ask if they could move her into a part-time position. The firm said yes, but Gloria told me, "When I walked in, I was placed in an intern desk, I wasn't given paperwork to fill out, so it was just kind of like I knew I wasn't getting paid." Gloria eventually had to quit because she could no longer afford an unpaid internship. While Gloria interned for a marketing company, her experience was like those who had more "stereotypical" English major internships. Christy, who interned at a local theater company, and Marne, a library intern, also had dead-end internships. In both cases, they knew their internships would not offer career conveyor belts. Rather, they went into the internships aiming to learn more about an interesting field where, if they were serious about it, would require sustained postgraduation effort to enter. Marne decided to take that path; Christy did not.

It was not common among the English and communications majors I interviewed for their internships to turn into jobs, even when the students interned in fields matched to their professional interests. Lana, an English major, wrote magazine articles for a publishing company at her internship, which did not offer an employment opportunity. Yet when I asked if she wanted to stay in publishing, she said, "Yes, in the near future, I hope to be in publishing, and I think I will be." She added, "That is my strongest interest right now." Despite working in publishing and wanting to stay in publishing, no pathway to employment was offered through her internship.

Communications majors occupied a unique space in this study, as communications is a social science that hews more closely to professional degrees than many other liberal arts disciplines. As such, communications students interned in industries matched to their degree more frequently than English majors. Yet even firms in industries tightly matched to communications degrees rarely offered employment opportunities through internships. For instance, Allison interned at TV Brothers, a well-known media firm. She hoped to apply for a position with them but told me, "No one was offered a job. But they said if I apply to TV Brothers, let them know as soon as possible." Clearly, this company did not have a career conveyor-belt process in place, a situation that was framed as a sector or industry issue by June, also a communications major: "Communications jobs, they don't hire, like I have a bunch of engineering friends, and they all have jobs and stuff, and that's great, but communications, they don't do that, and I talked to other majors, and they don't realize it, they're like, 'Why don't you have a job lined up?' And you're like, 'Ahh, I don't suck!' But yeah, most communications jobs, they don't hire you until a month or a few weeks before they want you to actually start." June expressed how the lack of organization in her major-related labor market frustrated her and was a source of stress; business and engineering students did not have to grapple with the same issue. The lack of organized labor markets also inhibits degree matching. Recall Jade, the communications major with a career conveyor-belt internship who had to accept a position in pharmaceutical sales. The timing and process of hiring created a large source of inter-major inequality in terms of finding a job that places students in a new organizational career right after college, and also with regard to attaining work that matches their degrees.

Career Conveyor-Belt Internships and Practical Arts Majors' Employment Advantages

In this chapter, I showed how the labor market trade-off I expose between majors starts early, while students are still in school and seeking internships. Students, usually liberal arts majors, who leveraged personal networks to find internships rarely received job opportunities, yet most students hoped to parlay their internships into permanent employment. Students who were recruited on campus, on the other hand, were mostly practical arts majors and often had access to career conveyor-belt internships. This uncovers the process through which many practical arts majors come to enjoy new organizational careers, which is in line with media narratives highlighting their superior initial labor market outcomes over liberal arts students by most employment measures.

Examining career conveyor-belt internships also helps expose some of the gender inequality inherent in degree-field segregation because in the practical arts, where men are overrepresented, students accessed career conveyor-belt internships at greater rates than students in the two women-dominated disciplines. However, race was less salient as 76 percent of respondents in my study with job opportunities were White, perfectly mirroring the overall sample of students. This is to say that, yes, White students are overrepresented in these fields and at the university, but they were not disproportionately likely to receive a job opportunity once interning. Ultimately, the differential access to career conveyor-belt internships by major has implications for racial and gender inequality in the labor market because of the demographic makeup of each major, both in my study and nationally.

There did not appear to be patterned differences in access to career conveyor-belt internships by social class background. Of course, I only interviewed students with internships, with the result that any students from low-SES backgrounds who could not find an internship were not included in this study.[12] Nonetheless, among the students I interviewed, social class did not seem to predict which students received career conveyor-belt internships and which did not. This was the case even among practical arts majors, which further illustrates the seemingly automatic processes captured by the conveyor-belt metaphor.

Hiring sector and firm size played a large role in student access to career conveyor-belt internships. However, sectors that recruit for internships clearly do so with cultural assumptions about fields of study. While engineering and business students tended to intern in larger, more profitable firms that matched their degrees, we can imagine career conveyor-belt internships in industries of interest to liberal arts majors and dominated by large employers like media, entertainment, advertising and marketing, telecommunications, or education, all sectors well represented in the *Fortune* 500. Of course, students at CSU were somewhat constrained by geography. Liberal arts students at colleges in Chicago or New York may have more access to internships with large publishing companies, for instance, which may incorporate career conveyor-belt internships. Moving to these cities to pursue an internship was not an option for many CSU liberal arts majors. Business and engineering students, on the other hand, were able to intern all over the country, in places like Jacksonville or Dallas, for example. These opportunities were full time and paid, which likely contributed to these students' ability to relocate for an internship or co-op. For liberal arts majors, opportunities for paid internships at large profitable firms were generally confined to the local labor market, usually in health care or financial services. This situation means that English and communications students who did have access to career conveyor-belt internships were limited to industries that did not match their degrees, and they were also competing with a large pool of students from other disciplines, which further suggests students from liberal arts majors are seen as somewhat interchangeable.[13] If this is indeed the case, an argument could be made that *liberal arts skills* are, in fact, in demand in the labor market and any college graduate, regardless of major, is eminently employable.

The connections between firms and the university created distinct advantages for ISE and business majors. Companies annually attended the career fair or posted on the department-specific career services websites and used internships as a pipeline for permanent hires. These networks proved more fruitful than personal connections and were only available to certain students, which contradicts accounts about elite universities where personal networks may be beneficial and it seems all students can take advantage of university-firm ties.[14] The data presented in this chapter also helps discount one potential alternative explanation to unequal labor market entry by field of study: Communications and English majors were not less career-oriented than business and engineering students.

Next, I discuss how students in this study used the content of their degrees at internships. I did not find evidence to support the stereotypes that practical arts graduates have "hard" skills and liberal arts graduates have "soft" skills, a key component of media narratives that cannot be extricated from degree fields' gender makeups.[15]

4: WORK TASKS AND CAREER CONVEYOR-BELT INTERNSHIPS

Chloe and Arthur, discussed in the opening of chapter 3, studied communications and industrial and systems engineering (ISE), respectively. Chloe, an upper-middle-class White woman interned in the PR industry, and Arthur, an upper-middle-class Asian American man, interned in manufacturing. Chloe was no less driven or career-oriented than Arthur, yet she had a dead-end internship while he had a career conveyor-belt internship with a firm he targeted for permanent employment. The previous chapter established that the differences in internship type were likely due to the students' majors and how they found the internships. Yet, internship task disparities could still potentially explain who obtained a career conveyor-belt internship and who did not.

In this chapter, I show that the proportion of students using their skills at internships was largely similar across all majors. Business and engineering students were thus not recruited on campus at higher rates for internships because employers required their major-specific skill set for these positions. This demonstrates that internship work tasks had no bearing on the type of internship students obtained and this fact undermines media narratives that practical arts majors are more desirable to employers, even for internships, because practical arts skills are in demand in ways liberal arts skills are not.

Neither Chloe nor Arthur used their major-specific skills at their internships. Chloe's internship, at Ravine Communications in London, involved a lot of what she called "random tasks." She would do "rippings, where you go into the big news conference room, and we would all just rip through all daily traditional print papers. Just looking to see if we had client-relevant news." When a client received media attention she had to "scan and compile into a folder," those mentions. She also "ran all over the city," doing chores such as delivering flowers to a client. She said, "If you could envision *Devil Wears Prada*, it's kind of like that." When I asked her if any of her tasks required skills she had learned in the classroom, she responded "not consciously." I confirmed this assessment by matching her internship tasks to the communications curriculum at CSU (derived from student reports of their classroom learning).[1] Chloe's situation is indicative of communications majors in this study, who, even when interning in a firm closely matching their degree, could end up completing mostly clerical tasks.

Arthur, like Chloe, did not use his degree skills in his internship at Downstate, the manufacturing conglomerate. He was assigned to a plant that had recently opened in Jacksonville, Florida. The company was moving manufacturing processes into the facility, and Arthur's team helped set up the assembly lines to make the plant operational. He said, "I got tasked with basically ordering anything that the shop floor guys were needing for builds and anything, like we ordered a bunch of different materials throughout the summer . . . just putting in orders in online [systems]." He would also sometimes meet the vendor representatives who "come in two days a week and see what was depleted, and then they would go and bring that stuff back." Besides ordering materials for the new assembly lines, "things were being moved around all the time so just like some of the general clean ups and like safety hazards were also on my plate." When I asked for further clarification, Arthur expanded, "They had this temporary paint booth that was not very safe and we [Arthur and the other intern] were over there a lot just cleaning it up, helping those guys out." He also said, "We actually did a little bit of manual labor putting some stuff together, some racks, putting parts on the binds, counting pieces." This last task was building shelving racks for the assembly lines.

Arthur mainly learned how to be a "working professional" at this internship, saying "once you figure out how to enter [orders] in through Downstate's workflow [program] and how to order something then it's kind of like a piece of cake." His job was neither difficult nor technical, and yet he told me that the company only hired ISE students. Though Arthur maintained that a non-engineer would struggle to learn how to order the various parts, this assertion seemed suspect because he responded in a hesitant and uncomfortable manner.

Not all interns did nonspecialized work or manual labor; many students had "substantive work tasks," which I conceptualize as related to skills students learned in their degrees. I counted clerical work, such as data entry or filing, as nonsubstantive. If interns did any relevant work, such as an engineering major doing statistics or an English major performing professional writing, I considered it a substantive task internship—a conservative measure.[2] There were no instances of interns doing substantive tasks without engaging their degree-specific skills. This makes sense considering that, when students were interning in a chosen field and given an assignment, they relied on their degree knowledge to complete the steps for which there were not specific instructions, as would be the case for clerical tasks. This will become clearer as I delve into what interns did at work.

In this chapter, I demonstrate internship task parity between majors. First, I give an overview of the relationship between task type and internship type. Then I show the substantive work students from all majors and internship types completed before concluding with the internship tasks for those who did exclusively clerical work.

Internship Task Parity between Majors

Much public and academic discourse tends to be critical of internships as short-term, precarious, and exploitative.[3] The few studies on the tasks that interns complete often find students engaging in clerical work and becoming disillusioned.[4] However, prior research on internships focuses almost exclusively on the nonprofit or aesthetic fields.[5] The rare exception is scholars who study one industry in-depth (e.g., marketing students and marketing internships).[6] In this book, to fully show how the trade-off between majors unfolds, I include internships across a range of industries and majors that are more representative of the kinds of internships most students have. To understand the relationship between skill use and career conveyor-belt internships, I investigated what interns do at work.[7] This follows a long tradition of sociologists who believe the only way to uncover what workers do is to examine them closely rather than rely on surveys or talk to employers.[8]

Students in all four majors secured internships that assigned them substantive work tasks. English and communications students were slightly more likely to do substantive work than business and engineering majors. About 55 percent of participants were assigned substantive tasks, which is similar to economist John Robst's finding that 54.8 percent of the US population report "their work and field of study are closely related."[9] These numbers are not necessarily representative of the general population, but we see there are not large differences between majors (although less than 50 percent of business majors were found to complete substantive tasks; this rate was over 50 percent for the other three majors). In general, the strongest indicator of substantive work was whether interns were assigned a project rather than a series of ad hoc tasks. I noted that such projects usually took the form of an internship-length assignment that was assigned at the beginning of the term, and it was therefore unlikely that a supervisor would decide to assign one based on the individual quality of the intern. Table 4.1 compares substantive versus clerical tasks by major. Table 4.2 confirms there is no relationship between substantive task assignment and career conveyor-belt internships.

TABLE 4.1 Internship Tasks by Major

	ISE	Business	Communications	English	Total
N	24	23	26	18	91
Tasks (%)					
Substantive	63	44	54	61	55
Clerical	37	56	46	39	45

TABLE 4.2 Internship Tasks by Major and Internship Type

	CCB internship	CCB clerical	CCB substantive	DE internship	DE clerical	DE substantive
ISE/business (*n* = 47)	68	40	28	32	19	13
Communications/ English (*n* = 44)	30	14	16	70	41	30
Total sample (*n* = 91)	49	21	28	51	24	26

Notes: CCB = career conveyor-belt; DE = dead-end. All counts listed are percentages. Some do not add up to 100 due to rounding.

Internship Projects and Substantive Work

Labor sociologists tend to view jobs, rather than people, as skilled or un-skilled.[10] Jobs require high levels of skill if they contain task complexity and high levels of autonomy, discretion, and responsibility.[11] With these attributes in mind, I determined that having a large project assigned to them was the best indicator for which interns used their degree skills. Projects were likely to be complex and autonomous rather than continuous tasks like the "rippings" Chloe conducted, which could be monotonous. Students from all majors completed substantive tasks at comparable rates, which further undermines the distinction between "practical" and "passion" majors that media narratives perpetuate.

Substantive Tasks for ISE and Business Interns

Stephen, an ISE major, had a career conveyor-belt internship at engine manufacturer Caraway, Inc., a *Fortune* 500 company headquartered in a state neighboring CSU. Stephen worked in the corporate quality department. His assignment provides a good example of an internship project; he was tasked with writing a report to determine how many quality engineers the firm should hire in emerging markets. This project required Stephen "to determine the drivers behind those staffing factors, to show how many people they should actually hire." Having an internship project was also a significant factor for why Stephen thought he had a positive internship experience; he said, "I had had two internships previous to Caraway, three actually, and all of them were rewarding in their own way but it never really had like a final project or a big deliverable at the end of it. So, I didn't really have an 'I made this impact with the company.'" His wording, "in their own way," implied that previous internships did not live up to his expectations. I asked, "And you really wanted to have that sort of experience?" To which Stephen replied, "Yes, I wanted to be able to say, 'I accomplished this.'"

To complete internship projects, interns leveraged their classroom skills. After all, to complete a big project in a field related to their major, classroom learning comprised students' primary source of knowledge on which to draw. Stephen continued, "I was able to use a lot of the statistical knowledge I learned [in class], a lot of the Lean Six Sigma skills and tool sets I learned in class, I really got to apply." When asked if another major would struggle to use those tools he said, "100 percent yes, if I had been mechanical [engineering], if I had been any other engineer, it would not have worked out." In contrast to Arthur, the ISE major who hesitantly claimed that he needed his degree to do his internship, Stephen pointed out specific processes, tools, and concepts from his ISE major he applied to his internship at Caraway.

The business students, all operations and logistics majors, had similar experiences to their ISE peers. Stacie was a business major with a career conveyor-belt internship at a firm called Moorhead Specialties, a manufacturer of diesel additives. Stacie had a large internship project to conduct "market research to determine which countries were potentially the best ones to get into." Her company concluded that Mexico would be a good market for expansion, and Stacie was given the opportunity to implement parts of the expansion strategy. This included constructing a new marketing campaign. Stacie said, "I created billboards for them to use in Mexico. . . . I also revamped the product labels. . . . I helped their web guy build the new website. . . . I helped them with Google AdWords later on, which was directing traffic to their website." All these tasks related to launching Moorhead's products in Mexico, so it was a cohesive project. When asked explicitly if this related to her major, she said, "I would say that I was the operations manager of their international effort, so I do think so." In fact, the internship related directly to an exporting course; Stacie reported that, if she had not taken that class, she would not have been well-prepared for her internship project.

Some business and engineering students had dead-end internships. When these students had substantive tasks, the content looked similar to that of students with career conveyor-belt internships. Adam sat for one of my earlier interviews in November of 2015. He had struggled to choose between business or engineering, but ultimately declared an engineering major. Adam interned at a medical device company in the state's largest metropolitan area. He worked as a quality engineer. Adam said the size of the company gave him opportunities to experience multiple areas of quality; he worked on the factory floor, with the state regulators, and with suppliers. He helped the quality engineering team prepare for a state audit that was coming up. This required leveraging his degree skills, he said, "I've taken a quality engineering class, last spring, and some of those concepts were definitely applicable." He used a program called Minitab at work, which he trained on in school. However, unlike many of his engineering counterparts, this small medical device company did not offer employment after its internship program.

Mickey, the business student who ended up with a dead-end internship in his preferred location in Colorado, was fortunate enough to have substantive tasks as an intern. Mickey interned in the distribution center of a manufacturer and had two "continuous improvement projects" that required him to draw on his logistics degree skills. First, he created a standard operation procedure for one of the jobs. To do this, Mickey said, "I analyzed how they were doing their jobs and all five of them were doing it slightly differently, and we came up with a standard operation procedure in writing." He also worked to cut down the number of databases used for outbound tracking. For his second big project, Mickey created the company's first supply balance scorecard. He did this by pulling information from all the different suppliers to hold them accountable. In conjunction with the managers at the distribution center, Mickey helped figure out how much weight should be applied to each data point, he analyzed the data, and he created the scorecards.

Ultimately, these four practical arts students, were given similarly technical tasks that drew on their degree skills, irrespective of whether they obtained career conveyor-belt or dead-end internships.

Substantive Internship Tasks for English and Communications Interns

Approximately half of the English majors who obtained career conveyor-belt internships used classroom skills as interns. Katie was unsure of what she would gain from an internship as an English major, saying, "I go, 'What does an English major do as an intern? Am I the coffee fetcher?' I didn't want to be that." Katie's initial expectations matched popular narratives about her abilities and internship prospects for English majors. However, she went on to say, "I was wrong. I was really wrong."

Katie's internship was with a retailer called Alpine Ski and Board. Her responsibilities included putting inventory onto the company's website from a spreadsheet of product specifications. This ended up being a substantive project; in addition to writing the descriptions from scratch, she had to "enter all of [the] keywords for SEO [search engine optimization], you enter the links, you enter the size specs, you enter the dimensions for the packages, you enter the photos, you write the descriptions. Meta-tagging. Everything. Everything. And once I was knowledgeable on that, it was, that was toward the end of the summer. We had a fully functioning site." Katie went on to say, "You have information you need to convey but it's up to you how to convey it. You get to put your own voice and your own spin on things. . . . I really like that aspect of it." Beyond her English classes that focused on writing mechanics or the study of composition and literature, Katie also reported that, in her professional writing cultures class, "we did an entire segment in class on how to blog for a company. . . . We did a whole segment in the class about content writing and how to do that properly." While professional writing cultures may not seem like a typical English course, Katie received specific training that facilitated her success at Alpine. While English curriculum at elite institutions may focus exclusively on literature and creative writing, English students at less prestigious schools also learn more "practical" skills like professional writing.[12] In Katie's case, an example of that is writing blogs and other corporate content. Katie's intern project clearly related to her English major skills.

English students who obtained career conveyor-belt internships for which they completed substantive tasks contradict media narratives about which majors teach occupationally relevant skills, so it is worth covering another example in-depth. Mort, like Katie, changed his mind about English majors after his internship. Both students initially held stereotyped views of how relevant English majors' skills would be for internships and jobs; recall from chapter 1 that Mort initially feared he would get an English degree and end up unemployed. Yet by the time we spoke during his senior year, he said, "I don't [have that fear] anymore. I did. I don't have that misconception anymore, it is a misconception. . . . If you really want to use your degree and be employed, you totally can." Many English majors in this study, like Katie and Mort, were easily able to articulate how specific skills or concepts from class related to their internships.

Mort's internship with a marketing firm required a lot of writing, mostly for corporate blogs. He said, "You do a lot of writing in an English degree, they had a pretty high threshold for the kind of writing you were expected to do." He went on to say, "I worked hard during my degree to become a really strong writer." Mort even said, "I don't imagine that a psych or a business major would have been as well suited for the job as I was." From the experience, he recognized that he had acquired occupationally relevant skills not taught in every other discipline.

Both of these cases were atypical because the internships offered employment opportunities; however, Mort and Katie were typical for liberal arts majors with career conveyor-belt internship in that their internships did not match their degrees even when their work required their major-specific skills. Katie worked in the web and tech support office of a retailer and Mort was a marketing intern. These positions would not qualify as degree-to-internship matches based on survey data alone.

Alonna, a communications major, was one of few students who had a career conveyor-belt internship in PR. One of her assignments was to write and edit articles for a client and then pitch them to magazines. Alonna also had to build relationships with media personnel, go to media events, and find an audience for their clients. She connected this to her communications skills, telling me she had learned a theory whereby persuasive communication involves getting someone to like what you tell them just a little bit—you do not need them to buy in completely. Alonna told me how she applied this at her internship: "We had come up with this idea and [the client] didn't like it but we had to, of course, rework it for them. We kept the things they did like so they could like it a little more. I feel like I said 'like' a lot, but basically this theory we learned in class, I was able to apply in my internship and kind of basic-level communications skills, theories, casework examples from class, all came up in my internship." Alonna's case is a clear example of substantive work relating to classroom skills, which she applied to her internship tasks.

But most English and communications majors had dead-end internships, even among those who did substantive work. Laura, an English major, had a dead-end internship at a small nonprofit. With only around ten employees and many interns, it is not surprising they lacked employment opportunities and relied on interns to complete many essential functions of the organization. On the first day, the director gave Laura a choice of three or four projects to work on. She decided to write the organization's newsletter and worked with the PR director to plan articles. She interviewed people, put together a newsletter template, and wrote the articles. Laura and I both assessed that her project closely matched her degree. She said, "I was writing and editing and doing interviews so I would say [the internship] relates pretty directly to what I was doing in the classroom."

Communications majors Allison and Mitchell also had substantive tasks in their dead-end internships. Allison had a project-based internship at TV Brothers, a large media company. Her primary responsibility was monitoring commercials for a list of clients advertising on television. She also had the opportunity to create a new client proposal. These projects related to her major and she said it was overall "really positive . . . I feel it was just a great learning experience." She said she "learned in the classroom a lot of aspects" of what she used to complete her project. For Allison, it was easy to see the connection between her chosen major and internship tasks.

Mitchell interned with an entertainment company. When I asked if this related to his major, he said, "Yes, my major is media communications and technology, and I've done a lot of classes in web design, and photography and video, and learning what I did at that internship, I was able to relate directly back to the classes that I was taking. Persuasive comm[unications]. I learned about persuading people, I would put that into clientele management, so put that to writing emails to clients and bosses and it was, I want to say the stuff that I learned was direct[ly] on par." Notice Mitchell mentioned the relevance of his persuasive communications course. Like Alonna, Mitchell related communications theory to effective workplace practices and emphasized this more than applied skills such as video editing.

Overall, most English or communications majors obtained dead-end internships, 58 percent of whom (eighteen out of thirty-one) demonstrated their ability to do substantive tasks in a professional workplace. Clearly, they were not denied career conveyor-belt internships due to lack of skills training.

While the majors may differ on the spectrum of most to least technical, students from all majors used their degree-learned skills to complete substantive tasks at their internships. For business and engineering students like Stephen and Stacie, substantive work involved research reports that included strategy implementation. For English students like Mort, Katie, and Laura, substantive work emphasized writing of one type or another. Communications majors relied on specific skills or strategies they had learned in class and applied them at work. This data counters the idea that practical arts majors are most likely to apply degree-specific skills at work and that this is why specifically these students are more likely to obtain career conveyor-belt internships.

Clerical Work at Internships

I now turn to the more than 40 percent of students I interviewed who were assigned clerical work during their internships. Key definitional components of clerical work include sorting and filing, recordkeeping, answering phones/interacting with customers, managing communication, and other similar tasks. Considering these tasks as clerical fit technical and lay definitions of the term.[13] The main difference between clerical and administrative work is that the former involves repetitive tasks, and the latter involves decision-making.[14] Because clerical work is both repetitive and does not require skills gained in college, interns often found this kind of work disappointing and developed a negative impression of the internship. This was especially the case if the internship did not offer employment opportunities. As in the previous section, I begin with business and engineering students before turning to English and communications majors.

Practical Arts Majors Completing Clerical Tasks at Internships

Readers might expect that, out of all majors, engineering students would engage their learned skills the most at their internships. However, like all the other students in this study, approximately 40 percent of ISE majors had clerical internships, including those who obtained career conveyor-belt internships. Marc, an ISE respondent with a career conveyor-belt internship at a consulting firm, said that he did "a lot of just sitting in meetings, taking notes, and they have their own internal like Google Docs thing and [I] just updated [it], making sure everything was there." These were clerical tasks unrelated to Marc's training as an engineer. When I asked him if he learned anything at his internship he said, "Not necessarily through, like, work, on a daily basis."

Roberta, another engineering major with a career conveyor-belt internship, worked in the packaging department of a cosmetics company. Her main responsibility was tracking how many bottles of shampoo were wasted. She explained:

ROBERTA: I was able to get their production plans of how many bottles they produced on each line, so then we would see how many bottles they threw away and then divided that by how many they actually produced, this was in decimal form, so you could see like, this is how many.
CMP: And you would keep track with, like, a spreadsheet?
ROBERTA: Yes, and then every week I would send an update email to our team.

While Roberta had to do some math, this was not a technical task that required an engineering background. Roberta also had to account for the defective bottles, but this did not require meaningful investigation; she asked the operators (assembly-line workers) to account for why bottles were thrown out. When asked if another major could have done her job, at first, she said if someone's major were "anything technical, I think you would have been OK doing it." I then followed-up by asking if she thinks a philosophy major could have done her job, to which she responded, "I think you could have, it would've just taken longer, maybe." Notice she qualified her reaction by saying "maybe" at the end, to suggest she may not have believed herself when she told me another student would have taken longer to accomplish the tasks.

Business students with career conveyor-belt internships were likewise not immune from clerical tasks. Clark interned at a manufacturing facility, where he had to standardize documents and write employee profiles. He called these tasks "busy work" saying they were "projects I hated." Thomas, another business major, was asked to work on a collaborative internship project with the other interns. He called this "a total waste of time," saying the work "was really boring for me," and was not "like a full-time job." Burt, also a business major interning with an automotive company, told me his job was "coordinating information between different buyers." I asked him to tell me exactly what this entailed. In practice, Burt received information from individuals and put them in an Excel column. He said of the experience, "I don't think it was challenging." These and other business majors were asked to perform clerical work that any student could accomplish, yet the business major reputation remains above others and many, including Clark, Thomas, and Burt, obtained career conveyor-belt internships with the prospect of permanent employment.

Engineers with dead-end internships could also have clerical assignments. Marly, the engineering major who was mentioned along with Mickey in chapter 3, found her internship at a manufacturing firm where her mother worked. Marly and Mickey both had dead-end internships in fields matched to their interests, but Mickey had a substantive assignment and Marly did not—further evidence that task assignment is not related to type of internship. Marly's main task was asking workers if their jobs matched the current standard operating procedure. Theoretically, this could relate to the data analysis or workflow process optimization parts of the engineering curriculum, but when I asked if her job required data collection or analysis, Marly said, "Not really because it was just subjective stuff. It was just asking them [the workers]." Marly did say her internship related to her major because it dealt with manufacturing processes and she drew on some of her soft skills, but her work tasks did not require her degree-specific skills. Moreover, the monotonous and nondiscretionary task of asking workers if they followed the standard operating procedure fits the definition of clerical work. Marly, Marc, and Roberta all majored in the most technical field in this study and acquired paid internships at large profitable companies, yet none of them were asked to do work that required their technical skills.

Frank, a business major, had a dead-end and clerical internship connected to a study abroad experience. Frank interned in Germany at a company called Josef Security, which makes monitors that track the conditions inside shipping containers. Frank was paid for his internship; however, there were no employment opportunities and Josef Security assigned him menial and manual work tasks. He performed troubleshooting with faulty devices and helped reorganize shelving in the warehouse, which he called "basically cleaning up the office." In fact, Frank wanted to do a market analysis as part of his internship, so he could challenge himself beyond the assigned tasks. He planned to collaborate on this project with the other intern but, he said, "We were asked not to do that during work hours." *Josef Security did not want him using his business major skills during work time.* When I asked Frank if his internship duties were connected to his business major classes, he said, "I actually haven't been in a situation where I've had to use any of that."

Another business major, Roger, like Frank had a dead-end internship. He had chosen to major in logistics because it sounded interesting, not because he had a career plan. When we spoke in November 2015, Roger was interning at a sports store. When I asked if this was related to his major, he said "no, not at all." Then he took a moment to step back and figure out ways it was related. I found it noteworthy that Roger said, "If I was to do college over again, I'd probably major in a skill." When asked what he meant by that he said, "Spanish, like a language that's useful . . . English, learn how to write. Learn a skill." He said, "I would rather spend my time learning something that I know I could use rather than I don't know if I'm going to use." Roger viewed English as a more practical and usable skill than business, which stands counter to media narratives about the practicality of business as a major.

Liberal Arts Majors Completing Clerical Tasks at Internships

Greta, the English major who wanted to work in publishing and practiced explaining her degree's relevancy, was one of the rare interns to obtain a career conveyor-belt internship in publishing, where she performed simple data entry and organization. She voiced her disappointment about this openly. She said of her internship, "They had a series of editors and contributors and authors and clients, so I spent a lot of time organizing them in spreadsheets. That was the least glamorous part, but it did take up a lot of my time." She would also call prospective clients, ask if they were currently using her firm's textbooks, offer them a free trial if not, and compile their responses. When asked how her major related to these tasks, she said, "Honestly, not to a huge extent." However, Greta noted many of the publisher's employees have English degrees, suggesting her major may have made her application attractive to the firm.

Communications majors with career conveyor-belt internships also performed clerical tasks. Jade, a communications major who interned at a health care company, said of her internship, "I helped with a lot of the day-to-day things because a lot of the big picture stuff had already been completed." In practice, Jade mostly made PowerPoint presentations from existing content. For example, an employee in the Chicago office who ran trainings asked Jade to make PowerPoints based on the curriculum materials. She also made a PowerPoint for the company's awards banquet, with slides on each nominee. Although "designing" PowerPoints could have drawn on Jade's communications skills, this work falls under the definition of clerical. Plus, when I asked Jade if she used anything specific from her major—"theories, concepts, terms, skills"—she said, "Nothing really jumps out."

Many communications and English majors with dead-end internships were also assigned clerical tasks. This intersection was particularly problematic for students, as 48 percent of these internships (dead-end and clerical) were unpaid, double the total for the full study sample (24 percent). Perhaps because the firms invested so little in their interns, they did not care to give them substantive projects. These internships tended to cluster in the nonprofit or creative sector, similar to previous case studies on internships.[15]

Vance, an English major, interned at a radio station, which he thought sounded like a "cool opportunity," although he was not interested in becoming a journalist or pursuing media. However, all he did was prepare cups of water for the guests, keep the studio neat, and call guests to prepare them for being on the air. He said, "I don't want to be there because I feel like . . . this is just the same thing kind of day in and day out," he reported. "It gets boring real fast."

Marne, on the other hand, had a passion for libraries. She had previously completed a degree in accounting but had trouble finding a job in a library because her degree did not signal enough interest in literature. To rectify this, Marne went back to school for a second bachelor's in English. To further bolster her competitiveness for a library position, Marne chose to intern at a small college's academic library in the same state as CSU. But during her internship, she kept inventory, scanned barcodes, and sent lists of books to her supervisor to be deleted from the system. Marne said, "I do wish they would give me more to do because sometimes I feel a little bored and sometimes it does get monotonous, because I mean, you got a cart of seventy books so you're just stamping 'deleted' on them and copy paste, it's not necessarily stimulating work." Marne and Vance were disappointed with the tasks they were asked to do for their internships, which comprised of work that did not draw on the human capital they had acquired in school.

In Marne's case, even an internship-to-degree match can signal interest or general ability but not apply specific human capital. Marne thought she needed an English degree to be taken seriously as a candidate for library jobs and internships. She said, "Because I got an English degree, they're like oh English she likes books, libraries make sense, but I feel like the knowledge I'm gaining from the degree itself in a lot of instances does not apply." Marne's experience seems to reinforce popular stereotypes about English majors, but the same pattern emerges from all disciplines, not English alone.

Sophie studied communications and had a dead-end internship. She interned at the Transplant Network, an organ donation nonprofit in the same city as CSU. The position was unpaid and Sophie's title, communications intern, matched her major. In practice, however, she mostly helped with event planning, which was not what she had anticipated and did not seem to her like a good use of her time and skills.

CMP: What are your general thoughts and feelings about being an intern there? About your experience?

SOPHIE: I don't know, I'm kind of indifferent about it, and I love the people that I work with, but I didn't think I gained as much as I could have out of that experience. I felt like I was kind of on a tight leash compared to other things I could've been doing.

CMP: Like what? What could you have been doing that they didn't let you do?

SOPHIE: I feel like I could have helped a lot more in social media or different aspects of our advertising instead of just doing event stuff. I think that's really what I could've helped on. Or even the education side of things, going to schools and help[ing] with that.

CMP: Why don't you think they did any of those things?

SOPHIE: I think it's just because this is what the interns have always done, they stayed with the events side of things, because that's probably where they need the most help. Where the lady in social media probably has most of it handled.

Notice Sophie said her assignment with the events side of things reflected what the interns have always done, not her specific skills or abilities. When I asked whether her duties related to her major, she said event planning was "part of communications in the broad sense of things," which suggested it was not closely related to her skill set. When I asked if a student in another major could have been equally successful at the "communications intern" position she said, "Yes, I think so," reinforcing the clerical nature of her assignment.

Overall, interns from all majors were assigned substantive and clerical tasks, irrespective of discipline. I did not find notable differences based on race or gender: 78 percent of the substantive task internships were held by White students and 62 percent were held by women, totals that closely reflect the overall study percentages.[16] There were also no social class differences in who was assigned substantive tasks, likely because students were not informed of the work tasks before selecting an internship. Chloe and Frank are both from upper-middle-class families, which may have afforded them international internships that others might not have had access to, yet both internships consisted exclusively of clerical work, as did many other internships across all majors.

Internship Tasks and the Transition into Entry-Level Work

Previous research posits that a good match between major and job is evidence of human capital mechanisms connecting school to work, and that the match explains why practical arts majors have superior initial employment outcomes.[17] The data from my study says otherwise. For internships at least, researchers cannot simply look to degree-job matching as confirmation that human capital acquired in school is applied at work. Recall Marne thought she needed an English degree to obtain her library internship, but not to complete her assigned tasks. In contrast, some liberal arts graduates used their degree-specific skills even when interning in fields that were not matched to their degree, as was the case for Mort and Katie. In general, English and communications majors were equally as likely as their practical arts peers to use occupational specific knowledge and should have demonstrated equivalent or better social and soft skills.[18] Yet, while my study reveals task parity between all four majors, engineering and business students received better employment opportunities from their internships. Thus, business and engineering students were more in demand for career conveyor-belt internships than English and communications students even though they did not need to demonstrate their skills at a greater rate.

It is important to note that dead-end internships were not necessarily bad internships. First, students can benefit from dead-end internships that require substantive work. In such contexts, students may grow and expand their skills, test if jobs related to their major are right for them, and make positive associations with firms and managers that may be useful down the line for mentorship or networking purposes. Second, even dead-end internships where students perform purely clerical tasks can have some of the same advantages as all internships. Students can learn about office cultures, experience regular working hours, get a sense of the industry they are working in, and add to their résumés professional experience that may be a prerequisite for a job after graduation. In sum, both types of internships can potentially be useful for students trying to navigate the college-to-work transition.

Ultimately, chapters 3 and 4 show that the trade-off students make when choosing a major begins with their internships. Often practical arts majors were recruited on campus for career conveyor-belt internships, which led to new organizational jobs. Liberal arts majors, on the other hand, were rarely recruited on campus and usually received dead-end internships. Many English and communications graduates ended up precariously employed after graduation. Internship types likely did not cause the postgraduation employment disparities, but internships are a key stage in the college-to-work transition, and I demonstrate their instrumental role in the process of how employment disparities unfold.

My evidence also undermines media narratives that may erroneously explain why practical arts majors have greater access to career conveyor-belt internships. It is, in fact, *not* that these students' skills are in greater demand at the internship stage nor that they needed to demonstrate those skills to receive an entry-level job.

*

Part 1 of this book reveals how the real trade-off students make when choosing a major starts during college. The movement from engineering or business major to a new organizational career begins with access to a career conveyor-belt internship, access most liberal arts majors are denied. The differences in internship types and this selective access reinforce misleading media narratives about the employability of college majors. Furthermore, part 1 also undermines the distinction between "practical" and "passion" majors that underlie much of this discourse. Chapter 2 shows that students from all four disciplines were similarly oriented toward the labor market and careers. Indeed, the curricula across majors are strikingly similar. Chapter 3 shows that liberal arts majors adopted similar approaches to internships as practical arts students. And chapter 4 shows that liberal arts majors were just as likely to use their classroom skills at internships. I also document that liberal arts degrees convey occupationally relevant skills that students deployed at internships. In all, part 1 undermines popular explanations for why practical arts majors enjoy better initial employment outcomes by traditional metrics.

Yet the evidence in part 1 would not fully disprove such media narratives if practical arts graduates actually went on to use career-specific skills in entry-level jobs at higher rates than liberal arts graduates. In part 2, I show that they do not and, in fact, English and communications majors had specific skills employers needed, although these graduates struggled to find full-time positions and were poorly remunerated for substantive work. In contrast, business and engineering majors overwhelmingly entered the labor market smoothly, found stable employment for good pay, yet conducted clerical tasks at work.

I reveal these outcomes by employing a method that labor sociologists have used since the earliest days of the discipline—conducting a microstudy of what individuals do at work.[19] Applying this method to an issue of contemporary importance, the connection between college and work, helps fully uncover the true trade-off between majors vis-à-vis the labor market.

PART 2: RECENT GRADUATES' ENTRY-LEVEL JOB EXPERIENCES

5: JOB SEARCHING AFTER COLLEGE

The transition from college into the labor market is an important moment in the stratification process, and, as such, has received much recent sociological attention.[1] In my study, liberal arts graduates, the majority of whom had dead-end internships, often struggled to find education-level appropriate work. Consider English major Laura. She makes $42,000 per year as a program adviser and product specialist for a software company. This was not her first choice of industry or occupation. Originally, Laura, like many English majors, wanted to work in publishing. She was a high-achieving student, finishing college with an impressive 3.89 GPA, and she had two internships in college. Yet, working in publishing did not seem realistic, as she told me publishing is "a really hard industry to be in. I think I got one interview request . . . but I sent out a ton of cover letters and stuff. And I read them carefully and I know that they were good cover letters." She attributed her lack of success to not being in New York or Chicago, the hubs of publishing in America. However, moving was "not really feasible when you don't have any money and you just graduated." Even if Laura had moved, in a competitive industry like publishing, there were likely more qualified graduates than job opportunities. Laura settled for work at the software company, which mostly requires online research, because finding a job was a struggle.

Two dead-end internships meant that Laura did not have a job lined up by graduation and she had to undertake a protracted job search with many rejections. She sent out "a lot of job applications. I think after about a month or two of just filling out job applications, I moved back home. . . . I moved back home because my lease was out." While she was sending out applications from home, Laura's grandparents died and she moved to Florida for a month, putting her job search on hold to be with family. While in Florida, Laura turned down a job because it only paid $12 an hour, which she found unacceptable for a college graduate. In December, four months after her August graduation, she received a call for the job interview that led to her current position. She found the position through an ad on LinkedIn, saying, "I just looked at it and I was like, 'I don't really know. I'm not 100 percent sure what this job is, first of all.' The description seemed really vague." However, LinkedIn made it easy to apply, so she did, and she ultimately accepted the job offer. I asked if she had any other offers, to which she replied, "No. I'm sure that was part of it. I was tired of looking for a job." The job search "got pretty frustrating" for Laura. She said "I think mostly because I was bored. Also, I think part of it looking back is because I just, I really wanted to be in the publishing industry." While many factors contributed to Laura's difficult labor market transition—few obvious matches between job postings and her college major, high competition for jobs in her desired field of publishing, and the timing of her personal loss—the fact remains that internships without employment opportunities force students who seek full-time postgraduation employment to begin searching right out of college.

Meanwhile, many practical arts graduates with career conveyor-belt internships leveraged their initial job offers to find further employment opportunities in a stress-free environment. Steve, an industrial and systems engineering (ISE) graduate, interned with a large multinational automotive firm. Steve currently works at Downstate, a large manufacturer that recruits heavily from CSU. He is in the Operations Management Leadership Program, a rotational position for recent college graduates where he will complete three eight-month rotations. Despite having a career conveyor-belt internship that came with a job offer, Steve conducted a job search *during his senior year*. He stayed in contact with his internship site, but he also went to the engineering career fair and applied to positions listed on the engineering career services (ECS) website. When I asked Steve how many jobs he applied for, his response was, "A lot. On ECS's page alone, probably about sixty." The job at Downstate was posted on the ECS website, but they have a strong connection with CSU and conducted interviews on campus. Following his initial interview, Steve had a second interview at their regional headquarters and the next day he received a job offer. At the time, he also had job offers from three other companies—two multinational automotive companies and a large manufacturer of farm and construction equipment. Given the labor market for industrial engineering, Steve used the university's connections to field multiple job offers *even after* knowing he could return to his internship site.

In contrast to Laura, Steve had multiple job offers lined up before graduation and was able to choose the position he most wanted. When I asked why he chose the offer from Downstate, he said, "I love [the former CEO's] culture of open, honest, direct communication." He also said he liked the "focus on making people great, that I loved." Steve's first rotation was in the same city that Laura lives in, where Downstate's regional headquarters are located. Steve said, "It was my first pick." When asked about the anxiety of postgraduation transitions to the workforce, Steve noted, "It was nice having the comfort of 'I've got a job.'" During our second interview in January 2017, roughly eight months after his graduation, I asked Steve again about his choice of Downstate. He responded, "Given the opportunity and knowing everything I knew at the time, and even knowing what I know now, I would stick with the same decision."

Steve had a career conveyor-belt internship and Laura did not. While neither one of them is currently working with the firm they interned with, nor even in the same industry, Steve leveraged his job offer into a smooth labor market transition. Due to the ease with which he entered his targeted field through a career conveyor-belt internship, Steve did not have as much stress or uncertainty as Laura during his labor market transition.

Ultimately, this chapter shows the media narratives around which students enter "good jobs" immediately after graduation is largely correct, illustrating a central component of the trade-off described in this book. It also demonstrates that the entry-level jobs found by the graduates in my study match expectations set by prior research, so I clearly did not interview outlier students who found jobs atypical for their fields. Indeed, this chapter is more myth-confirming than myth-busting: I show how labor market entry unfolds for recent college graduates. I discuss how graduates entered the labor market by internship type and describe labor market outcomes by major. Later in part 2 I disprove the reasons media narratives give for the discrepancy in employment outcomes between majors.

Finding a Job

How do students find jobs after they graduate from college? We know surprisingly little about this process outside of elite universities.[2] Audit studies are a common way to study hiring, where researchers send fake résumés to real job listings.[3] Although audit study researchers might manipulate fields of study, I found that students from different majors rarely applied to the same jobs or even searched for work in the same places. Further, audit studies only speak to one way that new college graduates search for employment—blind applications. Yet, many students in this study searched in other ways. Steve took advantage of the ECS website. Other students used personal or social networks to find work. Uncovering how students searched for work was vital to understanding why some graduates were successful in quickly entering the labor market and some were not.

Finding an entry-level job is the crucial first step in determining how much students will benefit from their college education over their lifetime because disparities in first jobs have long-term social and economic consequences.[4] I have already explained which students had access to career conveyor-belt internships, so I turn now to what happened to students after graduation. How did students with dead-end internships find jobs and decide which opportunity to pursue? What did it look like when students who had access to career conveyor-belt internships opted to find an alternative opportunity? This section answers those questions.

How Graduates with Dead-End Internships Entered the Labor Market

Despite not having employment opportunities from their internships, most students with dead-end internships successfully found employment.[5] However, as most of these students studied English or communications, many worked precariously, either in temporary jobs while searching for more permanent employment or more long term (i.e., without looking for stable work).

Graduates from the two liberal arts majors held a wide variety of jobs, partially because communications and English majors have two of the lowest rates of degree-to-job matching in the US.[6] In this study, graduates from these fields found work in firms that included nonprofits, PR, marketing, and other corporate organizations. Across all majors, graduates who had dead-end internships were also more likely to enroll in graduate school or remain un- or underemployed than those with career conveyor-belt internships. Five out of forty-six students with these kinds of internships were in graduate school, and seven out of the forty-six students were underemployed or unemployed at the time of their wave two interviews.[7]

The modal way graduates with dead-end internships found jobs was postgraduation job hunting that included internet searches and public job ads. Some alumni used school resources or personal networks, but this was less common. In general, it took most graduates of dead-end internships three to six stressful months searching for work after graduation before landing full-time jobs. The rest of this section lays out some of the college-to-work transition experiences and challenges often faced by graduates of dead-end internships.

Chloe, the communications major who had a dead-end internship as part of a study abroad experience in London, had a labor market entry typical of those in her discipline and similar to English major Laura's. After her study abroad internship, she did another internship at a fashion company during her final semester of college. Given her goal of working in PR, she considered moving to New York but, similarly to Laura, she said it was too expensive. At first, she struggled with the job search, saying, "It's tough, obviously. I felt like I worked my ass off in school, and I got a ton of experience, and I was ahead of the curve compared to a lot of my peers in terms of experience I had and the level of professionalism I felt I possessed." This quote shows Chloe was not unconcerned with her employment prospects but was actively trying to enhance her employability in college. Chloe, like Laura, moved back to her parents' house during her job search and had offers for less than she was anticipating, saying an "offer came in and I was like, I really don't want to take this for $12 an hour; I'm overqualified for this shit."

Chloe eventually secured a job she liked in her field, but it started in September, more than four months after her May graduation. She said of job searching, "It was stressful. I knew I was going to get a job. It was just a matter of what I was going to settle for. Because I wanted something really awesome, and I wanted something that I would be able to tell people [about] and be proud of." Chloe, an upper-middle-class White woman, had the luxury of waiting out the job search, the connections, and the ability to ultimately succeed. She found her job after a friend who works at that organization told her they were hiring. She read the job ad, thought it sounded interesting, and applied. Chloe's case demonstrates that, even when things work out well for communications graduates, it can be after a protracted and stressful experience. She interned through the end of college without any job offers. She then had a difficult job search, only finding employment in her field more than four months after graduation. For many communications and English majors, this constituted a best-case scenario.

Some liberal arts majors with dead-end internships accepted corporate jobs. This could mean eschewing their passion or putting it on hold. Emily studied communications and had an internship at a television station. She loves media and still aspires to become a television news reporter. However, she currently works at Thebes, a giant technology company, where four respondents are employed. Thebes pays Emily approximately $50,000, higher than the median salary for communications graduates (which was $40,000). Meanwhile, most business and engineering majors working in large bureaucracies, including at Thebes, earn appreciably higher salaries than Emily. Of course, they are not usually doing the same work, but clearly the opportunities available to graduates varied significantly even for those targeting similar types of firms for employment.

Also, unlike the many business and engineering graduates employed at large bureaucracies who found their jobs through career conveyor-belt internships, Emily found her job after an intensive postcollege job search, saying, "After school, I applied for tons of different jobs, internships, etc. . . . I got some interviews with some big companies, but I didn't make it all the way through." Emily interviewed with a production company, an opportunity she was excited about, but it didn't pay well enough. She interviewed with Thebes "as a backup and ending up getting it and toward the end, maybe mid-July, figured I couldn't hold off their offer very long." Her decision to take the job was more about cost-benefit analysis than interest. She said, "I spent a lot of money going to [CSU], so I was like why would I take a marketing job that doesn't even pay me enough? Like, I have bills to pay, eventually will have to pay back my loans." Like Chloe and Laura, Emily did not have the funds or opportunities to fully chase her dreams. Unlike Chloe, instead of holding out for over four months for the right opportunity, she took a corporate job she was not thrilled about a little over two months after graduation. Also unlike Chloe, Emily is a Black woman from a working-class background. Her positionality likely contributed to her need to find work more immediately and her lack of success in entering media, the industry she initially targeted.

A common thread running through the narratives of communications and English majors without career conveyor-belt internships involved decisions about whether to move to a new city without a job. Almost none of the respondents in this study chose to make that leap, which likely reflects the class location of those I interviewed. A strategy that women from privileged backgrounds use to reproduce their class position is moving to large urban centers, like New York City, after graduation.[8] When less privileged students, like many of those who attend CSU, graduate from college, they are more geographically restricted.

While the graduates mentioned above did not move mostly for financial reasons, some stayed close to home for personal reasons. For example, Rachel, a graduate with an English degree, interned at the local ballet company. After graduation, she considered an internship in Chicago and started working for the company remotely with the intention of moving there. Ultimately, she opted not to go to Chicago, saying, "I was kind of prepping to go to Chicago . . . [but] the editing internship didn't pay a lot . . . and I didn't like it very much." Rachel, like many English majors, was mostly interested in publishing. She decided to work at a local bookstore in the same city as CSU while conducting her job search, saying, "I just really liked the store, and I just went in and asked for an application. . . . I was just thinking it would just be a summer thing and I may go off and do a big publishing job. But the pull of, like, my boyfriend being here and my friends being here was a lot." As of our latest interview, Rachel was still working at the bookstore but planning to quit in the coming months to take a transcontinental road trip with her boyfriend. Although Rachel viewed her underemployment as temporary, her case shows the difficult choices English majors frequently have to make. Her options were to stay in the same city as CSU and face underemployment or move to a larger city with the uncertainty that comes from another internship or unemployment. Both options constitute forms of precarious work. She chose the former, partially because she did not like her internship and partially for her boyfriend.

One dual English and communications major who did take the leap to a move to a new city, Gloria, did so after waiting tables for the summer in her hometown. She moved to New York City to pursue an internship in communications with an ice cream company that she hoped would lead to employment in the PR industry. Waiting tables and participating in a post-graduation internship are both examples of precarious work. Meanwhile, unlike peers who had no safety net, Gloria noted that her mother's family was in New York, and she would be staying with her aunt. Research by sociologist Laura Hamilton shows this kind of familial involvement is crucial to student success at large public universities.[9] Still, the string of precarious jobs worried Gloria, who said, "I feel so behind sometimes. My best friend just bought a car and she's paying interest and has a job, and I'm over here like, 'I have an internship and I'm scared to go to New York City.'" Gloria was unsure if she would like New York, but she felt moving would be best for her career.

Some business and engineering majors had dead-end internships and struggled to enter the labor market as well. One example is Kim, who studied operations and logistics at CSU and had an internship at a logistics company. She did not like her internship, saying, "I thought they might have a job opening after that [ended]. Turns out by the end of the two months, I was super bored and didn't want to do it anymore." This led to a protracted job search similar to the English and communications majors mentioned above. She said, "I just went on LinkedIn, I went on ZipRecruiter, and I did set up quite a few interviews." She started working in September, four months after graduation. When I asked if the interim search was tough, she said, "For sure. Absolutely. Yeah, I had no income. Like, I'm a fresh grad right out of school. I'm freaking out. So really anything that I could get, I was just going to take." Kim currently works at a multilevel marketing company that people warn her is a pyramid scheme.

Kim's case demonstrates that *business students with dead-end internships can have postgraduation experiences like the communications and English students* who similarly did not have career conveyor-belt internships. Kim interned in her field but did not have a job opportunity, nor did she like the internship. Her lack of a career conveyor-belt internship contributed to her rough college-to-work transition despite her middle-class background (Kim's father is a dentist). Yet, Kim's class background alone was not sufficient to ensure her smooth labor market entry. For students already admitted to the competitive business and engineering majors I studied, there were no social class differences in access to career conveyor-belt internships.[10] Kim struggled for months to find a job, was willing to take anything, and found her current employment through online searches. Her case also shows that career conveyor-belt internships matter in conjunction with major even after graduation.

Some practical arts graduates with dead-end internships leveraged the career fair or other university-affiliated opportunities, which led to smooth labor market entries. Sonny is an ISE graduate who interned at a global non-profit where she conducted Skype calls with people all over the world. She completed this internship during the fall semester of her senior year, then had a summer internship at an automotive company. She knew she did not want to work at the car company, telling me, "My heart is really not in industrial engineering; like, I'm very glad that I chose that as a major, but I just don't love the whole cost-cutting of it. I would rather be on the creating value side." As a result, Sonny went to the career fair and solicited offers from multiple firms (as did many students who, unlike Sonny, were considering job offers from career conveyor-belt internships). She now works for a consulting firm she met at the engineering career fair. Sonny's case illustrates an interesting phenomenon: Even when engineering or business students pursued internships in areas outside their degree, this did not seem to adversely affect the efficacy of school connections for helping them find jobs.

Overall, graduates' college internship experiences were instrumental for entering the labor market smoothly. Most recent graduates who had dead-end internships had to use general job searches or personal connections to find entry-level work, and many of them ended up precariously employed, at least for a time. The job search often took several stressful months and graduates sometimes received job offers for which they felt overqualified. Many people contemplated taking the risk of moving to a new city and many had to live at home for financial reasons. They ultimately had to decide whether they wanted to hold out for a job they were passionate about, take a corporate job, or settle for underemployment while looking for a better position. The main factor at play was how long they could maintain the search for suitable employment and financial considerations always played a part in that decision. Graduates who could live at home or had parental support could hold out longer for jobs they wanted or do a postgraduation internship. Since most graduates with dead-end internships studied English or communications, this ultimately shows how class background manifests in inequalities for liberal arts majors even after college graduation.

How Graduates with Career Conveyor-Belt Internships
Entered the Labor Market

Graduates who had career conveyor-belt internships generally had less stressful labor market transitions than those with dead-end internships due to greater postgraduation certainty. They also, overwhelmingly, found new organizational careers—permanent employment with decent pay, full benefits, and opportunities for advancement.[11] Many stayed with their internship firm, while others used the job offer as leverage for exploring other opportunities. Mary is an example of a graduate who stayed with her internship firm. She had a career conveyor-belt internship at Republic Automotive, one of the biggest car manufacturers in the world. As an ISE graduate, Mary could choose from several engineering programs and departments within Republic for her entry-level job. When I asked Mary if she struggled when deciding on what to do after college, she said, "I just kind of avoided that." She went on to say, "I just knew I liked Republic since I had an internship with them." The decision that Mary needed to make was not about which firm to join, but which group. Originally, Mary considered going back to the group she interned with, but instead chose new model development, saying, "The new model job sounded way more fun and exciting and along with what I wanted to do." For Mary and many other graduates with career conveyor-belt internships, these were decisions they made before finishing college.

In general, a striking advantage graduates with career conveyor-belt internships enjoyed was the security to make decisions based on what they *wanted* to do. In the industries these students targeted for employment, there seemed to be a surplus of jobs, and the security of a job offer before graduation allowed them to pursue their interests, as Mary did. In another example, Arne, a business graduate, is a White man who grew up working class, but by the time he was a senior in college identified as upper-middle class after his father's employment situation changed. Arne is the exact kind of student large manufacturing corporations target for career conveyor-belt internships. He was willing to move to the South for a job at a major snack manufacturer and was offered a choice between a business rotation program or a supply chain job. Notably, moving with a secure job lined up is markedly less stressful than moving to a new city to search for a job, as many of his liberal arts peers were contemplating.

Arne decided on the supply chain engineer position, an opportunity similar to those ISE graduates receive. He said he was able to go "where I feel my strengths are." When I asked if he applied for any jobs outside of the snack company he interned with, he responded, "No, I didn't really need to. I based my career decisions off my internship selection. I knew for the most part wherever I was going for an internship, that was most likely going to be the company I was working for long term." This long-term commitment shows how these kinds of internships are an extension of organizational careers that have existed since the mid-twentieth century in some of America's biggest firms.[12]

Communications majors with career conveyor-belt internships had similarly smooth labor market entries as their peers from the practical arts. Derek graduated with a communications degree and now works at a government relations firm that companies hire to manage their relationship with the state government. I asked if he had a chance to apply for other jobs before he returned to the firm and he said, "I honestly wasn't looking." When I later asked if he had any reflections on his postgraduation decision-making, Derek responded, "I'm happy. I'm happy there. I was happy when I was interning, so I think that also applied to why I didn't look for other internships." Derek interned for this firm for several semesters hoping to receive a job offer, which eventually came.

Another communications major with a career conveyor-belt internship, Alan, had a less positive experience. Unlike Derek, Alan interned in a field he was not interested in and that matched less with his degree. He strategically chose to intern with Diamond Bank because he thought a large financial institution would pay their interns well. He was right and the internship turned into a full-time job offer. When I asked if his transition to work was stressful, Alan said, "It was stressful because I was worried about whether or not I made the right decision." Alan did not like his job and thought avoiding the job hunt allowed him not to think about what he hoped to do with his future. He said, "I feel like it would have been stressful to have to figure out what I wanted to do and find a job, but I think it would have forced me to think about what it is I actually want to do. So, I just sorta went into [the position at Diamond], and it's not great, but I don't particularly hate it either, it's just sort of a thing I go to every day." Alan's disappointment with his job was common among those with career conveyor-belt internships, but the opportunity shifted his stress from searching for a job to choosing the right one.

While neither Derek nor Alan applied to jobs beyond their internship sites, several students who had job offers from their internships applied to other positions. They were able to make career decisions based on their personal preferences. Esther, also a communications major, interned at a company that makes nutritional products. They offered her a position and she did not accept it. But before Esther turned the job down, she conducted a job search and found a position she preferred at a regional bank. She listed several reasons for choosing the bank. First, she said the position at the nutrition company "didn't pay nearly as well." Recall from chapter 3 that liberal arts majors with career conveyor-belt internships sometimes found internship-to-job pipelines that led to jobs with worse employment conditions than their practical arts counterparts. Second, Esther said, "I had made up my mind to the degree of 'I wanted to go back home.'" The regional bank position is located in her hometown, whereas the nutrition company offered her a job in another state. Finally, she saw it as a new experience, saying, "I wanted to do something different, do something a little more challenging. I've never been in banking so that was very different for me." Despite being a communications major, a discipline with worse employment outcomes by traditional indicators than business or engineering in this study and in the labor market overall,[13] Esther leveraged her internship-based job offer to find a more suitable position with the security of searching with a fallback option.

Thomas, a business major, also decided to pursue a job unrelated to his internship in the food and beverage industry. He now works for a manufacturing firm called Rochester Industrial. Thomas was mostly looking for a firm with a culture where he would fit in. Thomas said, "I ended up getting three or four job offers, and I narrowed it down to one because it's pretty much the only one I really, really wanted." He told me why he chose Rochester: "They apparently had a great culture so that is definitely why I picked Rochester." He even noted, "It wasn't necessarily like they were offering me more money or something like that." Some of Thomas's friends had interned or worked at Rochester Industrial before and they all told him it was a great place to work. This motivated Thomas to seek them out at the career fair. He went to the fair determined to speak with the representatives from Rochester Industrial. He was invited for an interview and they offered him a position.

Thomas's experience highlights another advantage of students who were recruited on campus. Almost all practical arts students with career conveyor-belt internships who sought alternative opportunities exclusively searched through their college's career fair or career services. Since firms make regular connections with colleges to recruit certain majors, students in those fields can share information about the firms, which helps the job seeker feel better informed and therefore confident. This exclusive situation suggests audit studies may not be generalizable to many college graduates, especially in business and engineering. The timing of this process is particularly advantageous as it allows students with career conveyor-belt internships to field and consider multiple offers well before graduation. Ultimately, although neither Thomas nor Esther wanted jobs with the firms they interned with, the process of career conveyor-belt internships and knowledge of the opportunities available to them still made their experiences with labor market entry smoother and more successful than many of their peers who had dead-end internships or could not access the same career search support services.

In sum, the labor market entry process was quite different for different students, mainly depending on type of major and internship. A significant manifestation of this appears with the conditions around mobility: whether graduates could move to a new location for work. Like Arne, business and engineering students with career conveyor-belt internships were able to move to new cities regardless of class background because they had job security. These students were not inherently more interested in moving for work than liberal arts majors with dead-end internships, but they were *able* to do it in the supportive context of having a job lined up, rather than as a first step in a job search of unknown length or even success. Given the assurance job stability provides, postcollege experiences were less divided by class background among practical arts majors than liberal arts majors.[14]

Recent College Graduates' Entry-Level Jobs

In addition to differences in how graduates found jobs, there was also variation in the jobs graduates secured, both within and between majors. An overview of the jobs obtained by graduates provides insights into each majors' marketability to different kinds of employers. These descriptive insights are valuable since researchers know little about college graduates' entry-level jobs, though data from my study matches prior research when it comes to traditional employment indicators.[15]

The next section discusses alumni jobs from each major in turn. I also present a summary in table 5.1, which shows a big part of the trade-off students make when choosing a major. One key distinction between the new organizational careers available to many ISE and business majors and the more precarious employment found by English and communications graduates was the large gulf in salaries. This, of course, has gendered implications as ISE and business majors are much more likely to be White middle-class men whereas communications and English graduates are more likely to be White middle-class women or men from less advantaged backgrounds.

Among ISE majors, the modal employment sector was manufacturing and the modal entry-level position was a rotational program. These programs last roughly two years and send recent graduates on a series of six- to eight-month rotations in various departments of the organization. In each rotation, ISE graduates usually have the job title of engineer. For example, they may spend six months as quality engineer and six months as design engineer. ISE majors also had the highest annual salary in the study, on average over

TABLE 5.1 Summary of Entry-Level Jobs by Major

	ISE (*n* = 22)	Business (*n* = 21)	Communications (*n* = 25)	English (*n* = 17)
Modal industry	Manufacturing	Manufacturing	Technology, marketing (tied)	Publishing, nonprofit (tied)
Modal job	Rotational program/engineer	Analyst	Communications coordinator/ specialist	Administrative
Modal way found job	Internship	Internship	Internet search	Internet search
Median salary	$63,100	$56,500	$40,000	$33,500
Occupation-degree match (%)				
Yes	83	76	38	47
No	17	24	62	53

Notes: For this table *n* = 85 because it only includes those who participated in wave two.

$60,000. Besides manufacturing, many ISE graduates worked for consulting or technology companies. Those not in rotational programs often entered jobs with engineer in the job title; examples include cost engineer, supply chain engineer, and manufacturing engineer. By traditional survey measures, over 80 percent of ISE graduates had jobs matched to their degree.[16]

Among business majors, over 75 percent found work related to their degree, and the median annual salary was $56,500, the second highest in my sample. The modal industry was manufacturing (with logistics as a close second) and the modal job title was analyst. The second most common job title was manager, such as account manager or area manager.

Business and engineering graduates had less variation in entry-level jobs than liberal arts alumni, which is unsurprising since communications and English graduates have much lower rates of degree-to-job matching in the general population.[17] Taken together, most business and engineering graduates entered stable well-paying jobs in large corporations that offered opportunities for advancement, clear indicators of new organizational careers.

Communications majors varied significantly in their postgraduation employment. Only 38 percent of communications graduates found a job matched to their degree, the lowest in the sample, providing further evidence against communications being a practical arts discipline at CSU. Their modal industries of employment included technology and marketing, but each industry employed only four graduates from my study. Three graduates worked in media companies and the rest were employed in a variety of industries ranging from nonprofit organizations to banking and health care. The median salary was $40,000. Many worked as a communications coordinator or a specialist and found their jobs through targeted internet searches. A few communications alumni were either unemployed or underemployed, including one graduate who worked as a concierge in an apartment complex.

And now we come to the English majors. The modal industries were nonprofit and publishing; however, only two English graduates worked in each of these fields. Like communications majors, fewer than half of English graduates found work matched to their degree. The rest worked in for-profit fields such as retail, health care, marketing, or logistics. Several English graduates had job titles with the word "manager," such as project manager and case manager, though these jobs were often administrative in nature. English majors had the lowest median salary in the study; half of them made less than $34,000. This calculation does not include the three English alumni who were in graduate school. Three other English graduates were underemployed during wave two interviews, and one was unemployed. Indeed, English majors had worse employment outcomes than communications graduates by some measures, which matches their respective placements on the spectrum of majors with English as least technical.

In sum, with comparatively low salaries, the normalcy of temporary or contract employment, and prevalence of underemployment, many English and communications graduates ended up precariously employed after graduation. Moreover, even if liberal arts graduates found stable work eventually, many still spent time precariously employed between graduation and finding that permanent position. That extended time before successfully entering the labor market could have all kinds of implications for liberal arts majors. A full accounting of how this transition affects other areas of graduates' lives is beyond the scope of this book; however, by virtue of their struggles with labor market entry, liberal arts graduates may tend to fall behind their peers in other respects as well, such as establishing long-term romantic partnerships, buying homes, or having children, all traditional markers of "adulthood" in American society.[18]

Internships and Labor Market Entries

This chapter revealed the process of *how* the graduates in this study entered the labor market, which is one manifestation of the trade-off students make when selecting a major. Many practical arts graduates leveraged career conveyor-belt internships directly into new organizational careers while many liberal arts graduates struggled to enter the labor market and were precariously employed. Of course, the internship structures do not cause labor market differences, but they show how students with different majors experience labor market entry. Due to the nature of their respective job markets, many English and communications competitively vie for jobs in industries where the supply of applicants exceeds demand. On the other end of the spectrum, many business and engineering graduates may choose to work for other firms in their industry besides the sites where they interned. In this situation, few business or engineering graduates found labor market entry difficult while many English and communications majors had taxing and prolonged job searches.

I noted in this chapter that fewer liberal arts graduates moved to a new city than practical arts graduates. This was mostly because the security or uncertainty varied considerably between major types. Many English and communications majors would consider moving to a new city out of necessity to look for work or complete another internship. In contrast, almost all business and engineering students who moved did so to start a stable job they had already secured, an assurance that makes moving far less personally and professionally risky.

For business and engineering graduates, it did not always matter much if their internships were career conveyor-belt or dead-end. Although a few practical arts graduates who had dead-end internships struggled to find jobs or became precariously employed, most were able to enter the labor market smoothly anyway thanks to the career services available exclusively to them. For liberal arts graduates, the type of internship they obtained mattered much more for labor market entry. Yet, there is no evidence that in any field students with career conveyor-belt internships were more organized, more career-oriented, or "better students" than those who had dead-end internships. Therefore, we cannot credit personal characteristics such as these for their smoother labor market entries.

Thus, although some of my evidence reinforces common media narratives about the employability of various degree fields, my data on how the process of labor market entry unfolds shows the pivotal importance of internship structures, especially for liberal arts students. The information in this chapter also validates my study sample by showing the jobs recent graduates received match expectations set by prior research for traditional employment indicators (e.g., salaries and rates of jobs matched to degrees).[19]

While chapter 4 shows that internship type is unrelated to internship work tasks and all majors completed substantive tasks at internships at comparable rates, in the next two chapters I show that *liberal arts graduates in this study were more likely to use their degree skills* and complete substantive tasks in their entry-level *jobs* than business and engineering graduates. This information strongly undermines key myths that suggest practical arts graduates receive an education that better prepares them for entry-level work than their liberal arts peers. Ultimately, I reveal the final sides of the trade-off in outcomes between college majors.

6: WHAT RECENT COLLEGE GRADUATES DO AT WORK

By their senior year of college, many of the students I interviewed expressed optimism about the job market and the skills they learned in school. A snapshot of that time in the 2015–2016 school year shows a higher education ecosystem working in sync: Academic department websites claim they teach students in-demand skills, and students think they will use their classroom skills in their future work. At the internship stage of the college-to-work transition, more than half of the respondents reported using their degree skills to complete substantive tasks. As discussed in chapter 4, the extent to which interns used learned skills was unrelated to whether the firm offered employment opportunities. This fact alone threatens the human capital theory explanation of the college-to-work transition and media narratives surrounding degree fields.

To briefly recap, the three media narratives I contend with in this book are: (1) practical arts degrees lead to better initial labor market success, (2) practical arts degrees provide more in-demand skills needed for entry-level work, and (3) liberal arts fields only provide "soft skills." These narratives reinforce ideas that some majors are "practical" majors and others are "passion" majors.[1]

The previous chapters help confirm the first narrative and begin to undermine narratives two and three. To fully disprove the latter two empirically, here and in chapter 7 I examine the entry-level work phase of the college-to-work transition. I uncover what graduates do at their jobs and show how this relates to their schooling. This close examination of work tasks further erodes myths that business and engineering graduates enjoy employment advantages over liberal arts alumni early in their careers because they learn in-demand skills that twenty-first-century employers need and that liberal arts graduates lack such skills.

The reality of entry-level work rarely met business and engineering graduates' expectations. Seventy percent of practical arts alumni I interviewed did exclusively clerical tasks in their entry-level jobs. I arrived at this

■ Substantive   ■ Clerical

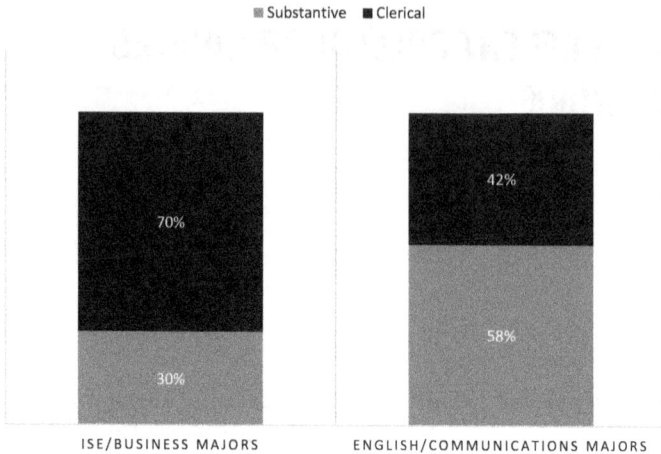

FIGURE 6.1 Substantive and Clerical Work Tasks Performed in Entry-Level Jobs by Major
Notes: For this graph *n* = 85 because it includes only those who participated in wave two. Clerical work percentages refer to graduates who performed *exclusively* clerical work. Substantive work percentages include graduates who were assigned *any* substantive work tasks.

number by asking people to list their job tasks and then list step-by-step how they completed those tasks.[2] In-depth interviews proved valuable in eliciting this information and for hearing graduates' subjective assessments of their work. Graduates tasked with clerical work expressed unhappiness or frustration. For the substantive tasks performed by 30 percent of business and engineering graduates at their entry-level jobs, I developed two categories: (1) complex problem-solving and (2) a specific project.[3] Like for those who had positive internship experiences, specific projects proved to be a source of satisfaction for new full-time employees.

At the other end of the spectrum, more than half of English and communications graduates I interviewed completed substantive tasks, commonly content creation, at their entry-level jobs. These alumni correspondingly expressed more positivity about their entry-level job tasks than practical arts graduates. They often seemed proud when describing their work assignments. Figure 6.1 gives a visual comparison of task type by major.

Given my sampling strategy, we cannot statistically generalize the difference I found between types of major. However, if the common explanation of practical arts graduates' employment advantages were correct, the numbers would, at best, be reversed. We would expect many more practical arts graduates to complete substantive tasks at work, especially since business and engineering graduates had better jobs than their liberal arts peers by traditional employment indicators (e.g., unemployment rates, salary, occupation-to-degree matching). While researchers have documented the degradation of white-collar work in the contemporary economy,[4] they often show job quality and task quality declining in tandem. Here I show that, in entry-level work, there is a decoupling between graduates' work tasks and employment conditions comparatively across industries.

Now I turn to examine in detail the types of tasks graduates from all four majors performed at their entry-level jobs.[5] Having already established that practical arts graduates were more likely to secure new organizational careers and liberal arts majors were more likely to be precariously employed, I start by investigating the types of work tasks assigned to business and engineering graduates before turning to communications and English graduates. By dispelling the myths about which skill sets are "in demand" or relevant, I show that liberal arts skills are more useful for entry-level work than media narratives allow.

Entry-Level Tasks for Business and Engineering Graduates

Despite the high prevalence of career conveyor-belt internships moving business and engineering students into jobs matched to their degrees, most practical arts graduates complete administrative or clerical work at their entry-level jobs. This evidence reveals a key side of the trade-off between majors: practical arts graduates with new organizational careers often have mundane jobs. Respondents found that, although many achieved the promised high salary and nice job title, the promise of technical work that required their degree skills remained unfulfilled.

Clerical, Administrative, or Liaison Work among Practical Arts Graduates

Many practical arts graduates were assigned administrative or clerical work in their first jobs out of college. Although, on occasion, the tasks could be technical or challenging, they did not require the new employees to use their degree skills. Most graduates engaged in "liaison work," which I define as coordinating information and recording it in a spreadsheet sheet or using it to generate a report for supervisors or project teams. Liaison work was neither interesting nor satisfying to respondents, who found their entry-level job tasks mundane, simple, or rote, despite their often-impressive job titles and high salaries.

Consider Jackie, an industrial and systems engineering (ISE) graduate working as an entry-level cost engineer for Syringa, a multinational car company. She has stable employment with many opportunities to advance and can see herself staying with Syringa long term. When I asked where she sees herself in ten years, she responded that she could still be at Syringa as a manager in either her department or an adjacent one. With an annual salary of $60,000, Jackie has high-paying, stable employment with room to grow in a large organization, typical attributes of a new organizational career.[6] By standard employment indicators, Jackie has achieved what many college graduates hope to obtain when entering the labor market.

Jackie was hired by Syringa through a career conveyor-belt internship. During her internship, Jackie helped estimate the costs associated with carpeting the trunks of Syringa's cars, which required running regressions and using other data analysis tools she learned in school. Now, as a cost engineer, Jackie estimates the costs of all electronics for the new model of one of Syringa's best-selling sedans. Syringa's buyers use her cost estimates as a guide before they attempt to purchase components from suppliers. In other words, Jackie provides an approximation of what buyers should pay for parts. In practice, Jackie simply asks others in the company (mostly design engineers) how much components should cost. For example, some parts are the same as they were for previous models, and Jackie asks her colleagues, "What is the part number you want? . . . I [then] go into a [computer] system, the system will tell me how much that part is going to cost, and I will write that cost down." For new parts, Jackie will ask, "Are there any other parts that use something similar, can we use that cost?" Remarkably, when I asked Jackie how close her estimates were to the actual costs of components, she did not know the answer. She even said, "No one actually knows what the true cost of anything is—for the most part, suppliers really dictate how much everything costs, so no one actually understands a cost for anything." Thus, despite her title of cost engineer, Jackie's actual work—getting a cost from a design engineer and updating a database for buyers—could more accurately be characterized as liaison work.

Respondents often found liaison work frustrating and unfulfilling. Jackie described her role as a "middleman," she said:

> We're always very reliant on talking to other people, like the buyers. We only get to see what they put in the system because we don't buy any of those parts, or we're not allowed to view the full details of the cost breakdown. . . . It's kinda frustrating because we're going back and forth with someone and they're like we can't tell you that. . . . I don't know what you want me to do. . . . *There are days when I feel like I'm an overpaid secretary and that doesn't make me feel good.* . . . All I'm doing is just managing this information that they're telling me. [italics mine]

This was not the case during her internship with Syringa. In her first interview, Jackie reported, "Overall I had a very positive [internship] experience. I think that it really showed me the ropes and I think it really gave me confidence that I could take what I learned [in school] and apply it to other fields." A year later, she described her entry-level role as an "overpaid secretary" completing clerical tasks. Jackie's experience, even as a major in the most technical discipline in the study, gets right at the fundamental trade-off between good stable jobs and interesting work.

Jackie was not alone in her experience. Valerie, also an ISE graduate, works in a rotational program for a multinational manufacturing company that employs many engineers. She conducts exclusively clerical tasks at work. Valerie's assignment is to streamline her unit's key performance indicators (KPIs). According to Valerie, KPIs are scattered throughout their computer system, and there is no central database that provides an overview of the organization's performance. She searches various documents to find KPIs and compiles them into an Excel file. She said of this work, "It's very trivial . . . it's not challenging." Valerie's experience is representative of many engineering graduates I interviewed who do nothing but mundane tasks in their work.

Business majors with occupation-to-degree matches also engaged in liaison work. Thomas works at Rochester Industries, where he was hired into the rotational program for recent business graduates. Thomas serves as the liaison between the planners and the suppliers, where his decision-making responsibilities are extremely limited: "My core responsibilities would be utilizing [the] MRP system [a production planning, scheduling, and inventory system] to purchase a product based on when the system is telling me I need it, based on parameters that are in the system, based on the demand that is being generated by our planning system, based on when our customers need those products. So, every day I have to buy things based on this planning system." Thomas's role involves some relationship building; if parts delivered by the supplier fail a quality check, Thomas must work with the supplier to fix the issue. But overall, Thomas's role is that of a middleman between those making production decisions and suppliers.

Sandy, another business graduate, was hired by Denoter, a large consulting firm with offices all over the US, following a career conveyor-belt internship with an import/export company. Sandy now creates PowerPoint presentations for other members of her team to deliver. She expressed dissatisfaction with these responsibilities, saying, "Basically, I do a lot of copying and pasting. I don't do a lot of creation of actual materials." She further noted that "for some people, it would be really cool, but I think I was spoiled by my last project." Sandy explained that her dissatisfaction stemmed in part from comparison with her internship experience:

I had such a great internship. It gave me this wonderful idea of what business is and I don't think that most businesses or teams are like that. I think the work I did there was a lot bigger than what I'm doing here at Denoter. . . . I think that now I'm much more of a secretary than before.

I actually had responsibilities [in my internship] and I was depended upon to perform well. . . . [My teammates] never treated me like an intern. . . . They valued my opinion on things just as much as anyone else.

Sandy's use of the word "spoiled" and her belief that she was now more of a secretary suggested that she now had generally low expectations of work.

All four of these graduates, Sandy, Thomas, Valerie, and Jackie, had career conveyor-belt internships. I now cover two business majors and one engineering graduate with dead-end internships to show that internship type was not related to entry-level job tasks for practical arts graduates.

Mickey, a business graduate, found work after a dead-end internship as an IT supply chain operations analyst, a clear match to his degree. When asked to describe his job in detail, Mickey said, "I'm in charge of all operational issues for our cloud-based visibility logistics tool called GT Nexus." In practice, this entailed two separate activities—running reports and troubleshooting. As an example of troubleshooting, Mickey said, "GT Nexus was not receiving the files MMS [another software] was supposed to be sending them. . . . I had to look into figuring out why things were getting stuck in MMS." When asked how he accomplished that, he said, "We contact different departments, and we finally end up talking to the MMS team. . . . We had to triage and just republish all [purchase orders]." Then I asked how he republished the purchase orders and Mickey responded, "I delegate that to our PO support team." Throughout our interview, it became clear that Mickey had two types of tasks, running reports and coordinating information between departments when an issue arose. According to Mickey, the reporting function was not more technical: *"Reporting is easy, I could be drunk and do it.* [italics mine] It's not that difficult. You have to be accurate, but it's more mind-numbing stuff." Mickey's example illustrates that business majors who had dead-end internships could still have a job that matches their preprofessional degree yet entails strictly clerical work.

Of course, business graduates with dead-end internships did not always end up in stable new organizational careers and even those precariously employed could conduct clerical tasks at work. For example, Kim interned at a transportation company where she essentially worked as a truck dispatcher. She did not enjoy the experience. After college, Kim found a job in a multilevel marketing firm, going door to door asking residents of a neighborhood if they wanted to switch their home energy provider. The firm recruited her through ZipRecruiter, and she receives a commission for customers who are willing to switch. In our first interview, Kim said she had a strong aversion to doing sales work. In the second interview she said, "I am doing sales. That's not what I want to be doing forever. . . . I wasn't looking forward to [accepting] it, but like I said, I really needed an interview."

Despite graduating with a business degree, Kim became frustrated with the job search and settled for the first job offer she got. Besides sales commissions, Kim can earn more money if she "recruits" or "trains people" under her. Kim said she must follow a script and her job was the same every day. Others in her social network warned Kim that her job is a pyramid scheme, though she did not see it that way. Kim's case is unusual for business majors; while many engaged in similarly menial tasks, they usually had new organizational careers. However, her case demonstrates that, for business and engineering majors, internship type and even job type rarely influence type of entry-level work tasks.

Finally, consider Sonny, an ISE graduate who had a dead-end internship with a nonprofit organization. Now, she works for Denoter, the same consulting firm that employs Sandy. Denoter offers a new organizational career, but with solely clerical tasks. Sonny described her work on a project implementing software for clients. Sonny's role involves obtaining a long list of documents specifying what Denoter will do for the client. Then her manager and the client map out the scope of the work. Sonny's job is to then go back through that list of documents. She said, "[My job is] saying, 'Okay we can do x, y, z, but we can't do the end of the list based off of what's in scope.' . . . It's based off of information we were already given." Notice that this task does not require analytical skill beyond comparing the work map to the initial documents. In addition, Sonny takes notes in meetings and keeps track of deadlines and action items.

The recent graduates described in this section all received work tasks representative of the majority of practical arts alumni, both men and women, who participated in my study. Many engaged in clerical, liaison, or administrative work that was menial and unrelated to the technical training they received as undergraduates. Of course, the structural inequalities inherent in higher education led to unequal outcomes by demographic cleavages in my study. However, graduates' race, gender, class background, specific major (business or engineering), internship type, and even job type, all varied independently of practical arts graduates' task assignments at work.[7]

The Business and Engineering Graduates Who Completed Substantive Tasks at Work

I now turn to the approximately 30 percent of business and engineering graduates whose entry-level jobs involved substantive tasks, either complex problem-solving or a project. Jordan, a business alum who works at Axios Airlines, the same company that provided him with a career conveyor-belt internship, engaged in complex problem-solving at work. Jordan's job title is domestic pricing analyst, and he is responsible for updating the prices of Axios flights in a certain region of the US. Essentially, Jordan sets fares by working off pricing strategies, sales, or promotions that Axios runs or off competitors' prices. Pricing fluctuates unpredictably throughout the day and Jordan found this stimulating. He said, "You really just never know, that makes it kind of cool, you just never know what's going to come through. It's like every couple of hours you get a new wave. So, it's like opening up a package and, 'All right, what's this one going to be?'" When asked if he was happy with his career progress so far, Jordan responded, "Yeah, absolutely." Pricing and the airline industry were both good matches for Jordan's operations and logistics degree, and the satisfying tasks reinforced that the job was a good fit for him personally.

While Jordan's tasks involved the complex problem-solving that many business and engineering majors enjoyed, Lesley's employment exemplifies substantive project work. Lesley studied ISE and she works for a large food and beverage company. Her title is supply chain engineer, so her job and sector match her degree well. Lesley's tasks involve a mixture of supervisory work, projects, and data analysis, but she said, "The project work is my favorite part." She gave me an overview of the projects she is working on:

> There is one that I'm extremely excited about doing. It's going to be affecting mostly the packers but also operators, and so it's going to be a rewards program. Basically, what's going to happen is they'll be told, "If you have less than 3 percent waste, you're going to get a star or something for the day. If you get so many stars, you can trade it in and get a free T-shirt or an umbrella or cooler or something really fun." That's going to hopefully help us meet our numbers better and then also reward the employees because you don't see that a lot. It's more like, "We expect you to do this, you better do it." I'm changing that culture at the plant by creating these rewards programs. Some of the other programs I'm working on involve automation, which we can't let leave the plant quite yet, but just to give you an idea of what it is, it's just creating a better line to run certain equipment using automation.

Like, Jordan, Lesley found her work exciting. For both, the job-to-degree match was evident and, notably, their assignments related to their learned skills.

Jordan and Lesley both had career conveyor-belt internships, but some business and engineering graduates with dead-end internships also found jobs where they used their human capital at work, further reinforcing that internship type and work tasks are unrelated among practical arts graduates. For example, Marly, the ISE major who had a dead-end internship for several summers at her mother's manufacturing firm, conducted a full job search and found a position at another manufacturing company. Marly was one of very few graduates in this study to do pure industrial engineering in her entry-level job. She creates standard operating procedures for a part of her employer's workflow. She explained how this works: "What I was doing for the first three weeks was observing the process, physically doing it myself, and then just kind of documenting everything I could see and taking time studies." Marly's job combines the complex problem-solving and project work that other practical arts majors found desirable. She described the work as engaging and challenging, saying, "It's definitely helped me grow a lot." Though her work might not sound substantive, workflow optimization projects and the specifics of doing time studies are both part of an industrial engineering curriculum. Further, this task differed from her clerical internship assignment where she simply asked workers how their job deviated from the standard operating procedures rather than collect data herself. In the end, Marly found work that directly used her degree skills.

The examples of Marly, Lesley, and Jordan illustrate that, as would be expected, some practical arts graduates used their degree skills and completed substantive work at their entry-level jobs. Surprisingly, and contrary to public narratives, these three cases were anomalies in my study. Moreover, these graduates and their peers who completed solely clerical tasks would appear the same according to traditional employment measures, yet pay, stability, benefits, occupation-to-degree match—none of these indicators reflect the type of work employees completed, substantive or clerical.

Entry-Level Tasks for Communications and English Graduates

More than half of the liberal arts majors in this study completed substantive tasks at their entry-level jobs. This is partially explained by the kinds of firms that hired English and communications graduates, most of which were smaller organizations than those who hired practical arts majors. Large companies, with a bigger division of labor, might have narrower clerical tasks for entry-level employees than smaller firms where employees are likely to have more task variety. Indeed, the few communications and English majors who worked in large firms, many of whom had career conveyor-belt internships, were more likely to conduct clerical tasks at work. And although a trade-off between stable employment and interesting work is often discussed, researchers and commentators rarely think of this compromise in terms of skill usage. Media narratives rarely suggest the liberal arts graduates working in smaller firms under more precarious employment conditions are the ones using their degree skills in the workplace.

Liberal Arts Graduates Who Completed Substantive Tasks at Work

Many liberal arts graduates found jobs that matched their field of study and required degree-relevant skills. Sophie works at Johnson Advertising, a marketing agency in the same city as CSU. She studied communications and, like many other graduates of her major, did not have a career conveyor-belt internship. Rather, Sophie interned at a nonprofit where she mostly organized events. When Sophie graduated, it took her a long time to find employment and she found the job search stressful. Ultimately, she found the job at Johnson online; she had no prior connection to the firm and knew no one who worked there.

Sophie's experience with Johnson Advertising encapsulates the trade-off between majors. Her job was not as stable or remunerative as most of her practical arts peers' positions, but her work mostly involved tasks directly related to skills she acquired for her degree. These responsibilities included creating and implementing a social media strategy for her clients. She recounted her experience with a new client: "I had just got a new client on Tuesday, so I did my call with him to go over all of his social media. So, I [then] started writing content for him to be posted." Beyond discussing strategy with the client, Sophie also went through her client's social media reviews to address specific strengths and concerns. Additionally, she tracked the success of her social media posts and used past experiences with other clients as a guide. For example, she told me, "We have a lot of dentists, so I kind of look back to see how other clients have performed with certain strategies." For each client, Sophie posted on Facebook, Twitter, and Google+. She found her work challenging, interesting, and she applied the skills she learned in her major that she had hoped to use professionally.

Another communications graduate, Lisa, works at Northern Brands, a PR/marketing firm. Lisa's job title, social media and digital content coordinator, matched her field of study and directly related to her work. Lisa said, "I probably manage about thirteen social [media] accounts right now. I write a ton of copy, I write blogs, web pages, every day." She even does higher order work, saying, "I'm dabbling in strategy work; I work to build marketing strategies." Writing copy and social media posts for clients are skills Lisa learned for her communications degree. She found the work fulfilling, saying, "All day I write about gas compressors, and yesterday I took a bit to write bubble wrap. . . . I really love it because I would never dabble into these industries without doing what I do." For Lisa, the connection between her degree and title extended to her work tasks, making her fortunate and happy. Notice that Lisa and Sophie mentioned writing about gas compressors, dentists, and bubble wrap, reflecting their more practical applications of PR skills rather than something more stereotypically glamorous.[8] These graduates also described work much more positively than their practical arts counterparts who were hired to perform clerical tasks.

Some jobs requiring substantive and fulfilling work may not match so well with graduates' degrees. Marty, a communications major who had substantive tasks in a job less related to his college major, interned for a professional sports team. After graduation he found a job in a small city working as the development coordinator for the regional office of a national nonprofit. Marty worked to fundraise for the organization and his job involved some clerical work, including event planning and responding to emails. However, he also worked closely with his boss on substantive projects. He explained, "We also do all the marketing stuff. For example, this is our 125th year in Granada,[9] and so we're kind of basing a lot of what we do around this milestone. We're doing a lot of extra marketing initiatives, and we created this milestone book." To construct the book, Marty gave the content to a graphic design company, and they put the book together. This form of content creation was common among communications graduates who were assigned substantive tasks at work. He went on to say that his job is very collaborative between him and his boss: "We make everything. And then, [there's] social media. I do the social media, as well, although we're mainly just on Facebook. But I do all the Facebook posts and everything like that, [all the] marketing materials." Despite his job title and employment in the nonprofit sector, Marty substantively applied his degree skills at work.

English graduates with substantive work tasks tended to have similar experiences as communications graduates. Jennifer also found a job matched to her degree. Unlike many liberal arts graduates, Jennifer only spent one month job searching; however, she took a risk that many of her peers did not: she moved to New York City without anything lined up and worked in a retail consignment shop until she found a suitable professional position. Now, Jennifer works as a social media writer for a digital marketing company that mostly promotes restaurants. In this role, Jennifer travels to restaurants, samples their food, and writes social media posts about the experience. This requires substantive work that uses her degree skills. Jennifer said, "My job is to have a relationship with the chefs and general managers and just make sure I'm getting the tone for the copy for Instagram captions right." Jennifer spends all day eating food, taking pictures of food, and writing social media posts about food. It was not very surprising when she said, "I enjoy that a lot." Jennifer's work involved photo editing and copywriting, substantive tasks quite different from the clerical work some of her peers are doing. However, Jennifer's example is also indicative of the trade-off students make. She was underemployed before finding this position, which pays $36,000 with no opportunities for advancement. Thus far in her career, all of Jennifer's postgraduation jobs are examples of precarious work.

Recall that Laura from the previous chapter had a difficult transition to the labor market. Like many English majors, she spent months job searching and had to move in with her parents. Eventually, she settled for a job unrelated to her degree. Laura works as a program adviser/product specialist for a firm that sells vendor management software. Clearly, her job is not matched to her English degree. However, her job aligns more closely with the new organizational careers of practical arts majors than the more precarious employment typical of English graduates. Laura's tasks are substantive and require degree skills. When discussing her work tasks, Laura said, "When I was first hired, I was doing a lot of research. Online research was pretty much my entire job." Laura has a list of clients, and she has to research news about their organizations. She explained, "Anything about mergers and acquisitions I'm going to want to look into more. If one of our vendors is being acquired by another company, that's going to be pretty big news . . . anything about leadership changes . . . any sort of financial risk or big organizational changes for a company. Any legal trouble, if somebody there broke the law and it's being reported on or if a government agency is investigating their company. Things like that." Beyond online research, Laura works on contract reporting. This differs from liaison work because she engages in problem-solving. She said, "Sometimes it's like solving a puzzle." Laura needs to see how documents uploaded into the system fit with other information already submitted. She said, "It can get really complicated with certain vendors." Despite not having a job matched to her degree, Laura uses her substantive research skills. Her tasks resemble the substantive work of business and engineering graduates more than the content creation her liberal arts peers perform.

All graduates in these examples entered the labor market after dead-end internships, demonstrating once again that career conveyor-belt internships do not necessarily lead to better jobs by all metrics of job quality. Nonetheless, here I give an example of a liberal arts graduate with a career conveyor-belt internship who completes substantive tasks at work. Katie, an English graduate, was one of the few liberal arts majors who had a career conveyor-belt internship and found a job that matched her degree. She works as a copywriter for an eyeglass retailer writing "brand descriptions," "product descriptions," and "blog posts." Writing brand descriptions for many pairs of eyeglasses is quite skilled work, as the descriptions must be distinct yet concisely written. This kind of writing is a substantive application of Katie's English major skills. Research finds that even college graduates struggle with writing well professionally,[10] which suggests other majors might be less successful in this position. Katie's situation was unique, however. Most English and communications graduates with career conveyor-belt internships ended up in corporate firms with jobs unrelated to their field of study and engaged in liaison or clerical work. This was likely because the types of jobs that required communications and English majors' skills rarely hired through career conveyor-belt internships, demonstrating once again the salience of internship type for entry-level job placement for those in this study.

Of the six recent graduates discussed in this section, four had occupation-to-degree matches. The other two, Marty and Laura, worked in positions that survey researchers would not consider a match to their degrees.[11] These six cases are representative of over twenty respondents who majored in liberal arts and now conduct substantive work in their entry-level jobs.

English and Communications Graduates Who Completed Clerical Work

Just under half of liberal arts graduates were assigned exclusively clerical work at their entry-level jobs. Usually these graduates worked at large corporations; however, some worked in smaller firms or had more precarious employment conditions. For example, English graduate Marne secured a part-time job at a library. She said 80 percent of her job was circulation desk and clerical tasks, such as checking books in and out. Despite having a job matched to her degree, the work tasks and employment conditions were disappointing to her.[12] When asked about her thoughts on the job, she said, "It's definitely not my favorite." Recall that Marne obtained a first undergraduate degree in accounting before returning to school to get a second degree in English. She hoped switching to this field would help her find work at a library. Although she was partially successful (she did find work, but it is part-time and therefore precarious), her day-to-day tasks were disappointing.

Colleen, another English alum, found a job in publishing, a sector that matches her degree. While her job title, project manager, sounds impressive, she mostly conducts liaison work. Colleen is responsible for "handling all the external [communications] between our clients with our in-house teams, making sure that everything gets done on time." In practice, this means Colleen spends most of her day emailing and participating in "status conference calls and stuff, just making sure everyone is on the same page with where things are." For Colleen, this seemed unrelated to her degree, even though she worked in publishing. She said that an English degree would only be relevant if she wrote more. And while many graduates write a lot in their entry-level jobs (e.g., by sending emails all day), those tasked with liaison work rarely create complex content that closely matches English or communications degrees. Therefore, while a survey researcher might uncover that employees like Colleen spend much of their work time writing emails, her own assessment of the work tasks reveals that this form of writing is not an application of substantive major-specific skills.

Colleen's work requires her to use time-management software that controls the steps and pacing of her duties: "Every single project has its own schedule in the program. . . . From when we get the manuscript all the way to when it gets sent out. So, you're constantly having to go in and sort of update where it's at, and as things get finished, mark them complete. So that way it tracks, accurately, how long we're spending on projects so that they know that they're estimating their bids correctly for our clients." While Colleen stated that the purpose of the time-management program is to estimate bids correctly, it also controls her task steps and deadlines and allows others in her organization to monitor her work. So, while Colleen is an English graduate working in publishing, her tasks are mundane and controlled by a computer program.

Alan, a communications graduate, works as a technology analyst for a cybersecurity team at Diamond Bank. When asked what he does every day, Alan responded, "Most of it is responding to emails and making Excel documents." When I pushed him to explain further, Alan said, "I do a lot of reporting to the broader groups about any security risks in our system. So, a lot of that is pulling data, organizing it, and then sending it out to a team somewhere else in the company, saying, 'Hey here are some of the things you need to work on, the deadline is this, and if you don't do it, we'll start talking to your bosses.'" While Alan produces the reports, he does not choose which ones to run and send, nor does he follow up on any responses to the security risks. Alan does not find this work interesting, engaging, or intellectually stimulating. Alan's tasks are unrelated to his major and typical of work done by graduates who had career conveyor-belt internships. Further, the repetitive and nondiscretionary nature of his tasks match the definition of clerical work, even though Alan's employment conditions qualify as a new organizational career.

For communications graduates working in large bureaucratic firms, clerical tasks were the norm, even if they did not enter the organization through career conveyor-belt internships. Emily earned one of the highest salaries for communications majors in this study despite having a dead-end internship at college. She makes $49,000 and works for the large technology company Thebes, in the kind of stable employment indicative of a new organizational career. She obtained this job when a recruiter reached out to her, and although it did not seem interesting to her at first, the salary drew her in. Emily has $100,000 in student loans, making a corporate job more attractive to her than it otherwise would have been. Unlike Alan, who was drawn to a bank because he did not know what he wanted to do, Emily was drawn to Thebes for the money. But similarly to Alan, she found the work boring.

Emily works in sales. She cold-calls businesses to ask if they would be interested in purchasing Thebes's products. Working down a list, Emily calls the contacts and asks if they would be interested in an introduction to the tools Thebes offers. This work is extremely repetitive. Emily asks if they want a "quick introduction," saying, "That's literally what I say every single time. If it's marketing, I'll say marketing analytics. If it's finance, I'll say finance analytics." Many respondents told me explicitly that they hoped to avoid working in sales after graduation, yet several felt they had to accept sales positions. These graduates, including Emily, did not enjoy their work. Emily said, "They want us to make fifty dials a day, but realistically, I don't do that many because I hate dialing and most times people don't want to talk to you. . . . I don't feel like calling that many people." Emily's tasks are boring, clerical, and unrelated to her degree skills.

The fifty dials per day metric is particularly stressful for Emily and likely matches others' experiences, as employers often monitor calls.[13] Emily told me, "Sometimes I make fake dials just because they monitor that stuff." When probed to explain further, she said, "The way they monitor our calls, they only see if you reach ten seconds then it counts as one. So, you can dial any number, let it sit there until it reaches ten and then you hang up." This strategy works particularly well if companies have automated phone systems with a menu of options when the call first connects. In those cases, Emily lets the automated message play for ten seconds before ending the call.

Alan and Emily, both communications majors, worked in corporate jobs unrelated to their degrees, while Marne and Collen, English majors, worked in occupations or sectors closely matched to their degrees, in a library and in publishing, respectively. However, none of these four graduates engaged in substantive tasks at their entry-level jobs. Rather, they all participated in rote clerical work similar to the tasks many ISE and business graduates performed. This is yet further evidence that an occupation-to-degree match does not indicate whether a graduate uses their degree-specific human capital or even much of their general human capital.

College Majors and Entry-Level Work Tasks

The evidence presented in this chapter offers important correctives to two of the common myths perpetuated by public narratives about why some college graduates are more "employable" early in their careers than others. First, I found no evidence that business and engineering graduates are in demand to employers because their degree skills are needed in entry-level work. In theory, matches between degrees and jobs are often understood as evidence of skill-matching or human capital explanations connecting school and work.[14] Theoretically, this is the reason why graduates of practical arts disciplines are more employable than liberal arts alumni and therefore, the reason behind the growth of these fields of study.[15] However, when I investigated the work tasks practical arts graduates are actually doing, I found that the data does not support the theory. On the contrary, the vast majority of practical arts graduates I interviewed conducted clerical work at their entry-level jobs, even at jobs considered good by traditional employment indicators.

The second myth this chapter dispels is that liberal arts majors only use "soft skills" at work rather than any degree skills. Data about the work these graduates do shows otherwise: roughly half of the English and communications majors I interviewed conducted substantive work that drew on their skills developed in college, usually in the form of content creation. Yet, despite the demand for these work-related skills, liberal arts graduates often struggle to find jobs and, when they do, their chances of finding a new organizational career (much less one matched to their degree) were markedly lower than those of practical arts graduates.[16]

In another twist, English graduates' initial median salary is $33,500, while ISE graduates in this study on average earn almost double that. Yet, the English and communications majors I spoke to are more likely to use their degree skills in their entry-level jobs while most business and engineering graduates perform exclusively clerical tasks in their work.

Lower remuneration for liberal arts degree skills is an important component of the trade-off between majors. The issue is particularly pernicious because of its race, class, and gender implications. English, communications, and many other liberal arts disciplines, and the skills they impart, such as writing and communications skills, are associated with women and less privileged men.[17] As a result, the fruits of the labor market go disproportionately to White, middle-class men, most of whom enter the labor market seamlessly via career conveyor-belt internships.

While many of the differences between graduates in the outcomes explored in this book may be attributable to the types of firms that employ them, it cannot easily explain the differences in skill usage. There is no reason to suspect that recent graduates' tasks would be primarily clerical in nature, even at large firms with a high division of labor. As for pay, Emily, the communications major who was employed by a large bureaucratic firm, earned less money than business and engineering graduates in comparable firms, yet they all conducted mostly clerical work. This suggests firm size is not the whole story, although it does play an important role. Large bureaucratic firms have cut the number of front-line and clerical workers in recent decades,[18] which may push these tasks onto entry-level workers. However, this same fact would likely affect smaller firms as well (i.e., fewer dedicated clerical or secretarial staff).

In sum, liberal arts majors are more likely than practical arts majors to do substantive tasks at work. This finding suggests that it is not, in fact, easy to classify what is "practical" and what is not when it comes to a college education. Liberal arts degrees can prove useful for entry-level work in ways more aligned with public narratives about practical arts.

Chapter 7 continues to invert the common distinction between "practical" and "passion" majors by showing more specifically how graduates' degree skills relate to their entry-level jobs, including how practical arts graduates use their degrees in ways media narratives often associate with liberal arts graduates.

7: THE RELEVANCE OF COLLEGE DEGREES FOR ENTRY-LEVEL WORK

Researchers and commentators often discuss liberal arts and practical arts degrees quite differently. They tend to say that the liberal arts provide a well-rounded education rather than job training. For example, those seeking to major in liberal arts disciplines are said to "regard their undergraduate education not simply as a training ground for jobs but as a time for learning and personal growth,"[1] and that "training in the liberal arts is believed to strengthen a student's character and to develop qualities such as reason, judgment, and a sense of social obligation."[2] To be sure, students should use their undergraduate years for personal growth, however, highlighting these attributes cedes the "practical" application of college to technical or vocational disciplines. Liberal arts majors at CSU, and likely at comparable universities, learn a mix of occupational and general liberal arts skills.[3] Meanwhile, job advertisements call for liberal arts competencies, yet they rarely list liberal arts majors as desirable fields of study for candidates.[4]

In contrast, public discourse exalts practical disciplines, like business or engineering, as the fields where students learn skills for the contemporary workforce. Vocational and preprofessional fields are "designed explicitly to provide a student with the practical and job-related competencies necessary for entry into a specific occupation or profession, including business, . . . engineering," and other similar fields.[5] Graduates of these fields are in demand to employers and transition seamlessly from college to high-paying, stable jobs.

My findings run counter to public discourse surrounding degree fields and instead reveal the final component of the true trade-off between majors: Practical arts degrees lead mainly to highly paid clerical work, and liberal arts degrees usually lead to relatively low-paid substantive work that draws on graduates' degree-specific skills.

Taken together, this and the previous chapter examine the substance of entry-level jobs. Chapter 6 shows liberal arts students in this study were more likely to complete substantive tasks in entry-level work. Here I go one step further and show that the liberal arts graduates I interviewed were more likely to use specific degree skills by applying major-related coursework in their entry-level jobs than the practical arts graduates who participated in this study. I discuss how all graduates—with variations by major—see their degree as either "just" a required credential, as providing specific skills for work, or as providing general skills.

Approximately 30 percent of business and engineering alumni engaged their degree skills in entry-level work. Since that number is low, practical arts graduates tended to think about their degrees in more pessimistic terms during our second interview than they had during their senior year of college. For example, many admitted they did not need a college degree to complete their work tasks, even if they needed a degree to get hired. Others suggested their degrees were mostly useful because of the general liberal arts skills they acquired. While a well-rounded education is important, if practical arts majors apply only their liberal arts skills at work, this undermines the main rationale commentators, policymakers, and educators use for funneling students and resources into "practical" disciplines.

Meanwhile, almost half of the liberal arts students in this study used degree-specific concepts, tools, or skills in their entry-level jobs. They often framed their degree's relevance more positively than the practical arts alumni. Of course, these numbers are not representative or applicable to the general population, yet they are meaningful because, based on popular narratives we would expect the engineering and business graduates to use their degree-specific skills at higher rates than communications and English graduates, especially given their higher rates of occupation-to-degree matching. Figure 7.1 shows these differences.

Recall from chapter 2 that I asked each student what they were learning in their major classes during senior year. I then aggregated this information into a curriculum for each discipline. In second-wave interviews, I asked each graduate what they were doing at work and explicitly asked them to document how each task was achieved (a process I describe more fully in the methodological appendix). As a result, the percentages of students who used their degree-specific skills in entry-level work is based on matching graduates' responses about entry-level work tasks to the aggregated curriculum *and* graduates' own self-assessment. In almost all cases, my assessment and the graduates' self-assessment matched.[6]

Here I delve into how degrees prepared graduates for their entry-level jobs. My findings show that, while practical arts students may have better initial employment outcomes by traditional indicators, they are less likely to deploy degree skills at work. In fact, liberal arts graduates are more likely to

■ Applies Coursework   ■ Does Not Apply Coursework

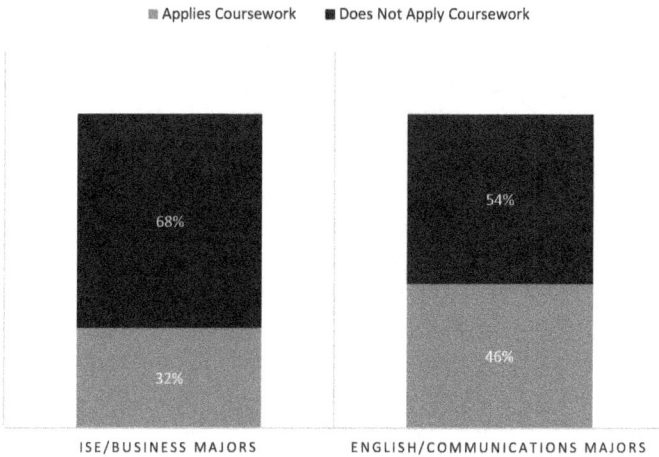

FIGURE 7.1 Degree-Specific Skill Use at Entry-Level Jobs by Major
Note: For this graph *n* = 85 because it includes only those who participated in wave two.

apply their degree-specific skills at work, particularly at jobs that are precarious and poorly paid.

Using Degree Skills in Entry-Level Work

Ostensibly, college prepares students for work,[7] and this is especially thought to be the case for students of the practical arts who receive training for specific professions, rather than students who study the liberal arts and supposedly receive only general training.[8] And though degrees from CSU provide both liberal arts competencies and pragmatic occupational skills, greater workforce preparation is often touted as the true advantage to choosing a practical arts major over a liberal arts major.

Evidence for this claim is often backed by survey research on occupation-to-degree matching. The extent to which majors match occupations is generally measured as a categorical distinction rather than along a continuum. Sociologists Josipa Roksa and Tania Levey break down degree fields into high, moderate, and low occupational specificity based on the number of alumni in those fields who find jobs related to their disciplines.[9] Business and engineering have two of the highest rates of matching in the moderate category (approximately 60 percent matching each) while communications and humanities students qualify as low matching (closer to 20 percent).[10]

Studies often argue that degree-to-job matching demonstrates that college graduates use their degree skills at work.[11] They assume, for example, that a logistics major who gets a job in logistics means the student learned logistics skills in college and applies them at work. On the other hand, if an English major gets a job in logistics, this is usually taken as evidence that the graduate's general skills (either learned in school or elsewhere) were sufficient to land the job.[12] Research on occupation-to-degree matching is often quantitative and based on survey data. Yet, through qualitative inquiry I show that occupation-to-degree matching is no guarantee that a graduate will use degree skills at work. Perhaps the hypothetical logistics major mentioned above is just getting coffee for managers in that entry-level job. After all, almost 40 percent of all employees in the economy consider their jobs to be "bullshit" or unnecessary for the functioning of the organization or the economy.[13] Indeed, this would suggest that my findings may well reflect work tasks even beyond entry-level jobs.

How Business and Engineering Graduates "Used" Their Degrees

Many business and engineering graduates I spoke to questioned whether they really needed a college degree to be successful at work. They discussed needing the degree to fulfill a requirement, but nothing more. The extent to which this reality bothered respondents varied. Ultimately, many graduates said they needed their specific degree to be employable at the level they wanted to work. When asked if their courses at CSU were useful, several participants mentioned using only their general liberal arts skills at work.

Burt and Kelly studied business and engineering, respectively. Both graduates had career conveyor-belt internships. Burt now works as an analyst for Syringa, a large automaker where he also interned. Burt does not use specific business skills in his entry-level job. When I asked Burt more about this, he said, "The whole point of a liberal arts education is the ability to be pliable, and the ability to think for yourself no matter what the situation, and to learn constantly." When I asked further questions about how his education connected to his job, Burt said, "If I had to put a percentage on it, I'd say maybe 5 percent of what I learned in school has been directly transferable to my position." The general, rather than specific, applicability of his degree goes against common notions of business majors' skills. Burt frequently referred to his "liberal arts" education, despite business being classified as a practical art.[14] Burt used this term somewhat pejoratively and is worth quoting at length:

BURT: The cynic in me says that school is, especially a liberal arts education, not about how much knowledge you accumulate. It's about the ability to show up on time, turn things in that are what's being asked of you, and gain knowledge when you're asked to. And so, I think in that vein, it all transfers really well [to working].

CMP: But why do you think that's cynical?

BURT: Because then you're saying content doesn't matter. *So even if it was that I went to school and learned about nothing but the English language or Arabic or did Hebrew poetry studies, then I could still go in and have a business career.* And I don't think that's too far off base. Obviously, exposure to certain principles and certain ideas like a Pareto chart is something that if you'd never seen a Pareto chart and you showed up for a business job day one, somebody's probably going to look at you sideways. But at the same time, if you have the ability to learn and understand, then the first time somebody explains 80/20 to you, then, [you say] "Okay, I get it." [italics mine]

CMP: Do you think you really need a degree to do your job?

BURT: No.

CMP: You could have done it before you went to college?

BURT: Yes.

Burt sounded disappointed that he could have majored in Hebrew poetry and been equally equipped to do his job at Syringa. In fact, one of the media narratives in the opening chapter explicitly stated that poetry won't "pay the bills."[15] Burt's account, however, reflects the idea that a business degree prepared him for entry-level work as well as a poetry degree would have. His experience differed considerably from what we would expect based on public narratives about practical arts majors.

Kelly is an account manager at Cloud Source, the large technology company where she previously held an internship. Like Burt, she also thought her degree had prepared her by providing general liberal arts skills, but she viewed this less negatively than Burt. To Kelly, an engineering degree did not provide her with useful technical skills, but instead taught her general competencies. She explained, "You know how to think. So that's what I think my degree prepared me for in this situation. Like, *I didn't learn anything in college that directly correlated with what I'm doing,* [italics mine] but I have a problem-solving logical mindset that I learned from engineering." She even told me explicitly, "I'm not using any industrial engineering . . . which is good, because I don't want to do that." Still, Cloud Source only considered engineering majors for the role Kelly holds. Kelly agreed with this policy, stating, "I just don't think an English major would have the right mindset to do this [job]. Maybe one in a few." Kelly suggested that school taught her how to think, which she saw as essential to being successful at her job. Regardless of whether an English major could do the work, she saw her degree as useful for the nontechnical skills it provided.

Ultimately, I found that most practical arts graduates gave two kinds of answers to how their degrees prepared them for working. Some said they did not need the degree at all. Others said they needed a degree for the general liberal arts skills they acquired. Only a small minority said they needed specific degree skills for their entry-level job. And although recent graduates may not be fully aware of how their degrees translate to entry-level work, since they have recently graduated, the classroom concepts should be fresh in thair minds. Yet their narratives departed considerably from the media narratives covered in chapter 1.

Degree as "Just" a Credential

Many respondents suggested their degrees were necessary to successfully *enter* the labor market, but not because of the skills gained from coursework. Sandy, a business graduate, works at a consulting firm. When asked if she needed a degree to do her job, she laughed and said "no." She espoused a view of credentialism for why education matters for employment—the degree is simply a requirement, but the content does not matter.[16] She said, "I think I need a piece of paper to get the job. I think they looked at me and saw someone who speaks a couple of different languages, but that's not something I learned in school." Sandy perhaps gave her degree more weight than others, suggesting that the credential represented her human capital. But Sandy did not think that school was where she built that human capital.[17] Besides saying she learned languages outside of school, Sandy added, "I think, had you put me in a job like this after high school, I would have totally crashed and failed. . . . I think people need to understand the value of working hard and they need the time to do that, and I don't think the classrooms are what teach that." For Sandy, college provided an opportunity for her to grow, mature, and learn valuable time-management and responsibility skills. However, she decoupled these skills from the classroom.

Sandy was disappointed by the lack of engagement with her degree. She regretted majoring in business; when asked if she would change anything about her education, she said, "I probably would have told myself to take some more time to get a degree I can actually use." Sandy's view that a business degree is not useful runs counter to narratives about the practical arts as advantageous degree fields. Overall, Sandy was not unusual among respondents; many participants reported that a degree was needed to get a job, but not necessarily to perform well at work.

Connie, an industrial and systems engineering (ISE) graduate, likewise said that she did not need a college degree to do her job at a technology firm. Despite graduating from a practical arts discipline and holding a job with the title technical consultant, when asked if she feels like she needs a college degree to do her job, Connie said, "In my personal opinion, no." She explained, "I think that higher education is a good and great and wonderful thing, but I don't think that a lack of it makes somebody incapable of doing the work." Yet, Connie told me everyone in her workplace has a college degree. She even mentioned part of her trouble adjusting to the workplace was based on a belief she expressed, saying, "My education was not the best way to prepare me for the job."

Connie's example, like Sandy's above, shows that, even in technical disciplines, graduates with an occupation-to-degree match may view a college degree as unnecessary to perform their work tasks. For these two graduates, their practical arts degrees did not provide specific skills or concepts they used in entry-level work.

Technical Degrees Provide Nontechnical Human Capital

Graduates may recognize the utility of their degrees even when not applying the skills they learned in their major at work. I highlight two representative engineering graduates who, despite having the most technical degree in this study, said their degrees applied to entry-level work exclusively by providing general competencies. Roberta works at Republic Automotive. When asked if she engaged her degree skills at work, she said, "Honestly, not a whole lot." She went on to say this made her feel "kinda bummed . . . I would like to do something more ISE related, as opposed to what I'm doing now." Roberta is now a packaging engineer, yet despite the word "engineer" in her title, she did not think her degree skills prepared her for the job. Roberta did, however, point out the recruitment advantages of studying engineering. She said, "I don't think you necessarily need an engineering degree, but I think now they hire in engineering. But I think a lot of people who aren't engineers could probably do it." Roberta told me Republic only hired engineers for positions like hers, but she did not use her engineering skills and thought nonengineers could do the work as well.

Further, Republic only hires from certain schools. Students had a sense of these recruitment advantages as interns and saw the full picture later as employees. Roberta explained, "A lot of people in my group went to Capital State, or Northern State, or Rolling State,[18] so it's kind of like the Midwestern [schools], because I think that's where Republic is going to be recruiting." While Republic Automotive has many facilities in the Midwest, they are a multinational corporation with offices and manufacturing facilities in many states. Roberta now saw how much difference career conveyor-belt internships make for college graduates. Her chances of getting a job with Republic, even one where she does not use any degree-specific skills, were greatly enhanced by her engineering degree from one of a select few schools where the firm recruits.

While Roberta reported that her engineering degree is not necessary for success in her position, she said that the college experience prepared her for working. Roberta was somewhat contradictory in her account of how school remained relevant saying, "I think it did a pretty good job. I mean, like I said, I'm not really using my degree a whole lot, so some of the classes that I struggled with, I'm like ugh, what a waste." What accounts for Roberta holding these contradictory views? Despite Roberta not using her engineering classes or degree, she thought school provided general competencies or skills that enhanced her ability. She said, "I think at the end of the day it's just more teaching you . . . the nontechnical skills, like how to work with different people, time management, and thinking through problems, stuff like that. So, I think it did prepare me well." Roberta espoused a direct liberal arts defense of her degree. *The greatest preparation Roberta said she received from her engineering degree for her engineering position was developing nontechnical skills.* Her perspective, like Burt's, was rampant throughout my sample of business and engineering graduates. It is possible that these alumni will use specific degree skills later in their careers, although working in highly technical jobs later may require skills far afield from past college courses. Nonetheless, at this early career stage, many said school prepared them for work only by providing general skills.

To show this is not a matter of gender sorting along technical and social roles in engineering, a common phenomenon found in prior research,[19] I present Steve, another engineering graduate who thought his general competencies better applied to his entry-level work than his technical training. Steve works in the Operations Management Leadership Program of a manufacturing firm. When I asked him if his coursework applied to his current duties, he said, "That's a good question," and then paused for four full seconds. He went on to say, "There are certain things [that apply], I think the thought process. Because that's one of the things they say, is that college isn't teaching you what to think, it's teaching you how to think, and how to approach things in a scientific method. I think that's what I really got out of college." When asked if any of his specific coursework applies to his tasks, Steve responded, "For what I'm doing now, no." Recall from chapter 2 that Steve thought his machine class and other concepts from school would apply when he entered the workforce. Yet Steve did not seem bothered about this disconnect between his initial expectations and current employment since he acknowledged credentialism as a component of higher education, saying of the rotation program he is in, "I think there's no other way to do it than to get a college degree," meaning it was a requirement for his job. Like Roberta and many others in this study, Steve had an engineering degree and an engineering job, yet he described general liberal arts competencies (in his case, learning how to think) as the most transferable skill from college.

Turning now to business graduates, Tonya also did not think her degree was needed for her job. Tonya had a career conveyor-belt internship and now works at Midwest Motors, a multinational car company. Tonya studied operations and said part of the reason she did not use her degree was that "every company is so unique in the way that they operate . . . I don't think there's any great blueprint that you could learn." Tonya explained that the specific concepts she learned in school were not applicable at work. When asked to what extent she used the skills she learned in her degree, Tonya said:

> I don't even know what to tell you, there's nothing great. . . . You know, it's like I wish I could say there were hard things that I learned that I can think back and say, "This material requirement and planning that we had to fill out for this one time," but it's like we don't use that in real life. We have systems that do that for us, and our systems suck, but we don't do it [ourselves]. Like I had a whole class on office controlling and planning . . . but those [are] things that I think you would have learned and picked up on when you got to whatever job you got to.

Tonya is yet another practical arts student whose specific training in school did not apply to her work, going so far as to say, "We don't use that in real life."

Like many other practical arts alumni in this study, Tonya noted the direct recruitment of CSU students by Midwest Motors as one the main ways her education connected to her work. When asked about this connection directly, Tonya said, "Recruiting-wise, yeah. That's actually a really big part of why I think I've been successful so far at Midwest Motors . . . being tied to CSU." Tonya even said, "I think 'What if?' sometimes, because if I hadn't met Elaine, who smiled at me at the career fair, if that had never happened, I don't even know what the heck I would've been doing." The career fair that led to the internship explicitly got Tonya in the door. She said, "The way that we hire now is really from our internship pool."

Tonya's reflections on the specific utility of her business degree aligned with Roberta's; both respondents felt the recruitment advantages of their disciplines mattered more for their employment status than the specific content of their coursework, showing how similar the career trajectories of business and engineering graduates were in this study.

Similarly to Roberta and Steve, Tonya discussed the general competencies she learned in school. She said, "I think if anything, the experiences [of school] and the discipline [it teaches], the time management, the maturing that you're supposed to do in college, that was to help me prepare, I think." Notice Tonya hedged by saying things like "if anything," and ending her answer with "I think." She was skeptical that school prepared her for working, but she acknowledged that maturing and learning time management may have increased her ability to work successfully. The responses from business and engineering graduates to questions about school preparation abounded with these kinds of answers. Some, like Burt, specifically mentioned the liberal arts education they received, but most followed the same narrative as Tonya and Roberta, stating that the general skills all college graduates acquired—time management, discipline, maturity, teamwork—combined as the biggest contribution school gave them for success in the workplace.

All of the graduates discussed in this section had career conveyor-belt internships. I now give one example of a practical arts graduate who had a dead-end internship to show that internship type had no bearing on skill usage at work. Similar to their counterparts with career conveyor-belt internships, only about a third of practical arts graduates with dead-end internships said their degrees specifically applied to their entry-level job tasks.

Nick, a business graduate, also works at Midwest Motors. His job involves liaison work. A buyer sends him a list of products the organization needs to buy. Nick inputs information about the products into a software system that delivers output for him to relay to others in his department. As Nick explains, "I just have to find the details and run it through the program and get that cost for the buyer." When I asked Nick how busy his work is, he said it depends on if he has all the information required to enter into the software system and how many products have been sent to him by buyers. He said when the buyers "get me all the information I need right away, I can have it turned around in fifteen minutes."

Despite conducting clerical tasks at work, like many of his peers with and without career conveyor-belt internships, Nick said he drew on general skills from college for his work. Although Nick claimed he learned many acronyms in school that helped him acclimate to the business world, the more salient takeaways from CSU are learned by all students. He said, "School definitely helped in that area [learning acronyms], communication, working with groups, I'd definitely say all those projects we had to do through school, knowing who has to take command, stepping up, just trying to get it done, working with different people, because I mean that's what you do in business." Though Nick explicitly says, "That's what you do in business," all college graduates should learn how to communicate with colleagues and work in groups. Responses like Nick's were the most common way practical arts graduates discussed how degrees helped them learn to do their jobs.

By using their general liberal arts competencies more than specific degree skills, even practical arts students' employment experiences reveal the true value of a well-rounded liberal arts education as perhaps the best preparation for workforce readiness.

Business and engineering students' reports of how their degrees prepared them for working provide an important corrective to understanding the college-to-work transition. Matches between degrees and jobs are often understood as evidence of skill-matching or human capital explanations connecting school and work.[20] Theoretically, this is the reason why graduates of practical arts disciplines are more employable than liberal arts alumni and therefore, the reason behind the growth of these fields of study.[21] However, this view does not align with graduates' actual work tasks or their own narratives about the relevance of their degrees at the beginning of their careers. Graduates of these disciplines saw their education as useful primarily through a liberal arts lens. They relied on the recruitment opportunities afforded to them for advantageous entry into the labor market but later used their general competencies more than the technical content of their education.

In some sense, this finding is intuitive, even if it goes against popular discourse. The technical learning in these fields becomes outdated relatively quickly and is subject to automation. If graduates use highly technical skills, they may be firm-specific and taught on the job rather than in college courses. All these reasons further reveal why it is essential to examine the entry-level work phase when course material should be most relevant and accessible to graduates. General liberal arts competencies, on the other hand, give students tools that they can use indefinitely and cannot easily be automated.

Few Business and Engineering Graduates Apply Degree Skills at Work

Roughly a third of practical arts graduates in this study *did* use degree-specific tools, skills, or concepts in their entry-level work. There is no apparent pattern as to which students used degree skills. This makes sense since most practical arts majors found jobs through career conveyor-belt internships, which often ended with a job offer for an undetermined role that was assigned later.[22] However, among the practical arts graduates I interviewed, those who had dead-end internships did not necessarily use their degree skills more frequently in entry-level work.

Marly, an ISE major mentioned in the previous chapter, does time studies at work, which is a classic component of an industrial engineering curriculum. When I asked how her job differed from her internship, she said, "I'm doing more work that is related to what I learned in school." She went on to say of her job, "Everything that we talk about [at work] I've seen at some point before from college." For Marly this was an important and positive aspect of her job. She said, "It's important [to me] to find a job where I can, based on my education, apply those things [I learned]." Marly's responses differed from most business and engineering graduates, who largely spoke less positively and with less specificity about the relevance of their degrees. In fact, her response echoed those who reported feeling fulfillment from substantive tasks while interning.

Perhaps because the presence of internship projects best predicted which students completed substantive tasks at their internship and these types of long-term projects were largely absent from entry-level job assignments, much fewer practical arts graduates reported using specific concepts or tools from their major in entry-level work than they reported during their internships. This provides evidence that perhaps studies on the mundane or clerical nature of internships are also more indicative of the next career phase (i.e., entry-level work) than is usually discussed.[23]

How Liberal Arts Graduates Used Their Degrees

In today's world, college coursework is supposed to prepare students for working.[24] Researchers and commentators suggest that liberal arts prepare students in a general way rather than by instilling employable skills related to specific occupations.[25] Some liberal arts majors who participated in my study would agree with this narrative; others had very different experiences.

More precisely, respondents fell into one of three camps. First, almost half of all liberal arts graduates I interviewed used degree-specific skills or concepts in the workplace. Second, some said school provided liberal arts competencies in a general sense, but not specific skills they could use. Third, some bemoaned their degrees only provided a formal credential, but no skills necessary for their jobs. Ultimately, most students either used degree-specific skills or general liberal arts competencies. This shows that a liberal arts education is, in fact, useful for entry-level work, including in ways heretofore written off by many researchers and commentators.

English and Communications Graduates Drew on Degree-Specific Skills

Approximately half of liberal arts gradates completed tasks at their entry-level jobs that called for the skills they learned in their majors. English majors most often applied their writing skills to create content. Jennifer, an English graduate working as a social media writer for a media company exemplifies this outcome. When asked how her degree contributed to how she does her job, she mentioned writing skills: "I took a lot of grammar classes, and that's been really helpful in writing Instagram captions. And thinking about branding for the different types of restaurants, so like one of the restaurants, we want it to be masculine, we want it to be classic, we're trying to get an older crowd, so writing a masculine caption as opposed to a caption for a younger, hipper, even feminine, restaurant or something—I don't think I would've been prepared to do that without some of the classes I had." Jennifer's employer was not necessarily looking to hire an English major and was not explicitly recruiting from CSU (the job is in New York City), yet Jennifer found specific concepts from her classes that she incorporated into her work.

This is worth expanding on because Jennifer's specific skills—the ability to write in different voices and her knowledge of grammar—are not general skills, and graduates of most disciplines would likely struggle with her work tasks. In fact, even among college graduates, most writing is strewn with grammatical (and other) errors.[26] Yet, recruitment for Jennifer's position was not restricted to English majors the way some firms recruit exclusively from among business and engineering students.

In general, many English majors said the writing and editing skills they learned in college directly translated to their entry-level work tasks. They could use other degree skills as well. When I asked Vance, who works at an African American community center, to what extent he used skills learned in his degree, he replied, "A good amount of time because I have a lot of reading [and] a lot of research." He even connected the African American and Asian American literature classes he took with his workplace success. For example, Vance wrote an op-ed about a James Baldwin documentary that came out during his time at the community center. Writing the op-ed required English major skills and knowledge of common themes in Asian and Black literature. He said that work assignment was "pretty English major-y." Although Vance, like many other English majors with dead-end internships, struggled to enter the labor market, he eventually found work that drew on the skills he picked up as an English major. This was important to Vance. He told me, "What I should be learning in school should interest me, that should transfer to what I'm doing at work. Because your life's work ends up being your work's work. You have to go towards that. School is a good starting point." Vance's job title is office associate, and he is precariously employed, earning one of the lowest salaries in the study at $23,000 with no opportunities for advancement at the community center. Nonetheless, he wanted a job that used his degree, and he was able to find one.

It may seem unsurprising that so many English majors use their degree skills at work, given how much call there is for professional writing.

Ironically, popular media focuses especially on English degrees in narratives about the decline of the liberal arts (especially the humanities), specifically on how disconnected the discipline is from the needs of the contemporary economy.[27]

Communications majors mentioned writing press releases as the degree skill they use most. Here it becomes relevant that communications degrees are more technical than English degrees. While both communications and English majors create content, communications majors do so in a more focused way. Consider June, who works for the manufacturing conglomerate Downstate. Her job title is communications specialist, which directly matches with her major. When asked how she learned to do her job, June responded, "Luckily, I did have a really solid foundation going into it, you know, the writing and everything." She told me she is "definitely" using skills learned in her degree. She said, "You take classes, and you learn some of the same things over and over, but a lot of those things are the basics and things that you need to know. So, I think I got all the basics down from school." Specifically, she said, "Writing the press releases, the media kits. All that stuff I did in school—it's all stepping stones." June described specific tasks she performed in school and at work, even mentioning certain classes. It was clear her degree prepared her for the work she found.

June's example is also notable partially because she works at a large bureaucratic manufacturing firm yet earns $30,000. Despite her employer's size and profitability, she is paid significantly less than business and engineering graduates at the same and similar companies. This shows that firm size or profitability cannot alone account for salary differences between majors.[28]

Finally, I consider Marty, a communications graduate who works in the nonprofit sector, to show that work task types did not vary by gender for the liberal arts majors. He mentioned school before I even asked if he used his degree skills at work. He said, "PR is essentially what I was learning in school . . . writing press releases, building a bigger media list, that's stuff I have experience in, something that my professors taught me, and how to build a PR plan for an entire year or two years or however long it may be. All that stuff I've learned in school, and so I've been able to use some of that." Using his degree skills was important to Marty, as he explained, "I didn't really want to graduate and end up doing something that had nothing to do with my degree [. . .] in communications. I could have seen myself doing something totally different because it is so broad." Marty thought of communications as a broad degree field, and it is included in the social sciences at CSU, yet he described specific skills that prepared him for his current employment.

The cases presented here show that English and communications majors used degree-specific skills in their entry-level jobs. While some scholars suggest that college students no longer learn much in school,[29] these respondents told a different story (although I cannot say for certain these skills were acquired in school, only that they were covered in the curriculum). These graduates expressed a human capital view of how college prepared them for work.[30] It is possible that liberal arts majors may have foregrounded their specific skills in order to justify their choice of major, a discursive strategy practical arts graduates had no need to deploy. However, I compared what these students learned in school to their actual work tasks, and this explanation is unlikely. Liberal arts graduates pointed to specific concepts and practices that transferred from school to work. This was often quite different from the business and engineering majors I interviewed who often had trouble pointing to specific tools or competencies they had learned in school and used at work.

I am not arguing that English and communications majors learned more "hard skills" than business and engineering graduates. Rather, I want to call attention to the idea that college graduates used their degrees at work in different ways depending on major, and these differences do not align with public narratives about why graduates of certain disciplines have superior labor market outcomes over others. Liberal arts graduates used their degrees in ways that we might expect from graduates of practical arts disciplines, and practical arts graduates often engaged their degrees in ways that we would expect from liberal arts majors. This shows that it is misguided to think about liberal arts and practical arts degrees in stark dichotomous terms that fail to capture the true distinctions between the fields. In fact, organizational and cultural processes may be as relevant for our understanding of employment disparities between fields as the relationship between degree-specific skills and entry-level work tasks.

The Liberal Arts Competencies of English and Communications Graduates

Like all college students, English and communications majors learned a set of general skills while in school and these general liberal arts competencies were sometimes displayed at work. For English majors, this usually meant engaging in professional writing in ways that did not require complex writing or content creation skills. Graduates considered these general rather than specific skills because the writing they did, either in emails or reports, required prespecified content.

Greta, the English graduate who works for a higher education technology company, said she frequently writes emails and instructions to clients. She did say that being an effective writer makes her better at her job than some of her colleagues. However, she was reticent to say that her degree prepared her or was very applicable to her job. She said, "I'm writing frequently, but the type of writing that I'm doing is not what I necessarily pictured myself doing, nor is it necessarily where my passion lies. Writing a good professional email sure is effective and great, but I don't get the same sort of feeling, like I'm truly applying my degree like I did when I was writing big profiles on nonprofit organizations [a project she was tasked with at an internship]." She went on, "As far the applications of writing at my current job, I feel like there's something to be desired there." When pressed on how her degree best prepared her for the job, she mentioned liberal arts competencies not specific to English majors. She told me, "Being able to communicate effectively and think critically" prepared her for working. She explained, "These sorts of skills you can get without having a college degree, but they're really reinforced in college, especially in the humanities fields." Greta's example shows the ambivalence of some English majors; they sometimes wrote for their jobs but did not say their writing connected to their major if it was neither difficult nor reflected the kinds of assignments they had in school. Recall for comparison, Jennifer's work tasks were more substantive, requiring writing in different voices. Since Greta was completing less substantive writing tasks, she cited liberal arts competencies like critical thinking or communication skills as most relevant to her job. Interestingly, she directly related these skills to the humanities. Her responses were similar to other English majors who said that, while doing some writing in their entry-level jobs, they did not see this as a direct outgrowth of their English degree skills. English majors also mentioned additional general skills, the most common being "time management."

Communications graduates likewise could be tasked with writing, but not necessarily creating content. Esther, a communications graduate who works at a large regional bank, discussed how her degree prepared her for work in a way similar to how business and engineering graduates spoke about their degrees. Although she technically writes marketing material, all the copy comes from the creative services department. In theory, her job in marketing should relate to her communications degree, yet when asked if she used skills from her degree at work, Esther said, "I wouldn't say it was my degree that I learned the most from, it was more my college experience. Learning how to manage time, and learning how to manage my time effectively, and how to prioritize your workload." For Esther, the general skills that she said "you learn in college just from being a student" best prepared her for working, not any specific communications classes. Her responses mirrored other communications graduates who likewise said general skills most prepared them for working.

Note many liberal arts students who mentioned general skills had career conveyor-belt internships and worked at large corporations. This could partially explain why their responses sounded similar to the practical arts graduates who also worked at large firms. It is possible that at large organizations with a fine-grained divisions of labor, employees rely more on their general skills than their peers who work for smaller firms where a larger variety of tasks are assigned and allow graduates to use more degree-specific skills.

Most graduates from all four majors reported that general liberal arts competencies proved useful for entry-level work, especially time management and working in teams. The extent to which the different disciplines teach these skills versus how much students gain from their college's general curriculum is an open question.[31] This is not a negative outcome, but rather suggests that all the majors prepare students well for the workforce. Rather than thinking majors are narrowly technical or broadly general, this finding helps break down the idea that the kinds of competencies taught in each major are radically different in terms of employable skills students can acquire.

Degree as "Just" a Credential

Like many practical arts graduates, some communications and English majors saw no connection between their degree skills and their jobs. These respondents felt they only needed their degree to fulfill a formal qualification. However, their responses differed in a key way from their practical arts counterparts. Engineering and business students with career conveyor-belt internships often said they needed their specific degree to get their position. In contrast, English and communications graduates said their job required a BA of any major, since they rarely enjoyed recruitment advantages specific to their school or majors.

Vicky provides an example of a liberal arts graduate who questioned the utility of her communications degree. After a dead-end internship with a start-up, she now works as a cloud application consultant for Thebes, the same large technology firm that hired Emily. Vicky laughed when I asked if there were any specific skills she learned in school that she uses at her job. She said, "Nope, I think I could have done this without college." Vicky's attitude toward her education undermines human capital theory.[32] Of course, Vicky may have learned skills in school that were necessary for her job that she did not recognize, but nevertheless, she did not view the skills she gained in college as necessary for this particular job. Vicky did, however, see the value of credentialism in her education.[33] When asked if it bothered her that she could do her job without a degree, Vicky responded, "Not really, because I didn't need college to do my job, but I did need a college degree to get my job." Vicky understood that Thebes would not have hired her if she did not have a college degree.

Many graduates who saw their degree as just a necessary credential had career conveyor-belt internships. Jade, another communications graduate, works at a large health care company that offered her a job while she was interning there. She said some older members of her team had not gone to college but that a degree is "just so expected now." Jade even said, "I can't really tell you exactly what kind of training they'd be looking for from your degree that requires them to ask for it." For Jade, the substance of her undergraduate degree did not seem connected to her job. This shows how credential inflation leads to an increase in requirements to get a job, but not necessarily an increase in skill level to do that job.[34]

Finally, Colleen, an English major with a career conveyor-belt internship who now works in publishing, does not think a college degree is necessary to do her job. She said, "Your classes aren't actually that applicable." Colleen took an undergraduate publishing course, similar to courses that practical arts students take connected to specific professions or industries, yet she said of this course, "I don't think it greatly captured what you do every day." For Colleen, like many in this study with career conveyor-belt internships, it was difficult to see the direct connection between the content of her education and her work tasks, even though she had a tight occupation-to-degree match and took a course on the specific industry where she is now employed.

Although Vicky, Jade, and Colleen questioned the need for their degree skills, they were not representative of many English and communications graduates. Most liberal arts majors applied their degrees by drawing on either the general liberal arts competencies that all college graduates should obtain or their degree-specific skills.

The Value of Graduates' Degrees in the Labor Market

Despite being more likely to have new organizational careers in large bureaucratic firms, the practical arts graduates I interviewed rarely used specific tools, concepts, or skills from their degrees in entry-level work. Meanwhile, the liberal arts graduates in this study often used specific degree skills in their entry-level jobs, yet were also more likely to be precariously employed. This evidence clearly shows the real trade-off between majors in labor market entry. It also dispels two common myths about college majors that are perpetuated in the popular press—that practical arts graduates' skills are immediately in demand and that liberal arts students do not learn specific occupationally relevant skills. As discussed in the previous chapter, and covered somewhat here as well, the kinds of firms hiring recent graduates may account for a large part of this trade-off. Regardless, the outcomes still run counter to popular narratives surrounding degree fields that frame much of the public debate on higher education and the relationship between college majors and employment outcomes.

The above discussion raises the question: What if students do not realize they are using their skills or define skills differently by major? Perhaps liberal arts students were so inundated with public messages about how "useless" their degrees were they became defensive and overestimated skill use. Perhaps practical arts graduates often heard their degrees would be useful, so their disappointment actually reflects inflated expectations. This explanation is unlikely, because I asked for graduates' opinions about their skill usage during the interviews *and* I also matched their work tasks to their degree curricula. This kind of triangulation makes the above explanation unlikely. Further, matching curriculum to job tasks was not a difficult interpretive endeavor. When employees conducted exclusively rote clerical work and bemoaned that it is not related to their degree, the disconnect was quite clear.

The second question raised by the evidence in this chapter is: Will practical arts graduates utilize their degree skills later in their careers? And although the focus of this book is the immediate college-to-work transition and entry-level jobs, if the answer to this is yes, then perhaps human capital theory still explains the differences in employability between majors, only the difference shows up later. While I cannot say definitively that this will not happen, I note that, at both the internship stage and entry-level job stage, practical arts graduates benefit from their credentials without having to display technical competency. Further, many of the business and engineering students tasked with liaison work were on separate employment tracks from those who were doing more substantive entry-level work. For example, they might be in technical sales or consulting. This fits with statistics that show, in the US economy overall, only about one-third of "scientists and engineers" are employed in "science and engineering."[35] In these jobs, the industry knowledge practical arts graduates gain and technical background from school could provide satisfaction and some utility, but it seems unlikely they will use their specific degree skills at work later in their careers.

Even if higher level employees do use their degree skills, there is limited space at the top (i.e., if one hundred entry-level engineers compete for twenty-five managerial roles, the number of graduates who end up using their skills remains small). Managers also might make use of technical knowledge but rarely engage in technical work. Besides, the technical skills learned in the engineering curriculum become outdated quickly and can be subject to automation. Taken together, my evidence gives very little indication that engineering and business graduates will use their technical skills later on in their careers at much higher rates than they do at their entry-level jobs even if they stay in business or engineering, which is not guaranteed.

In line with media narratives, practical arts degrees from CSU are useful credentials for entering the labor market successfully by traditional employment indicators. However, these credentials did not appear useful for the underlying skills they provided, at least upon labor market entry. On the other hand, liberal arts degrees were less useful as credentials for securing well-paying work quickly but provided degree skills graduates used for fulfilling work. And all students from all disciplines found their general liberal arts competencies very useful for work. These findings run counter to the way many researchers, even those defending the liberal arts, typically explain differences between degree fields. In fact, the evidence I uncovered provides an unexpected defense of the social sciences and humanities: liberal arts majors, including English majors, use degree-specific skills and practical arts graduates (even those working in technical occupations) primarily rely on their general liberal arts competencies in their entry-level work. In the concluding chapter, I tie all the empirical evidence together and chart a new way forward for higher education and the labor market.

8: CONCLUSION

Rethinking the College-to-Work Transition

This book exposes the real trade-off young people make when selecting a college major and career path, and it is *not* the choice between "practical" or "passion" major. In reality, students can opt to declare a practical arts major, move smoothly into a new organizational career, and likely end up doing mundane, clerical work at jobs with impressive titles. Or they can choose to major in the liberal arts, struggle to enter the labor market, possibly end up underemployed or in precarious work, and yet find purpose and fulfillment in jobs where they use the degree-specific skills they went to college to get.

As the term trade-off signifies, there are benefits to each major or career pathway. Some practical arts graduates pejoratively compared their tasks to secretarial work and others discussed having little to do during the day, yet they were often happy with their salaries and could live comfortably. English and communications graduates were rarely pleased with their salaries or employment conditions but were often satisfied that their work related to their schooling. The broad pathways my research uncovered are shown in table 8.1. My study reveals how the college-to-work transition really unfolds, adding insights into our understanding of internships, entry-level jobs, and the role of higher education in the contemporary economy.

The trade-off I describe in this book also allows me to separate myth from reality in media narratives around the employability of various college majors, thus exposing surprising truths about the college-to-work transition. I confirm one common media narrative but undermine two others. Narratives two and three relate to the second outcome of interest—entry-level work tasks. My research debunks them both.

Reality: Degrees in practical arts disciplines lead to better initial labor market success.

A common justification for suggesting students major, and colleges invest, in the practical arts is graduates' superior labor market outcomes relative

TABLE 8.1 Common College-to-Work Pathways among CSU Students

	Liberal arts majors	Practical arts majors
Typical student	White middle-class woman	White middle-class man
Ambitions	Corporate job related to major	Corporate job related to major
Internship search	Online and networks	Career fair and career services
Internship type	Dead-end	Career conveyor-belt
Job search	Online and networks	Career fair and career services
Job search stress	High	Low
Job type	Low-paid/precarious	High-paid/new organizational career
Task type	Substantive	Clerical

to other fields.[1] In line with media narratives and previous research, I too found that practical arts majors often enter highly paid permanent employment matched to their degrees after graduation. Thus, regarding the key outcome of entry into middle-class jobs, practical arts graduates outperformed liberal arts graduates.

Myth: Practical arts degrees provide in-demand skills needed for entry-level work.

The second common media narrative is that practical arts degrees immediately pay off because they provide in-demand skills employers need.[2] I found no relationship between graduates' skill use and employment conditions. In fact, roughly 70 percent of the practical arts graduates I interviewed conducted exclusively clerical work in their entry-level jobs. Beyond my own assessment, many practical arts graduates reported not using any degree content, concepts, or tools in their work. Students and professors in engineering or business programs, or employers, might not question how little technical skills are deployed in actual work (i.e., they may say classrooms primarily prepare students for the labor market by providing a problem-solving mindset or putting them through a tough major). Regardless, this is not how media narratives portray the utility of practical arts degrees.

Myth: Liberal arts fields only provide soft skills.

Media narratives claim liberal arts degrees pay off in the long run because they teach soft skills that can be useful in graduate school or for management positions rather than technical skills that are immediately applicable in entry-level work.[3] Yet, as I have shown in this book, around half of the liberal arts majors I interviewed used degree-specific skills in their entry-level jobs. English and communications are not "passion" majors that students choose because they are unconcerned with acquiring employable skills, as media narratives suggest.[4] At CSU (and likely at other similar schools), students in these fields learned a mix of occupationally relevant skills and general competencies. At non-elite universities, English majors do not exclusively read and analyze great works of literature; they learn elements of style and practice writing targeted to social media posts and technical reports. Many graduates use these skills in their entry-level jobs.

Furthermore, my findings undermine a key theme that runs through all three media narratives: skill discrepancies between majors cause disparities in employment conditions.

*

The three media narratives are indicative of general popular narratives in cultural discourse. As mentioned in chapter 1, a Burning Glass Technologies report shows that public perceptions of majors align with the media narratives.[5] Further, policymakers from both parties support investment in STEM precisely because of a perceived skill premium that is rewarded in the labor market.[6] Finally, some students' narratives in this book reflected an initial internalization of these narratives before embarking on internships and finding jobs. These narratives almost certainly inform how students (de) value one another's majors, how they talk to parents about majors, and how administrators perceive the various units of their colleges and universities.

Yet, these media narratives do not conform to empirical reality. During wave two interviews, one year after college graduation, it became quite clear *how* graduates' labor market trajectories diverged so considerably. Prior to the internship stage, and despite popular narratives, college students were quite similar in many respects. They all attended the same public university, the majority came from in-state, most were White, and many had middle-class backgrounds. Additionally, students in all majors learned a mix of practical and general skills, and most wanted stable middle-class jobs related to their majors. And yet, these students ended up in very different places as working graduates. This divergence begins with channeling students by major into dead-end versus career conveyor-belt internships, which lead to either a stressful, protracted job search or seamless entry into the labor market. Internship type proved critical to understanding the *process* through which students entered the labor market.

Of course, there were counter-cases. Some students with practical arts degrees were paid well *and* used their skills, and some liberal arts graduates similarly found gainful employment requiring substantive tasks. Yet I observed no patterned differences in the types of people or students who achieved these maximally beneficial outcomes. Taken together, it is important for students to realize that it is not always true (or even usually the case) that ability or effort will determine how they enter the labor market, their salary, or their skill usage at work. Rather, it is their majors, how fields are organized, and perhaps perceptions of fields by employers, schools, commentators, and even researchers, that play a larger role in determining students' eventual employment outcomes.

The pathways identified in this study also have important gender, race, and class implications. In the US, majors are gender imbalanced and the fields and skills associated with women are devalued in the labor market.[7] Research shows middle-class White women who major in English or communications may continue to rely on their parents financially or need to marry a higher earning partner to reproduce their class position, even after they find enjoyable jobs matched to their degree.[8] I found that middle-class men, however, can often reproduce their class position solely through work because men-dominated practical arts majors, like engineering, allowed even students with modest ambitions to find career conveyor-belt internships that lead directly to gainful employment in new organizational careers.

Nationally, students from working-class backgrounds, including many students of color, often end up at universities with employment outcomes inferior to those of CSU, or with employment outcomes inferior to their privileged peers at the same schools.[9] Within majors at CSU, and likely at similar schools, class inequality contributed to graduates' variable labor market trajectories but at different times for the two sets of majors. Since English and communications are open admit majors, class sorting occurred after graduation when students from higher-class backgrounds could hold out for jobs they desired or had an easier time securing their targeted jobs. Since business and engineering are competitive-admit majors, class sorting likely happened at the point of entry as differences in prerequisites, letters of recommendation, GPA, and other similar factors can make it harder for individuals from lower-class backgrounds to successfully enter these disciplines. Once in these majors, however, students seemed to have similar trajectories.

The empirical findings of this book suggest we rethink common media narratives about degrees and the very value of the liberal arts in American society. Recall that even business and engineering students often exclusively drew on their liberal arts competences in their entry-level work. People who advocate for the liberal arts in the public sphere often emphasize their nonpecuniary benefits, such as a well-rounded education.[10] The nonpecuniary benefits of the liberal arts are, indeed, tremendously important to personal fulfillment and a democratic society, and those who defend the liberal arts on these grounds should be lauded. Yet, these arguments do not seem to motivate students to major in liberal arts or institutions to invest in them. As a recent essay in the *New York Review of Books* by Pace University English Professor Sarah Blackwood highlights, even when the number of students majoring in English grows, university administrators still cut the department's staff and budget.[11] We may have more success in curtailing the decline of the liberal arts if we can demonstrate that all fields of study at a school like CSU prepare students with practical and liberal arts competencies, and the dichotomous understanding of the two kinds of degrees is misguided.

In this book, I show that the liberal arts can be defended on the grounds usually ceded to proponents of the practical arts: the liberal arts endow students with precisely the skills needed for the contemporary workforce. It was not my intention to write a book defending the liberal arts. Rather, I was aiming to undertake a comparative investigation of college majors to better understand how and why engineering and business majors come to enter the labor market more successfully than liberal arts majors. But in the process, my evidence pointed repeatedly to the value of liberal arts skills (major-specific and general) in the labor market while the primary benefit of the practical arts resides in stable job acquisition independent of skill acquisition.

In the remainder of the conclusion, I provide an overview of my contribution to our understanding of the college-to-work transition, give some potential explanations for the findings I uncovered, and discuss strategies and takeaways for firms, educators, and students, before offering a vision for the future of higher education and the labor market.

How the College-to-Work Transition Really Unfolds

My study provides important new insights into the largely understudied processes that connect people with postsecondary credentials to jobs, and to the cultural and organizational scaffolding that binds higher education with other social institutions. While it is well-known that universities serve as important hubs connecting to other social institutions,[12] two innovative methods I used in my study enabled me to reveal how, exactly, the college-to-work transition unfolds.

First, in using an *interinstitutional* approach[13] to examine the connections and processes that link higher education to the labor market, I uncovered that career conveyor-belt internships are the first step in a process whereby some students move seamlessly from college to stable employment while others struggle with stressful job searches to find precarious employment. This approach breaks important new ground by moving the higher education literature beyond its focus on sorting students differentially by institutions (e.g., students from elite schools have different opportunities than students from less selective colleges), toward the importance of examining intra-university labor market sorting processes as a source of inequality among students from the same school, specifically among students from different majors.

Second, by closely examining the actual tasks graduates performed in their entry-level jobs, I identified a new type of degree-job mismatching that should be of particular interest to scholars of the college-to-work transition. While majoring in practical arts disciplines mitigated against certain kinds of "mismatched" workers (e.g., college graduates working at Starbucks),[14] the entry-level jobs these students obtained—while better paid—were usually poorly matched to employees' skills or, in the case of liberal arts students, their interests.

This close examination of work tasks also exposed weaknesses in the human capital approach to understanding how people match to jobs. Despite myriad other studies on networks, culture, and organizations in hiring, the notion persists that human capital and skills are the major driver in placing college graduates into jobs.[15] Perhaps this is because, in contrast to this study, human capital theory often skips over how matching people with jobs really occurs and fails to focus on what those jobs entail. While human capital theory is, of course, a nuanced theory that means different things in different disciplines and contexts, when it comes to the college-to-work transition, researchers use occupation-to-degree matching as evidence of human capital theory.[16] I show definitively in this book that occupation-to-degree matching is not sufficient evidence for human capital theory explaining the college-to-work transition. In my study, there was no connection at all between occupation-to-degree match and whether graduates used major-specific coursework in their entry-level jobs. In fact, it is possible that differences in the early career outcomes of graduates I interviewed can be explained entirely without reference to major-specific human capital.

The evidence presented in this book also adds to our understanding of institutional theories of higher education. Researchers in this tradition look at how students build the correct cultural capital in school to be successful in the labor market.[17] However, without an inquiry into entry-level work tasks, scholars cannot fully disentangle cultural capital from human capital mechanisms explaining the college-to-work transition. In other words, they cannot discount a real connection between cultural competencies and job-specific skills. Through examining the economic returns to work tasks from prestigious disciplines (i.e., that business and engineering degrees pay off independent of skill-utilization), I add evidence to what institutional theorists have asserted but not demonstrated empirically. I also extend these theories by taking seriously the role of degree fields (i.e., majors) as sites of cultural value, rather than focusing on students' class backgrounds or the selectivity and prestige of the university, as research in this tradition normally does. Despite earlier calls to examine fields of study as important sites of inequality between students, research focusing on college majors remains underdeveloped in sociology.[18] Educators, employers, researchers, and commentators' perceptions of the skills majors offer (supposed "hard" and "soft" skills) are imbued with cultural valuation, which cannot be disentangled from their gender typing, making the extension of institutional theories to fields of study vital for understanding stratification outcomes among college graduates.

By assessing human capital and institutional theories of the college-to-work transition, I have also been able to demonstrate that the way schools match some students with jobs may be unrelated to employers' demand for particular skills. I have shown that it is not so much the skills students have that "earn" them "good" jobs, but rather the cultural and organizational infrastructure that defines their worth and value and matches them with opportunities. Students do have skills. But media narratives about the specialness of engineering and business skills is overwrought while the skills of English and communications tend to be minimized.

The trade-off I expose shows a decoupling of many students' skill use from their employment conditions. Documenting this trade-off adds to a burgeoning literature in the sociology of work and economic sociology on the degradation of white-collar work. Much of this literature looks at the de-skilling of work in tandem with the decline of employment conditions.[19] For example, Robert Brooks' work on lawyers performing document review reveals that some lawyers are precariously employed and also find their tasks relegated to one simple component of legal work.[20] In the case of entry-level work for recent college graduates, I found each type of job had downsides or, put differently, was degraded in different ways (i.e., business and engineering graduates not using their skills and communications and English majors doing substantive work while precariously employed). Thus, the decoupling of employment conditions from job tasks is one of the most significant contributions of this research to the sociology of work and economic sociology.

In addition to enhancing our understanding of entry-level jobs, I also clarify the role of internships in the college-to-work transition. To many researchers and commentators, internships are a form of precarious work that may exploit vulnerable students.[21] I show that some internships may fit that profile, but many do not. Career conveyor-belt internships can be an on-ramp into a new organizational career. But any internship may give students opportunities to tackle projects that allow them to use learned skills in ways many entry-level jobs do not.[22] In fact, internships can be students' *best* chance to use their degree skills in a workplace early in their careers. We now know that many entry-level employees complete exclusively clerical tasks, so we should rethink our assumption that internships are the primary domain of mundane clerical work.

In today's economy, where there are fewer "good jobs,"[23] how these jobs are allocated becomes an ever more pressing question. As the media makes clear, a college degree no longer guarantees stable middle-class employment (although employees with college degrees on average still fare better in the US economy than those without).[24] A recent Associated Press headline reads, "Overqualified, Underutilized: Many College Grads Facing Underemployment, Joblessness."[25] This concern represents a new empirical reality—the employment demand for highly skilled, educated workers, has been declining since at least 2000.[26] The rise of precarious and insecure work has permeated the labor market, even among educated, white-collar professionals.[27] And, if the economy cannot or will not provide good jobs to all who get a bachelor's degree, we must be able to better assess which types of bachelor's degrees are most likely to translate into good jobs and what these jobs entail.

Explaining Unequal Opportunities Available to Students

Graduates of schools like CSU are more likely to be differentiated by their majors than are graduates of elite universities, for whom the name of the college is enough of a credential to attract employers. And while my study cannot give a full accounting of *why* liberal arts graduates have initial inferior labor market outcomes by traditional measures, I can consider other contributing factors beyond the cultural devaluation posited by institutional theories, which is both cause and consequence of misleading media narratives. Three reasons I highlight here are: (1) school policies and practices, (2) local labor market conditions, and (3) the structure of the American economy.

School Policies and Practices

Colleges and universities play a large role in helping some students, but not others, obtain career conveyor-belt internships. This is especially evident at large public universities like CSU. Practical arts disciplines at CSU have their own colleges replete with specialized career services staff who coordinate connections with employers in areas of interest to their students. By contrast, liberal arts majors do not have access to the same level of career services. The arts and sciences career services and support staff have a far larger and more diverse set of students to accommodate, which makes it especially difficult to target employers to recruit on campus.

As I noted earlier, this disparity does not exist at elite universities, which can and do establish career conveyor-belt internships for all their students regardless of major (e.g., an art history major can connect with an investment banking firm).[28] At non-elite institutions, career conveyor-belt internships do not necessarily cause labor market disparities, but it is helpful to question the role of schools in labor market sorting where students' access to internship types is strikingly variable. Schools should make every effort to have career services as robust for liberal arts students as they have for practical arts majors.

Local Labor Market Conditions

The fact that so many practical arts students in this study landed jobs with large regional or national firms helps explain why career conveyor-belt internships exist where they do and for whom. Large bureaucratic firms hire lots of entry-level employees, have a steady need for more personnel, and often are highly profitable. To reduce the costs of looking for new hires, it makes sense for large firms to form connections with universities, recruit practical arts students for internships, and offer entry-level jobs to a percentage of those interns.

Local labor market conditions help explain why some firms only recruit students from certain fields. In the American Midwest, legacy car companies and large industrial manufacturers still employ many workers. These firms seek to disproportionately hire engineering graduates and business majors specializing in operations and logistics. Likewise, multinational companies without a large local presence but with a desire for technical workers, recruit students at engineering and business career fairs. Some firms active in local labor markets outside manufacturing or logistics—such as health care and finance—also attend the arts and sciences career fair at CSU and offer career conveyor-belt internships leading to new organizational careers. However, none of these types of employers routinely offer opportunities specifically for liberal arts majors. In general, we can imagine that the composition of local sectors and industries likely contribute to graduates' unequal employment outcomes.

Broader Structure of the Economy

School policies and local labor market conditions explain variation in internship types better than they account for the actual employment outcomes for graduates. Certain features of the broader American economy can explain both. First, many industries and sectors in the US—from credit cards to tech to corn seed production—are characterized by a few large monopolies controlling the industry.[29] As noted above, large firms are more likely to establish career conveyor-belt internships than are smaller regional companies due to more consistent staffing needs.

The domination of large monopolistic firms can also explain the trade-off I uncovered between employment indicators and entry-level tasks. A common misconception is that US firms are becoming "lean and mean." In fact, bureaucratic corporations outside of the retail industry have become what the late economist David Gordon referred to as "fat and mean." These firms have cut a large percentage of front-line workers (e.g., tellers at banks or automotive assembly-line operators) while bloating middle-management.[30] As the white-collar professional services class has grown, so has the percentage of these employees who view their jobs as mundane, meaningless, or both.[31] Growing white-collar ranks may lead to a greater division of labor, or more workers with nothing to do, potentially furthering the trade-off uncovered in this book (i.e., well-paid workers in profitable corporations complete clerical work because of the high division of labor). This outcome may also be because tasks previously done by the now-gutted secretarial staff have to be transferred to entry-level professional workers.

Why would these firms want to hire such graduates and pay them a college wage premium? Why would a firm "overpay" practical arts graduates to complete mostly clerical work? While fully answering these questions is beyond the scope of my study, I provide some speculative explanations. First, firms could be acting in their economic self-interest by hiring graduates to conduct clerical work. Data entry, technical sales, or other kinds of liaison work, while relatively simple tasks, potentially generate substantial revenue for the same reason any other fine-grained division of labor is more efficient and therefore profitable. Thus, even if they are not using technical skills, engineering or business graduates may contribute to a firm's "bottom line" and, as such, graduates "earn" their wages in a purely economic sense. Second, firms may be solving an information problem. Organizations may use entry-level hiring to find talented people who will be given more complex jobs later in their careers. In this scenario, firms might hire many more entry-level workers than they can promote, and then use entry-level work to determine who will move up in the organization.

There are also possible cultural explanations for "overpayment" of clerical workers, although these also have tangible implications for how firms operate and for their profits. First, people with certain characteristics have higher cultural worth in society than others and, therefore, hiring them requires firms to pay a premium. Firms will often seek to signal to customers that they have a large cache of employees who hold high cultural value. For example, Wall Street investment banks impress their clients with large teams of Ivy League–educated bankers.[32] In an analogous way, some companies may benefit from employing college graduates from high-prestige disciplines. Specifically engineering and business majors may have higher cultural worth than communications and English majors. A firm may win more business or be able to charge higher prices if it can boast a large team of "highly trained engineers" working on the project. Finally, hiring many workers to complete clerical work could be the result of power struggles within the organization.[33] One way departments or managers in organizations gain power or prestige is by securing higher staffing levels or resources in general.[34] Departments or units in an organization may fight for more personnel to gain (or avoid losing) status even if there is no substantive work to give new hires.

And, of course, these explanations also relate to the cultural "value" associated with people based on ascriptive characteristics, such as race, class, and gender. For example, a college-educated White man from a prestigious university has high cultural value independent of his observed skills.[35] This value seeps into the gendered associations we make with organizations as well. Firms doing economically well-compensated things that are considered masculine may have more money to pay employees than organizations that provide feminine-typed services. For example, car companies may have more profits to spend on entry-level engineers than a childcare organization can afford to pay teachers.

How Employers, Educators, and Students Can Maximize Internships and Jobs

Employers

Although firms may be happy with their current internship and hiring practices, reforming internship and hiring programs may allow companies to access more students, giving them a stronger talent pool. First, large firms should open their internship programs to students of any major. While the expected technical competency of business and engineering students is alluring, many liberal arts students would be successful in jobs that are now monopolized by business and engineering majors. After all, job ads for business and engineering positions list liberal arts competencies such as teamwork and critical thinking as vital to successful completion of work tasks. If firms recruit liberal arts students, many of them may be attracted to the stable employment offered.

Second, employers should acknowledge that liberal arts skills are important and that all graduates, regardless of major, are equally likely to have these skills. This means valuing general liberal arts competencies for seemingly technical jobs and emphasizing the degree-specific skills many liberal arts majors have when recruiting liberal arts graduates. By realizing that all degrees offer a blend of skills with a lot of overlap, we can move away from thinking of degree fields as either narrow or general.

Third, employers should have formal plans or policies in place for hiring and using interns. Large firms offering career conveyor-belt internships already meet this criterion. However, smaller firms should institutionalize the conditions under which they hire interns. This ensures they retain talented workers and have equitable employment practices.

Fourth, firms of all sizes should work to make connections with local colleges and universities. This would help firms maximize efficient hiring practices while spreading the benefits of career fairs to a wider range of students.

Finally, organizations should try to give their interns and employees big projects rather than (or in addition to) ad hoc tasks. Projects enhance employees' and interns' experiences while likely increasing their value to their organization. Overall, these changes would likely not affect which firms are able to hire recent graduates, but they could create a more level playing field for students of various majors and provide students interested in internships with more information about their job prospects.

Educators

Many schools actively encourage or require students to complete internships. At CSU, many English majors participate in an internship class through the professional writing program. These classes almost never connect students with internships that lead directly to full-time employment. While internship classes may be beneficial, the best way for schools to institutionalize internships is through connections with employers, through career services or career fairs. Career services should also share resources throughout the university to ensure equitable employment opportunities to students of every major. And schools should require firms to attend all their university career fairs, not only those exclusive to specific practical arts colleges. Although some firms may bristle at this last requirement, schools are not powerless actors. Many colleges and universities, especially large public research universities, have strong regional, or even national, influence.

Additionally, as this book shows, firms actively recruiting interns are more likely to hire those interns after graduation than firms that passively accept interns (although the recruitment strategy is of course not necessarily *the reason* these firms are hiring interns for full-time employment after graduation). Thus, schools should encourage students to seek internships in firms that show evidence that they are hiring, rather than encouraging students to use their own networks or launch their own searches. Schools can aggregate information on internships that routinely hire and share that information with students. In some sense this is already happening in colleges that serve practical arts students, but the liberal arts majors I interviewed received much less information on how to find paid internships that lead to long-term employment. Colleges can also better leverage alumni networks to share information with students to help them connect with and learn more about employers before choosing positions. Again, these changes might not affect the availability of jobs, but they will give students more information about options and better access to stable employment.

Finally, colleges and universities should make it easier for students from less advantaged backgrounds to access majors like business and engineering. Currently, these majors set students up for smooth labor market entry, so disparities in access continue to translate directly into inequities in early employment opportunities.

Students

Students should be aware that some internships lead to stable employment and some do not. They should also receive information about the respective rewards and drawbacks of each type. Students, regardless of major, who prioritize stable employment over uncertainty could then specifically seek career conveyor-belt internships in corporate firms. These students should prioritize career fairs and preexisting connections between their university and employers instead of seeking internships through personal networks. While practical arts majors are better positioned to do this than are their liberal arts peers, most English and communications majors in this study who were able to access career conveyor-belt internships—and subsequently new organizational careers—did so through the arts and sciences career fair. Students wishing to take the higher risk–higher reward pathway through dead-end internships should be aware that their internships will rarely lead directly to employment, and it may take several months, or longer, beyond graduation to find a fitting job. And the work they do find, even matched to their degree and requiring their skills, may be poorly paid.

Having said that, these students can maximize their chances of employment success by interning in as many firms as possible, starting early in their undergraduate careers. For all students in "less employable" majors, interning at small local establishments in their freshman or sophomore year might open doors to bigger firms in their junior or senior year.[36] Practical arts students can often wait until junior or senior year and still find career conveyor-belt internships at large prestigious firms. Practical arts students should also be aware that *the primary benefit of majoring in these fields is access to employment opportunities, not the acquisition of skills* (as shown, practical arts graduates rarely use degree-specific skills in entry-level work).

Students should also not be afraid to major in a liberal arts discipline. While labor market entry can be more stressful and success less assured, liberal arts graduates in this study had a significantly greater likelihood of using their skills early in their careers and, likely, will eventually catch up, at least somewhat, with their practical arts peers on other measures such as salary and job security. This information should help students avoid pressures to select a major based on perceptions of "employability" and instead encourage them to pursue their interests with realistic expectations.

Making Work Matter

In the early to mid-twentieth century, collective action by industrial workers led to mass unionization and the creation of the American middle class.[37] At that time, rampant strikes were not solely about pay and benefits. Industrial workers all over the economy, tired of boring assembly-line work, went on strike for less monotonous work.[38] Today, as American workers are squeezed and the middle class declines, employees have become more desperate for stable income and health insurance.[39] In this context, workers appear to have forgotten that *interesting work matters and should be rewarded*.

In the wake of the COVID-19 pandemic, workers are once again questioning their employment conditions. Strikes are up and the "Great Resignation" has seen workers leaving their jobs in record numbers, especially in the low-wage service sector.[40] With record-low rates of unemployment, workers have more leverage than they have had in recent decades. Will this current context usher in a period of renewed demands for work that matters, alongside demands for improved stability, pay, and working conditions? If so, how might employers respond? Would they recognize the benefits for both them and employees that can be reaped from creating jobs that require employees to draw on a broad set of skills? What might those new jobs look like? What effect would these changes have on higher education and what role could schools play to further these types of changes?

This book offers a partial—and admittedly aspirational—perspective for answering some of these questions. New jobs dually benefiting firms and their workers would require employees to use a broad and flexible set of skills drawing on all parts of their degrees. An increase in such jobs, combined with increased recognition that skills associated with technical degrees often go unused, might even begin to reverse the decades-long decline of the liberal arts and rise of niche credentials.[41]

In response to the rise in the number of college graduates experiencing career-long labor market uncertainty and the accompanying questioning of higher education's capacity to prepare students for work, a number of institutions have appeared that provide credentials or certificates for a fraction of the cost (e.g., coding boot camps). Yet by stripping away the traditional liberal arts core curriculum, new alternative credentials provide an education that is *too narrow* for the contemporary workforce. Employers are increasingly seeking improved written and verbal communication skills, which may be a signal of their own increasing awareness of the value of a broad liberal arts education. With luck, firms will progressively recognize that all high performing graduates—regardless of major—are qualified for on-the-job training, which is the best way to meet any corporation's needs.

When we recognize that liberal arts competencies are necessary workforce preparation *and* that universities are the institutions to provide them, we can reassert the liberal arts as central to the economy and society *and* re-center colleges and universities as vital social institutions. For this reason, I argue that it is time for schools to invest *more heavily* in liberal arts programs and do everything in their power to erode perceived differences between the liberal and practical arts. Indeed, perhaps paradoxically, this moment of broad questioning of the fundamental value of higher education may provide a unique opportunity to reestablish the value of a liberal arts education in preparing graduates for the workforce.

ACKNOWLEDGMENTS

I am extremely grateful to the ninety-one participants in this study who generously gave me access to their time, experiences, and opinions, and for putting up with my probing questions about their education, work, and lives. This book would not have been possible without them.

This project has been almost ten years in the making, and I would like to thank all the mentors, friends, and colleagues who supported me from the time I was a graduate student. Vinnie Roscigno, Claudia Buchmann, and Timothy Bartley provided direction from the study's inception and helped me turn my early ideas into a complete work. I am grateful to my graduate school officemate and coauthor, Davon Norris, who has been my dear friend and cheerleader throughout my career. I would also like to acknowledge the National Science Foundation, the sociology department at The Ohio State University, and the graduate school at The Ohio State University for providing funding that enabled me to complete such a time- and resource-intensive project.

Turning research into a book is challenging work. I'd like to thank Rachel Sherman, Jessi Streib, and Jenny Stuber for sharing their book proposals with me and providing formative feedback on my own proposal at a critical time in the development of the book. I would also like to express appreciation for the four anonymous reviewers who gave remarkably detailed and astute comments that helped me strengthen and better clarify my arguments. My editor at the University of Chicago Press, Elizabeth Branch Dyson, pushed me to make the book proposal and each draft of the complete manuscript stronger that the prior version. She consistently challenged me to think about the bigger picture, and her insights and belief in the project have made the final product more successful than it otherwise could have been.

With invaluable support from the University of Michigan and the National Science Foundation, I received time, financial resources, and access to a network of mentors, colleagues, and friends that allowed me to transform my research into the resulting manuscript. In addition to the myriad friends and colleagues I have discussed this book with during my time at the University of Michigan, I'd like to thank my summer book writing group: Paige Sweet, Jonah Stuart Brundage, Jamie Budnick, Pablo Gaston, and Luciana de Souza Leão for all their encouragement, accountability, and feedback. Jonah also read several iterations of the book's introduction, and I thank him for that. With the support of Fabian Pfeffer, Melissa Bora, and the Center for Inequality Dynamics at the University of Michigan, I hosted a book workshop that brought together four brilliant scholars to give me transformative feedback on the argument and structure of the book. I would like to extend deep gratitude to Beth Berman, Ofer Sharone, Amy Binder, and Elizabeth Armstrong, the four attendees, for being so generous with their time and intellect.

The biggest influences I've had in my career are Steven Lopez, Elizabeth Armstrong, and Erin Cech. Steve has lent his enthusiasm and keen insight to this project to an extent that cannot be overstated. I am truly grateful for his unflagging belief in me and in the book from graduate school through publication. Likewise, Elizabeth has offered unending support and engagement with my work, and I am continually blown away by her brilliance and generosity. Finally, Erin has enthusiastically provided critical feedback and professional guidance during the book's final revision process. I feel extremely fortunate to have had these three exceptional mentors who have together changed the trajectory of the book and my career.

Finally, books are not written in social isolation. I was kept sane and optimistic by my network of friends and family outside the academy. I would like to thank my parents, Sidney Pech, Beth Raiola, and Anthony Raiola, and many of the aforementioned colleagues, who have become dear friends, for their endless support. Most of all, I would like to thank Sara Moss-Pech. I am not nearly a good enough writer to properly express my gratitude and admiration for Sara. She is the most amazing person I've ever met and has contributed to this project by being a fantastic life partner and an intellectually curious interlocutor, and by always pushing and believing in me.

I began this project in the spring of 2015. At the time I was interested in the "value" of internships, partially motivated by my own experience as an unpaid intern during college. As I made progress on this project, it became clear that the broader story was about inequality between fields of study in the college-to-work transition. My study evolved into an inquiry into the different labor market opportunities for students in four majors. To understand these differences required a longitudinal design and an evaluation of interns' and employees' schooling and work tasks. In this appendix, I discuss the research design and practices, recruitment and sample of respondents, the interview process, data analysis and coding processes/decisions, and conclude with a note on generalizability in qualitative research.

Research Design and Practices

I chose to conduct longitudinal interviews with college seniors at a large Midwestern public research university instead of an ethnography or a survey. Qualitative interviews allowed me to combine individual perspectives into coherent social narratives.[1] Additionally, this style of interview is an excellent way to study life transitions, such as graduating from college and adjusting to entry-level work.[2] Many internship sites hire one intern or assign only one or two interns to each department. A participant observation would not have allowed me to observe many interns, and it would have made it hard to follow up on the longitudinal component since I could not work at the firm. A survey also would have been insufficient since when people are asked what they do at work they usually give vague euphemisms. Only through sustained probing can you uncover people's work experiences. This is discussed further in the interview process section.

I chose a large Midwestern public research university partially because many scholars who study higher education and its immediate outcomes focus on elite colleges. Yet almost 10 percent of all undergraduate students nationally attend public research universities.[3] Investigating students from this school ensures their educational and labor market entry experiences are likely similar to many undergraduates and recent alumni of comparable institutions.

Due to the anticipated scope of the project, I decided to complete a longitudinal study at one university rather than compare students across universities. As a result, I can only speak to processes at CSU, which is located in the Midwest. However, following others who do in-depth case studies of one university, I was able to theorize the trade-off students make when selecting a major as central to understanding between-field inequality. With specific reference to the differential internship structures, as a large Midwestern public research university, CSU graduates who accessed career conveyor-belt internships tended to work in manufacturing firms or for other large regional employers. Given the multinational reach of many of these manufacturing firms, I suspect many engineering and business graduates in other geographic locations find similar employment. I further suspect that the career conveyor-belt process would apply to many other large public universities that try to serve varied constituencies and offer a multitude of majors. Of course, the content of career conveyor-belt internships might change (i.e., the kinds of students with access and the types of firms recruiting them), but the form likely applies to many other universities in the United States. Though I make no claims of statistical generalizability, the fact that so many engineering and business students find gainful employment requiring menial job tasks is enough to substantiate the arguments in this book.

Another key decision was whether to interview employers and internship supervisors. I decided not to do this. As a result, I cannot speak to the logic behind why firms only hire certain majors or how employers decide to make connections with CSU instead of, or in addition to, other institutions. However, this is not germane to the research questions in this study. Interviewing students and graduates is sufficient for understanding what they learn in school, how they find jobs and internships, and what they do at work. Research in labor sociology has demonstrated that management never fully knows how workers do their jobs.[4] Additionally, employers cannot know if workers learned relevant skills in school without some type of assessment that is rare in white-collar hiring. Ultimately, employees have the best knowledge of their employment conditions and capabilities.

Before data collection, I completed preinterviews with academic/internship advisers in several majors. I did this to learn which students choose internships, what kinds of internships they do, and what kind of institutional policies facilitate them. I chose to conduct research with students in four majors: industrial and systems engineering (ISE) (n = 24), business with a specialization in operations and logistics (n = 23), communications (n = 26), and English (n = 18).[5] These were chosen because they cover a STEM field, professional field, humanities discipline, and social science and fall along a spectrum of most to least technical (engineering, business, communications, English). This design also allows for a study of internships in more common sectors of the economy, not just those in the aesthetic or nonprofit fields as is common.[6] Additionally, ISE and operations/logistics majors do similar jobs and internships focusing on business operations or supply chain management. ISE majors combine computer science and data analytics with traditional manufacturing and operations, so in some ways it is comparable to all other types of engineering. English and communications majors also complete similar writing- or communications-focused internships and jobs that are in analogous industries. Further, each pair of majors (business and engineering, English and communications) have similar unemployment rates and comparable rates of finding employment matched to their major.[7] Finally, we know that gender and race are significant factors in both choosing a major and subsequent employment outcomes.[8] Two of the disciplines included (ISE and business) are ones where men are overrepresented (though ISE majors have gender parity in my study sample) and the other two disciplines (English and communications) are women-dominated.

While communications is considered a practical art at some schools and a liberal art at others, at CSU communications is considered a liberal art. Additionally, my findings that communications majors' internships and labor market entries are more like English majors than business and engineering majors suggests that graduates of other social sciences disciplines will likely have more in common with the liberal arts disciplines I studied than the practical arts disciplines.

In addition to interviews, I attended one arts and sciences career fair at CSU. The career fair was central to understanding career conveyor-belt internships, but attendance was not widespread among English and communications students. I went to see which employers attended, to informally interview students and employers, and to gauge how well-attended the event was. Field notes from the career fair were not part of the formal data analysis or evidence presented in this book. However, it confirmed many of the processes I uncovered. First, employers in these settings did not restrict applications to specific majors, meaning all liberal arts students competed for the same positions. Second, attendance was sparse, and many students I talked to left disappointed because there were no opportunities specific to their majors. Finally, large regional professional services firms attended, the same firms that offer career conveyor-belt internships to the English and communications majors I interviewed. However, there were few manufacturing or industrial firms present.

Sample and Recruitment

I used quota sampling to recruit students in the four majors, a method that is effective for finding differences among populations.[9] While each major had a relatively small number of respondents, the overall sample of ninety-one participants created a medium-N study that was large enough to identify social processes.[10] Initial participants were found by emailing classes, professors, or major listservs. Respondents were asked to refer others or to send an email to classes they were taking in their major. Two forms of possible bias from this sampling method are homophily (all volunteers are from the same social network) and overrepresentation of certain kinds of volunteers.[11] Homophily was addressed by limiting the number of referrals for each individual, but also by asking participants to send an email to class lists rather than personal contacts. Overrepresentation was handled by providing a $20 gift card. The incentive mitigated overrepresentation and ensured some socioeconomic diversity; this was successful as study participants came from a range of class backgrounds. Overall, recruitment was effective for business, engineering, and communications majors. However, a more sustained effort was needed to find English majors, requiring me to pitch my research to four English classes. This led to the recruitment of several students.

During recruitment and at the end of the first interview, I informed respondents they were participating in a longitudinal study. After graduation, I emailed participants asking them to fill out a brief survey. This survey gathered updated contact information and asked them about their immediate postgraduation plans. Ninety of the ninety-one respondents completed the survey. Once all respondents had been out of school for at least six months I began collecting wave two data. Participants received an email asking them to participate in the next wave. If they did not respond, I sent a follow-up email two weeks later. If that garnered no response, I texted the participant. If they did not respond to the text, I stopped attempting to recruit them. In the end, I had a response rate of eighty-five of ninety-one, or 93 percent, for wave two. Of the six individuals who did not sit for second-wave interviews, no more than two came from the same major. In total, when added to the wave one interviews, I completed 176 interviews. However, three of the second-wave interviews occurred between a respondent accepting and beginning a new job. As such, these three graduates participated in a second wave-two interview resulting in 179 discrete interviews. Before finishing this book, I once again reached out to all participants asking them for updated contact information and their current employment status. I was able to secure written information on the entry-level jobs from two of the six participants who did not participate in wave two.

Interview Process

Wave one interviews occurred during the 2015–2016 school year. I conducted the first interview on November 11, 2015, and the last interview on August 10, 2016. Though interviews ended with the school year, there were enough respondents to make meaningful comparisons across groups. Interviews primarily took place in my office, though some occurred at a library, coffee shop, or eatery. All interviews were recorded using a digital recorder and subsequently transcribed by either an undergraduate research assistant or professional transcription service.

Interviews followed a semistructured approach. I utilized a standardized interview guide to make sure questions were consistent across interviews, but I also asked probes and follow-ups, as necessary. Wave one interviews were approximately an hour, with most being sixty-five to seventy-five minutes. Topics included why students chose their college and major, what they were learning in their classes, their internship experiences, how these experiences related to their schooling, and their career ambitions/future plans.[12] This process is consistent with Cohen's career narrative approach to learning about workplace experiences.[13] As part of this interview, I asked the students what they were learning in their major classes. I asked them to list specific concepts and ideas and then evaluate how useful they thought those classes would be for their internships or professional lives. These records allowed me to make a comprehensive list of what students learned in their majors while simultaneously capturing students' subjective understandings of the utility of their coursework.

Wave two interviews occurred during the 2016–2017 academic year and continued into fall 2017. The first interview took place on November 12, 2016, and I conducted the last interview on December 6, 2017. Before the interview, I reviewed the wave one transcript to refamiliarize myself with their case. I made notes about areas I should follow up on and specific topics I should cover. As a result, these interviews tended to be slightly longer than wave one interviews, with most lasting in the seventy- to eighty-minute range. On rare occasions, interviews lasted two hours or more. Very few of these interviews took place on campus in my office. Rather, most took place at coffee shops, eateries, or via Skype. Skype interviews presented a challenge since body language and conversational rapport were not as easy to read.

However, even Skype interviews lasted roughly an hour and provided all the necessary information. Once again, interviews were recorded on a digital recorder and transcribed by a professional service.

Second-wave interviews included questions about adjusting to the labor market, what respondents did at work, and how their work tasks related to their education and internship experiences; then they were once again asked about their future plans and ambitions.[14] In this interview, I collected detailed information on what individuals did at work and how they accomplished these tasks. Survey questions would not have revealed the same level of detail. Since at least the 1950s, research on labor sociology has shown that microstudies of work reveal that asking people detailed questions about what they do at their job lessens obscurity, making interviews an essential technique for this research.[15] For example, the below exchange with business graduate Mickey who worked as an IT supply chain operations analyst for a prominent fashion retailer reveals the importance of the interview at probing for details about the substance of respondents work tasks in a way that a survey could not capture.[16] Below is the unedited transcript.

CMP: Can you tell me, in as much detail as you can, what it is specifically that you do every day?

MICKEY: I'm in charge of all operational issues for our cloud-based visibility logistics tool called GT Nexus. It tracks inventory at SKU level, from vendor all the way through to in our DC.

CMP: Which is what—the distribution center?

MICKEY: The distribution centers.

CMP: And the vendors are the stores?

MICKEY: The vendors are China, Bangladesh . . .

CMP: The vendors are who make it [the clothes/attire]?

MICKEY: Factories.

CMP: They have a cloud-based—

MICKEY: Inbound logistics, visibility tool to see every single milestone.

CMP: And you work on IT on that, correct?

MICKEY: Cloud service.

CMP: Who is using it? The distribution center? To track things?

MICKEY: I use it to track the goods. I run a report that tells them "Hey, in two weeks you're going to get this stuff, or a week or you're going to get this stuff, tomorrow you're going to see this truck." All of that inbound visibility is tracked through GT Nexus, which is a cloud-based tool.

CMP: That you maintain?

MICKEY: That I maintain.

CMP: What sort of tasks do you have to do that are associated with it? What did you do today at work?

MICKEY: Today at work, this is going to go completely over your head.

CMP: That's fine. . . . Tell me what you did today. Try to say it in a way that I can understand, the best that you can.

MICKEY: Today we had an issue. I run a report that tells our Netherlands DC all of the items that are coming in for the next two weeks.

CMP: Okay so you run that report and you send it to them?

MICKEY: Yeah. That's just one thing. What I don't think you're going to get is, we have a PM management system, that's called Trade Stem, that sends POs and files and orders to MMS, which is another one of our systems. Then it sends that to GT Nexus, which is the system that I am in charge of.

There's an interface between those two systems called AS2. It's an AS2 connector and that connector went down. Which means, GT Nexus was not receiving the files that MMS was supposed to be sending them.

I had to then look into figuring out why things were getting stuck in MMS or, if they were getting stuck in the AS2 or, if possibly it was just getting started because there's a discrepancy in the information and Trade Stem to go all the way through.

So we were trying to basically figure out "Where is the link in the chain that's gone wrong and how to do we fix it?"

CMP: How did you do that?

MICKEY: We contacted diffcrent departments and we finally ended up talking to the MMS team, MMS team support and we had to triage and just republish all POs from Trade Stem that weren't flowing through GT Nexus. It was a system glitch that, if there's twenty errors in a row, it'll just drop every order.

CMP: How did you, when you say republish, you went in and entered these orders?

MICKEY: I delegate to our PO support team.

CMP: So they did that?

MICKEY: Yep.

The above shows that, through probes, it became clear that Mickey's job is to run reports (which he later said was so easy he could be drunk and doing it) and if there is an issue to contact other departments to fix those issues. I would not have ascertained the true nature of these tasks if we only had Mickey's initial impressive-sounding description of his job, which is being "in charge of all operational issues" for one of his company's computer systems. And while this is just one example, Mickey's case is representative of how countless interviews with students and graduates doing clerical work went, proving how essential interview methodology was to uncovering patterns across respondents' work tasks.

Data Analysis and Coding

Wave One

Data analysis included a combination of inductive and deductive methods, a strength of qualitative research. I coded and organized data using NVivo qualitative analysis software. As interviews were completed, I would review the audio and transcript, upload the transcript into NVivo, and link them to each respondent. Participants and all affiliated organizations were given pseudonyms to ensure confidentiality. The coding scheme initially followed the interview guide as I added top-level coding for themes such as "internship experiences," "school learning," and other themes deemed salient during data collection. Another set of deductive themes came from existing literature, such as coding for when students used network connections to find jobs. Organizing and coding the data around the deductive themes were the first steps in data analysis.

Next, a team of undergraduate research assistants and I wrote case summaries for each wave one transcript. My approach to data analysis was to treat each respondent as a case rather than analyze decontextualized text. To do this successfully required these succinct case summaries for each respondent. The case summary, one page long, had a background section on the student's biography, a summary of their internship placement, detailed information on their internship experience, a section capturing their thoughts and feelings on their internship and major, and a short paragraph on their future plans. Research assistants and I then used these case summaries to make an Excel spreadsheet to visualize important variables (e.g., race, gender, how the student found an internship). This spreadsheet was uploaded to NVivo and linked to the cases so transcripts could easily be sorted by any variable. At this stage, the two internship types began to emerge. I noticed distinct patterns of how students found internships (recruitment for engineering and business students and networks for English and communications students) and how these related to employment outcomes.

Next, I began inductively coding the transcripts by college major. I read through all the transcripts and wrote down themes as they emerged. At this stage, I began to realize the patterned differences between students given internship projects versus ad hoc tasks. I compared sections of transcripts both between and among majors on a range of demographic axes, for example, women engineering majors versus men engineering majors and women engineering majors versus women business majors. Once wave one interviews were coded, I used the emergent knowledge to inform the crafting of the wave two interview guide.

Wave Two

Data analysis for second-wave interviews proceeded similarly to wave one interviews. First, I reviewed transcripts as they came in and uploaded them into NVivo. I linked each transcript with the case summary and first wave interview. Second, top-level coding was based on themes from the interview guide and relevant literature. Third, undergraduate research assistants and I wrote case summaries for the wave two interviews. The case summaries again were one page each and included a background section, a synopsis of their current employment situation and future plans, and a section on their recollections of school and internship experiences. Finally, at the end of the case summary, we listed "survey" information about the respondent—their student loans, final GPA, salary, and any missing data from their first interview, such as their parents' jobs and income. The summaries then served as the basis of a second Excel spreadsheet containing wave two variables. This spreadsheet included analytically relevant information, such as whether the student stayed with their internship firm after graduation.

Next, transcripts were grouped and compared again to allow inductive themes to emerge. At this stage the full scope of the trade-off students make when selecting a major became clear. As I was reading through the engineering and business graduates' transcript sections on their work tasks, I could see that the vast majority of these graduates completed clerical work at their jobs. After fully analyzing the differences between graduates by major and looking at that data in relation to wave one findings, I began to outline the overall argument.

Finally, undergraduate research assistants and I completed a final combined case summary so that each respondent had a one-page summary that neatly mapped their entire college-to-work transition. The combined case summary has a heading with each person's pseudonym, major, internship placement, current employer, and internship type. The summary includes three sections. First, on the respondent's internship, how they found it, what their responsibilities were, and the relationship between their internship and their degree (including skill usage). Second, a section that covers the same ground but for their entry-level job (or graduate school if they were not in the labor force yet). Finally, a section detailing how their future plans have stayed consistent or changed between the two interviews.

Assessing Skills and Comparing Them to Classroom Learning

The most important coding decisions occurred while evaluating mismatches between the skills students learned in school and the tasks of their entry-level job. This is especially the case because many scholars see skills as a social construct whereby ideology and social structure influence how we view jobs or people as skilled.[17] Further, students might not realize they are using their skills at work or define skills differently by discipline. In this scenario, work expectations would be different for each major, and that would influence my interpretation of the data. Engineering and business graduates may receive messages about how useful their degrees are, only to be disappointed by entry-level work. On the other hand, communications and English majors might be told their degrees are useless and therefore are pleasantly surprised by what entry-level work entails. I addressed these two issues (social construction of skills and student awareness) by including subjective and "objective" measures of skill use.

Though I included students' subjective understanding of both their degree and their job, human capital theory rests on an assumption that the actual skills learned in school match up with entry-level job tasks. All first wave interviews asked respondents what they learned in their major classes. I combined that information into themes for each field of study (e.g., logistics analytics for business majors, probability and statistics for engineering majors, professional writing for English majors, and organizational communications for communications majors—see table 2.3 for engineering and business majors and table 2.4 for communications and English majors).

I then compared these themes with the actual tasks that respondents were assigned in their internships and entry-level jobs. I could then objectively assess whether internship or work tasks reflected the classroom learning students received at CSU. As mentioned above, these tasks were broken down into component parts. For communications majors writing press material, there was a direct link between a classroom learning category (writing press releases, media kits, and other content) with their work tasks. If a business major spent all day getting information from one person and reporting it to another, this was not considered a match. Generally, internships and work tasks were considered clerical if they were repetitive and required little discretion.[18] I marked as substantive any internship or work tasks that required more than this definition of clerical work. Rarely did these decisions require complex interpretive decisions or differ from respondents' opinions of their tasks because it was clear based on definitional standards when students performed clerical work. I am therefore confident that I did not mislabel interviewees' tasks.

A Final Note on Generalizability

The research findings presented in this book are neither meant to be generalizable to the entire population of US college graduates nor all practical arts or liberal arts disciplines.[19] The aim of my analysis is to demonstrate social processes and likely outcomes for individuals and fields similar to those I included in this study. By similar individuals and fields, I mean as a total suite of characteristics, not along specific variables. For this reason, and others, I did not take a variable-centric approach to data collection and analysis. For example, I did not choose to include a "women-dominated practical art" to compare to a "men-dominated practical art" to isolate the gender-coding of the discipline as a specific variable.[20] Rather, to better reflect the social world as experienced by students, I selected fields with common sets of characteristics (highly remunerative men-dominated practical arts and less-well-remunerative women-dominated liberal arts).[21]

Choosing these fields actually makes the results *more* generalizable than a variable-centric approach in several ways. I do not mean statistically generalizable, but generalizable in the sense that social experiences and processes are widely applicable. They apply to a broader range of disciplines (i.e., more fields will be similar to one of the four I've chosen than if the four fields were more narrowly defined), they apply to a larger swath of college graduates, and they therefore reflect the kinds of fields many men and women in higher education actually enter.[22] The only caveat is that for the results to be generalizable, fields must match on the totality of characteristics of each major. In other words, I use a case-based rather than sample-based logic, meaning results would apply to similar *cases*. I suspect the trade-off I documented in this book applies to many men-dominated practical arts fields that train individuals for white-collar office work *and* women-dominated liberal arts disciplines that teach feminine-coded skills at comparable universities. By taking a case-based approach that highlights the combined characteristics rather than a sample-population approach, I uncovered social processes and mechanisms that likely apply to the experiences millions of college graduates in the United States.

APPENDIX B: LIST OF PARTICIPANTS

TABLE B.1 Study Participants

Pseudonym	Major	Gender	Race/ethnicity	Social class
Alan	Communications	Man	White	Upper-middle
Allie	Communications	Woman	Asian/Pacific Islander	Working → middle
Allison	Communications	Woman	White	Upper-middle
Alonna	Communications	Woman	White	Upper-middle
Amanda	Communications	Woman	Hispanic	Lower
Carrie	Communications	Woman	Hispanic	Upper-middle
Chloe	Communications	Woman	White	Upper-middle
Derek	Communications	Man	Hispanic	Middle
Donald	Communications	Man	Asian/Pacific Islander	Upper-middle
Donna	Communications	Woman	White	Middle
Emily	Communications	Woman	Black	Lower
Esther	Communications	Woman	White	Middle
Isaac	Communications	Man	White	Upper-middle
Jade	Communications	Woman	Black	Middle
Jenna	Communications	Woman	Middle Eastern	Middle
June	Communications	Woman	White	Middle
Katherine	Communications	Woman	White	Middle
Lena	Communications	Woman	Asian/Pacific Islander	Working
Lisa	Communications	Woman	White	Middle
Marty	Communications	Man	White	Middle
Melanie	Communications	Woman	White	Middle
Mia	Communications	Woman	Black	Middle
Mindy	Communications	Woman	White	Middle
Mitchell	Communications	Man	White	Middle
Sophie	Communications	Woman	White	Middle
Vicky	Communications	Woman	Asian/Pacific Islander	Middle
Brett	English	Man	White	Working
Catherine	English	Woman	White	Lower-middle
Chris	English	Man	Black	Working
Christy	English	Woman	White	Working

Internship type	Internship industry	Entry-level occupation–degree match	Entry-level salary (thousands)
CCB	Finance	No	63
DE	Website	No	30
DE	Media	Yes	43
CCB	Public relations	No	0 (unemployed)
DE	Health care	N/A	16 (grad school)
DE	Retail	No	50
DE	Public relations	Yes	42
CCB	Public relations	Yes	33
DE	Media	N/A	0 (grad school)
DE	Nonprofit	Yes	38.5
DE	Media	No	49
CCB	Food/beverage	No	56
DE	Nonprofit	N/A	16 (grad school)
CCB	Health care	No	78
CCB	Government	No	60
DE	Automotive	Yes	30
DE	Manufacturing	Yes	40
DE	Media	No	42
DE	Public relations	Yes	38
DE	Professional sports	No	40
CCB	Packaging	No	36
CCB	Health care	Yes	39
DE	Museum	No	26
DE	Entertainment	Yes	0 (started own business)
DE	Nonprofit	Yes	40
DE	Start-up	No	60
DE	Education	No	0 (unemployed)
DE	Government	N/A	0 (grad school)
DE	Education	N/A	N/A
DE	Nonprofit	No	14 (part-time)

(continues)

TABLE B.1 (*Continued*)

Pseudonym	Major	Gender	Race/ethnicity	Social class
Colleen	English	Woman	White	Working
Eloise	English	Woman	White	Upper
Genna	English	Woman	White	Middle
Gloria	English	Woman	White	Middle
Greta	English	Woman	White	Upper-middle
Jennifer	English	Woman	White	Lower-middle
Katie	English	Woman	White	Middle
Lana	English	Woman	White	Upper-middle
Laura	English	Woman	White	Middle
Linda	English	Woman	White	Middle
Marne	English	Woman	White	Upper-middle
Mort	English	Man	White	Upper-middle
Rachel	English	Woman	White	Middle
Vance	English	Man	Black	Middle
Adam	ISE	Man	White	Middle
Andi	ISE	Woman	White	Working
Annabelle	ISE	Woman	White	Middle
Arthur	ISE	Man	Asian/Pacific Islander	Upper-middle
Artie	ISE	Man	White	Lower-middle
Brian	ISE	Man	White	Middle
Connie	ISE	Woman	Asian/Pacific Islander	Upper/upper-middle
Daniel	ISE	Man	White	Upper-middle
Dominic	ISE	Man	White	Upper
Jackie	ISE	Woman	Asian/Pacific Islander	Working
Juniper	ISE	Woman	White	Middle
Kelly	ISE	Woman	White	Middle
Lesley	ISE	Woman	White	Upper-middle
Marc	ISE	Man	White	Middle
Marly	ISE	Woman	White	Middle
Mary	ISE	Woman	White	Upper-middle

Internship type	Internship industry	Entry-level occupation–degree match	Entry-level salary (thousands)
CCB	Publishing	Yes	38
DE	Education	N/A	0 (grad school)
CCB	Media	No	33
DE	Marketing	Yes	42
CCB	Publishing	Yes	34
DE	Media	Yes	36
CCB	Retail	Yes	42.6
DE	Publishing	No	60
DE	Nonprofit	No	42
DE	Nonprofit	Yes	18
DE	Library	Yes	18
CCB	Marketing	N/A	0 (grad school)
DE	Performing arts	Yes	20
DE	Media	No	23
DE	Health care	No	85
CCB	Airline	Yes	79.59
CCB	Technology	Yes	69.2
CCB	Manufacturing	Yes	69
CCB	Manufacturing	Yes	67
CCB	Automotive	N/A	N/A
CCB	Technology	Yes	62
DE	Education	No	0 (unemployed)
DE	Insurance	Yes	90
CCB	Automotive	Yes	58
DE	Retail	Yes	68
CCB	Technology	Yes	63.1
CCB	Manufacturing	Yes	42
CCB	Consulting	Yes	60
DE	Manufacturing	Yes	61
CCB	Manufacturing	Yes	60

(continues)

TABLE B.1 (*Continued*)

Pseudonym	Major	Gender	Race/ethnicity	Social class
Mike	ISE	Man	Asian/Pacific Islander	Middle
Quincy	ISE	Man	Asian/Pacific Islander	Middle
Roberta	ISE	Woman	Asian/Pacific Islander	Middle
Sonny	ISE	Woman	Asian/Pacific Islander	Middle
Stephen	ISE	Man	White	Middle
Steve	ISE	Man	White	Lower-middle
Valerie	ISE	Woman	White	Upper-middle
Wilson	ISE	Man	White	Upper-middle
Andy	Ops/logs	Man	Asian/Pacific Islander	Middle
Arne	Ops/logs	Man	White	Working
Burt	Ops/logs	Man	White	Working
Clark	Ops/logs	Man	White	Moved from lower to middle when adopted
Courtney	Ops/logs	Woman	Mixed race	Upper-middle
Danny	Ops/logs	Man	White	Upper-middle
Dustin	Ops/logs	Man	White	Lower-middle
Edward	Ops/logs	Man	White	Middle
Frank	Ops/logs	Man	White	Middle
Jake	Ops/logs	Man	Asian/Pacific Islander	Working
Jordan	Ops/logs	Man	White	Upper
Kim	Ops/logs	Woman	White	Middle
Luke	Ops/logs	Man	White	Lower-middle
Max	Ops/logs	Man	White	Upper-middle
Mickey	Ops/logs	Man	White	Middle → upper-middle
Nick	Ops/logs	Man	White	Middle
Roger	Ops/logs	Man	White	Upper-middle
Samantha	Ops/logs	Woman	White	Upper
Sandy	Ops/logs	Woman	White	Upper-middle
Shawn	Ops/logs	Man	White	Middle
Stacie	Ops/logs	Woman	White	Lower-middle

Internship type	Internship industry	Entry-level occupation–degree match	Entry-level salary (thousands)
DE	Automotive	Yes	65
DE	Manufacturing	Yes	24 (works overseas)
CCB	Manufacturing	Yes	65
DE	Nonprofit	No	77.5
CCB	Manufacturing	Yes	62
CCB	Automotive	Yes	69
CCB	Manufacturing	Yes	65
DE	Defense/military	No	53
CCB	Education	No	0 (grad school)
CCB	Food/beverage	Yes	61
CCB	Automotive	Yes	70
CCB	Manufacturing	Yes	58
CCB	Greeting card	Yes	50
CCB	Retail	Yes	70
CCB	Logistics provider	Yes	53
CCB	Automotive	Yes	52
DE	Manufacturing	No	0 (grad school)
CCB	Retail	N/A	N/A
CCB	Airline	Yes	52
DE	Logistics	No	19.2
CCB	Consulting	Yes	72.5
DE	Retail	Yes	54
DE	Manufacturing	Yes	53
DE	Manufacturing	Yes	65
DE	Sports complex	Yes	69
CCB	Retail	Yes	60
CCB	Chemical	Yes	75
CCB	Energy	N/A	N/A
CCB	Manufacturing	No	50

(continues)

TABLE B.1 (*Continued*)

Pseudonym	Major	Gender	Race/ethnicity	Social class
Thomas	Ops/logs	Man	White	Middle
Tonya	Ops/logs	Woman	White	Upper

Notes: Internship types are career conveyor-belt (CCB) and dead-end (DE).

Internship type	Internship industry	Entry-level occupation–degree match	Entry-level salary (thousands)
CCB	Food/beverage	Yes	55
CCB	Automotive	No	75

APPENDIX C: WAVE ONE INTERVIEW GUIDE

RAPPORT/BACKGROUND/CLASSROOM LEARNING

1. Where are you from?
2. Why did you decide to come to CSU? Were you considering anywhere else?
3. So, you are majoring in [business/engineering/English/communications], why did you choose that major?
4. Tell me about the classes you are taking this semester. What are you learning in them? For each class or concept, do you think this will be useful to you in the future?
5. So, you're doing an internship. Can you tell me where, how many hours per week, whether it is paid or unpaid, and any other basic details?
6. How did you come to choose this internship? How did you decide what to do?

INTERNSHIP EXPERIENCE

1. Can you tell me what you do at your internship in as detailed a way as possible?
   a. What are your specific/regular tasks?
   b. How did they change over time?
   c. What's your level of self-direction?
   d. How do you collaborate with staff?
   e. How is your work similar and different from entry-level employees?
2. How do you do your job at your internship?
   a. What are you learning?
   b. How easy is it to pick up? (Determining where "skills" come from)
   c. Do you find learning these things useful? Why or why not?
3. What are your thoughts and feelings about being an intern?
   a. Do you consider this internship successful? What would determine that?
   b. Is the internship what you expected it would be? Why or why not?
   c. What do you enjoy most about interning? Least?
   d. Are you treated the same as regular employees? How so?

     e. What is your relationship like with your supervisor? What kind of mentoring do you receive?

     f. Have you ever experienced maltreatment or discrimination?

4. Does your internship relate to your major?

     a. Do you use things you learned in the classroom at your internship?

     b. Is there anything you wished you'd learned in the classroom before starting?

     c. What do you see as the relationship between your major and internship?

     d. What do you see as the relationship between your major and your career?

5. Overall, how is your internship an educational experience? A work experience?

FUTURE PLANS

1. What are your plans after graduating?
2. How will you attempt to find a job? Who will you reach out to?
3. Do you think you'll obtain another internship?
4. How has your internship informed or altered your future plans?
5. How has your major informed or altered your future plans?
6. Where do you see yourself in five years? Ten years? What do you think will get you there?

BACKGROUND QUESTIONS

1. Employment history

     a. Dates

     b. Pay

     c. Details

2. All majors (including dual majors, minors, and previously declared majors)
3. High school's characteristics
4. College GPA
5. Family history
6. Socioeconomic class
7. Age
8. Race
9. Gender

APPENDIX D: WAVE TWO INTERVIEW GUIDE

Review the first interview and note details to follow up on. Mention them where they fit below; if not applicable, bring them up at the beginning or end of the second interview.

RAPPORT/BACKGROUND

1. So, fill me in on what you did between when we talked last and graduation. Did you do another internship? You graduated [semester/year], right?
2. Are you working or in school, where for what? Tell me about it.
   a. If YES (have a job or are in school):
      i. How did you make the decision what to do? Offers? How'd you find them?
      ii. Thoughts and feelings about the decision process? Broad challenges facing you after school is over? Like most/least about being out of school?
   b. If NO (still figuring out what to do after graduation):
      i. Tell me about the transition after school. What challenges do you face? Enjoy most or least?
      ii. What do you see as the big decisions ahead? How do you plan on making them? What networks will you use to find a job?

MORE ON CURRENT JOB

1. So, tell me in as detailed a way as possible what it is that you do now.
   a. Specific/regular tasks
   b. Changes over time
   c. Self-direction
   d. Collaboration
   e. Do they have interns? How does your job differ from theirs?
2. How did you learn how to do your current job?
   a. What are you learning? How easy was it to pick up?

    b. To what extent are you using skills learned in your degree? Thoughts/feelings about that?
3. Back to general thoughts/feelings about the current job.
    a. Expectations
    b. Enjoy most/least
    c. Boss/supervisor
    d. Maltreatment/discrimination
    e. Room for advancement/career building

FUTURE PLANS

1. How long do you plan on being in the current job?
2. Do you have a specific career aspiration? What will it take to achieve? Will the skills you learned in college help you achieve that?
3. Where do you see yourself in five/ten years?

SCHOOL

1. How do you think your education affects what you're doing now?
    a. Prep for the current job? Helped get current job? Relates in any way to the current job?
    b. Still in contact with anyone?
2. Knowing what you know now, what would you do differently in college? Different school, major, etc.?

INTERNSHIP

1. So, when we last spoke, you interned at [company/employer]. Thinking back on it, what do you think/feel about the internship?
    a. Prep for the current job? Did it help you get current job? Relates in any way to the current job?
    b. Still in contact with anyone? Will help with a future job?
2. Would you do it again? What would you do differently knowing what you know now?

FINANCIAL SITUATION

1. How much are you earning now? How do you feel about that? Did you negotiate your salary?
2. Do you have any student loans or other debt? How do you feel about that?

OVERALL ASSESSMENT

How would you assess the current path your career is on? What are your feelings about it?

FINAL BACKGROUND QUESTIONS

1. Employment history since the last interview, final college GPA
2. Relationship status and current living situation
3. Push more on class background from the last interview. Has this changed? Parents' income?

NOTES

Chapter One

1. Mort and Capital State University are pseudonyms. All names of respondents, their employers, and their schools have been changed to ensure confidentiality.
2. Many English majors attempted to enter the labor market directly and struggled to find satisfactory work rather than enter graduate school.
3. Thompson (2015).
4. Redden (2020).
5. Burning Glass Institute and Strada Institute for the Future of Work (2024).
6. Garcia-Navarro (2018); Kalleberg (2007).
7. Ashworth and Ransom (2019).
8. Mullen (2014, 294).
9. See Brint et al. (2005).
10. Brint et al. (2005, 172).
11. Pearson (n.d.).
12. Burning Glass Institute (2018, 15).
13. Burning Glass Institute (2018).
14. Burning Glass Institute (2018); Burning Glass Institute and Strada Institute for the Future of Work (2024).
15. Thompson (2016).
16. Ibid.
17. Ibid.
18. Van Dam (2022).
19. Ibid.
20. Heller (2023).
21. Van Dam (2022).
22. Feder (2012).
23. Bessner (2023).
24. Townsend (2012).
25. Deming (2019).
26. Levenson (2013).
27. Schmidt (2018).

28. Anders (2017).
29. Levenson (2013).
30. See Hill and Pisacreta (2019) for a good summary of the mixed evidence of the economic returns to a liberal arts education.
31. Deming (2019).
32. Ibid.
33. Ibid.
34. Herrity (2023).
35. Selingo (2017); Van Dam (2022).
36. Carnevale, Cheah, and Strohl (2012); Han, Tumin, and Qian (2016); Kim, Tamborini, and Sakamoto (2015); Roksa and Levey (2010).
37. I define stable middle-class work as a "new organizational career." See the section "Variations in Entry-Level Jobs by College Major" for discussion of that term.
38. Although I uncover an important social process moving some students into entry-level work more easily than others, it is of course possible (even likely) that recent graduates would still end up in very different entry-level jobs, depending on major, absent these internship structures.
39. A limitation of my method is that I cannot speak to what motivates employers' actions. However, see chap. 1n63 for information on how employers tend to list liberal arts competencies as desirable in job ads despite liberal arts graduates having, on average, inferior labor market outcomes by traditional measures than practical arts graduates.
40. National Center for Education Statistics (2020).
41. Pitt and Zhu (2019).
42. Blackwood (2023); Heller (2023).
43. For more on generalizability, see "A Final Note on Generalizability" in the methodological appendix. I also discuss the rationale for choosing these majors in chap. 2.
44. Pitt and Zhu (2019).
45. Brint (2002).
46. National Center for Education Statistics (2020).
47. McCaughey (2019).
48. Ibid.
49. White (2019).
50. O'Connor (2020).
51. Brighouse (2019).
52. Dickler (2020); The Hechinger Report (2018).
53. Hubler (2020).
54. Hamilton and Nielsen (2021, chap. 4).
55. Hamilton and Nielsen (2021, 111–12).
56. To maintain anonymity, enrollment reports are not cited.
57. This is more fully explored in chap. 2, but also see Indeed Editorial Team (2023) for skills commonly listed in job ads.
58. Arum and Roksa (2011, 202). Note in their work: Communications majors do not have a statistically significant difference in scores from business majors.

59. Competitive admit majors refers to majors that students must apply for, and be accepted into, even after they are admitted to the university. This is opposed to open admit majors that anyone can declare once they have been accepted into the university.

60. Although occupational segregation literature often refers to fields as "male-dominated" or "female-dominated," following contemporary best practices in the Sociology of Gender, I have removed sex-reductive language and refer to "men" and "women" dominated fields/majors.

61. American Academy of Arts and Sciences (2020).

62. Wright, Roscigno, and Quadlin (2023).

63. See Ridgeway (2011).

64. Quadlin (2018); Pech, Klainot-Hess, and Norris (2020); Ridgeway (2011).

65. I give a fuller accounting of the effects of race, class, and gender in subsequent chapters throughout book.

66. Human capital theory assumes students *learn* these skills in school. In this book, I make no distinction between whether students learn the skills in school or acquire them independently. Rather, I focus on whether the curriculum of students' majors match their entry-level work tasks.

67. Becker (1964).

68. See Kim, Tamborini, and Sakamoto (2015, 321).

69. Di Stasio and van de Werfhorst (2016); Humburg and van der Velden (2015); Nunley et al. (2016).

70. Bills (2003); Nunley et al. (2016).

71. Roksa and Levey (2010).

72. Meyer (1977). Many consider Meyer and his intellectual descendants "neo-institutionalist"; however, when particularly referencing education, "chartering" this theory is often referred to as simply "institutionalist." "Neo-institutionalism" in education tends to refer to schools or organizations adopting the same practices or policies to appear legitimate to others in a field (and the subsequent decoupling between formal policies and on-the-ground actions). In practical terms for this book, the distinction between institutional and neo-institutional theory is not salient.

73. Armstrong and Masse (2014); Bills (2003); Bourdieu and Passeron (1990).

74. Bourdieu (1997).

75. Binder, Davis, and Bloom (2016); Rivera (2015).

76. Davis and Binder (2019).

77. Binder, Davis, and Bloom (2016); Ho (2009); Rivera (2015).

78. Armstrong and Hamilton (2013); Hamilton (2016); Mullen (2011).

79. Pitt and Zhu (2019).

80. Bills (2003, 451).

81. Bills (2003, 452).

82. Of course, other theories of the college-to-work transition exist, but most of them are designed to explain differences between those with a college degree and those without. As a result, they are not salient for our attempt to understand differences in labor market entry by degree field. One worth mentioning is signaling theory, most often associated with the economist Michael Spence (1974). Declaring a practical

arts major may signal to employers that students have the skills needed to be successful employees. Usually, researchers use signaling theory to mean students signal to employers that they have the innate or general ability necessary to be trained by the firm to accomplish their tasks (see Bills 2003). However, when all students come from the same institution, given that liberal arts majors tend to score higher on standardized tests of general competencies than practical arts students, if practical arts disciplines are signals to employers that their students are more employable because they signal more general ability, this is likely the result of the cultural bias suggested by institutionalists. Signaling theory could also potentially mean degree-specific skills will be used later on (i.e., a signal to firms that students have the skills needed to move up into higher roles in the organization eventually). However, that understanding of signaling is not as germane to the focus of this book on entry-level work and initial employment disparities by major.

83. Hanson and Gulish (2016).
84. Gault, Redington, and Schlager (2000); Parker et al. (2016); Smith (2010).
85. Perlin (2012); Shade and Jacobson (2015).
86. Shandra (2022).
87. For anonymity reasons I withhold the citation/link for the graduation survey.
88. Crain (2016).
89. Di Stasio and van de Werfhorst (2016); Nunley et al. (2016).
90. Stevens, Armstrong, and Arum (2008).
91. Davis and Binder (2016).
92. Of course, the connections do not explain *why* some firms offer career conveyor-belt internships or why some majors have better employment outcomes than others. Rather, the connections describe how the disparities between majors emerge.
93. See Rivera (2020, 219) for an overview.
94. At elite private universities, access to employers via internships are likely available to students from all majors (see Binder, Davis, and Bloom 2016; Rivera 2015).
95. Carnevale, Cheah, and Strohl (2012); Han, Tumin, and Qian (2016); Kim, Tamborini, and Sakamoto (2015); Roksa and Levey (2010).
96. Roksa and Levey (2010).
97. Mullen (2014); Pitt and Zhu (2019).
98. Binder, Davis, and Bloom (2016); Rivera (2015).
99. Moss-Pech (2021).
100. Clarke (2013).
101. Clarke (2013); Pech (2017).
102. Clarke (2013); Whitford (2005).
103. Kalleberg and Vallas (2018).
104. Kalleberg and Vallas (2018); Pugh (2014).
105. Graeber (2018).
106. Brooks (2011); Christin (2018); Graeber (2018); Kalleberg (2011); Lebovitz, Lifshitz-Assaf, and Levina (2022); Sitkin, Long, and Cardinal (2020).
107. Bills, Di Stasio, and Gërxhani (2017).
108. Mullen (2014, 294).

109. Brown (2015).
110. Mellon Foundation (2019).
111. Hill and Pisacreta (2019).
112. Ryff (2019).
113. Toor (2022).
114. Students may not be making the trade-off I discuss consciously as their information about labor market opportunities and college majors is often incomplete at best.
115. Roksa and Levey (2010).
116. Davis and Binder (2019).
117. O'Shaughnessy (2011).
118. College enrollment report, source confidential to protect anonymity of respondents.
119. Hanson (2024).
120. College enrollment report.
121. Ibid.
122. Hanson (2024).
123. Ibid.
124. See Armstrong and Hamilton (2013, chap. 2).
125. Mullen (2011).
126. See Binder, Davis, and Bloom (2016); Cottom (2017).
127. For those outside the United States, senior year means a student's final year in college, which is typically their fourth year.
128. I discuss the majors and the rationale for choosing them in chap. 2.
129. Di Stasio and van de Werfhorst (2016); Nunley et al. (2016).
130. Frenette (2013); Leonard, Halford, and Bruce (2015); Shade and Jacobson (2015); Taylor and de Laat (2013).
131. Frenette (2013); Gault, Redington, and Schlager (2000); Matthew, Taylor, and Ellis (2012).
132. See appendix B for full list of respondents. All respondents graduated and were therefore eligible to sit for a second wave interview.
133. Most research focuses substantively on either school or work, even if they include variables of interest from the other domain.
134. When I refer to practical arts majors' "liberal arts competencies," I am referring to the general skills acquired in college that are not major-specific.

Chapter Two

1. Cech (2021).
2. Binder and Abel (2019); Binder, Davis, and Bloom (2016); Mullen (2011).
3. American Academy of Arts and Sciences (2020).
4. Mullen (2011); Quadlin (2018; 2020); Shauman (2016); Roksa (2005).
5. Monaghan and Jang (2017).
6. Ibid.
7. Wingfield (2009); Woodhams, Lupton, and Cowling (2015); Yavorsky, Cohen, and Qian (2016).

8.   I use students' self-reported social class, although I have information on their parents' education levels, jobs, and income to corroborate their reports. If there was a discrepancy or a change in students' class over their lifetime, it is noted in the text.

9.   There is no general business track at CSU, all students pick a narrow specialization—others include marketing, accounting, and finance.

10.   Monaghan and Jang (2017).

11.   Many women-dominated practical arts majors offered at universities prepare students for careers in feminine-coded trade occupations like dental hygiene whereas masculine-coded trades (e.g., HVAC) tend to be taught at community colleges or vocational schools.

12.   Hamilton et al. (2019); Hill Collins (1990).

13.   See Pitt and Zhu (2019).

14.   See Blackwood (2023); Heller (2023).

15.   Because I did not over-sample for racialized minorities, I cannot make strong claims about the effects of race within the confines of the school. However, I can discuss how, as a racialized organization, the effects of the processes I uncover affect the students at CSU, who are mostly (but not exclusively of course) White and middle class.

16.   National Center for Education Statistics (2020).

17.   Carnevale, Strohl, and Melton (2014).

18.   See Armstrong and Hamilton (2013).

19.   Binder, Davis, and Bloom (2016).

20.   Mullen (2014).

21.   Cech (2021).

22.   Very few students in this study came from truly "upper class" backgrounds, which is not an anomaly given the type of institution CSU is and the populations it typically serves.

23.   Cech (2021).

24.   I read program requirements for two Ivy League English departments and the only courses mentioned were in literature, diversity, creative writing, and literary theory/criticism.

25.   Cech (2015).

26.   Ridgeway (2011); Kilbourne et al. (1994).

27.   CSU English department webpage not linked for anonymity, but see National Association of Colleges and Employers (n.d.).

28.   Indeed Editorial Team (2023).

29.   Daneva, Wang, and Hoener (2017).

30.   Sodhi and Son (2010).

31.   Brunner, Zarkin, and Yates (2018).

Chapter Three

1.   Some business and engineering students completed co-ops. Co-ops are not functionally different from full-time internships; the major logistical difference is that

they take place during a fall or spring semester (or two consecutive semesters) rather than over one summer. For students participating in co-ops, they either take extra courses to graduate on time (often over the summer) or delay graduation by one semester.

2. Frenette (2013); Perlin (2012); Taylor and de Laat (2013).
3. See Nunley et al. (2016) for an example of using audit studies to research internships.
4. Even at elite universities, students' background can influence their opportunities (see Jack 2016; 2019).
5. Damaske (2009); Davis and Binder (2016).
6. Damaske (2009); Davis and Binder (2016).
7. Clarke (2013); Pech (2017).
8. See chap. 4 for a more in-depth discussion of internship task assignments.
9. Bills, Di Stasio, and Gërxhani (2017); Yakubovich (2006).
10. Rosenbaum and Binder (1997).
11. Frenette (2013).
12. See Shandra (2022) on the demographics of who completes internships while in school.
13. It is possible some firms preferred hiring certain majors. I cannot know employers' preferences. However, firms recruiting at the Arts and Sciences career fair interact with students from a wide cross section of majors.
14. Binder, Davis, and Bloom (2016); Rivera (2015); Tholen et al. (2013).
15. See Roksa (2005), which shows that occupationally specific degrees that are women-dominated (such as education) do not have the same labor market outcomes as those that are men-dominated.

Chapter Four

1. See chap. 2 on what students learned in their fields of study.
2. For further details on how these terms were coded and what interview questions uncovered the answers that led to the typology, see the methodological appendix (appendix A).
3. Frenette (2013); Perlin (2012).
4. Frenette (2013); Taylor and de Laat (2013).
5. Frenette (2013); Leonard, Halford, and Bruce (2015); Shade and Jacobson (2015); Taylor and de Laat (2013).
6. Frenette (2013); Matthew, Taylor, and Ellis (2012).
7. This is a sociology of work approach to examining the microconditions of internships.
8. See Burawoy (1979); Roy (1954); Sherman (2007).
9. Robst (2007, 42).
10. Vallas (1990).
11. Fine (1996); Hodson (2001); Ikeler (2016); Vallas (1990).
12. Claim based on reading curriculum at Ivy League English departments' websites.

13. Learn.org (n.d.); US Bureau of Labor Statistics (n.d.).
14. Indeed.com (n.d.).
15. See Frenette (2013); Taylor and de Laat (2013).
16. For full sample demographics and characteristics see chap. 2.
17. Di Stasio and van de Werfhorst (2016); Roksa and Levey (2010).
18. Arum and Roksa (2011).
19. See Roy (1954) for an early example, also Burawoy (1979); Sherman (2007).

Chapter Five

1. Bills (2003); Binder, Davis, and Bloom (2016); Quadlin (2018); Rivera (2015).
2. Some studies that examine how elite students get elite jobs include Binder, Davis, and Bloom (2016); Rivera (2015); Tholen et al. (2013). For one counter example from a less elite school see Streib (2023). Also see Arum and Roksa's (2014) study of almost a thousand college graduates from a diverse range of colleges and universities.
3. For good examples of audit studies see Nunley et al. (2016) and Quadlin (2018).
4. Bills (2003); Bills, Di Stasio, and Gërxhani (2017).
5. Six of the students with dead-end internships went directly to graduate school. The rest entered the labor market. In general, graduates' unemployment rates closely matched the US average for college graduates (US Bureau of Labor Statistics n.d.).
6. Robst (2007); Roksa and Levey (2010).
7. See Kalleberg (2007) on mismatched workers and underemployment.
8. Hamilton and Armstrong (2021).
9. Hamilton (2016).
10. This makes sense given that business and engineering are "competitive admit majors" so most demographic sorting likely occurs at entrance into the major rather than in experiences once in the major where opportunities for students seem plentiful (although, of course, there could be patterned differences between those who had internships and those who did not complete an internship). This finding is in line with recent work by sociologist Jessi Streib, which finds parity among business graduates of the same university regardless of class background (Streib 2023).
11. See Clarke (2013) and Pech (2017) on new organizational careers.
12. See Kalleberg and Vallas (2018) and Clarke (2013).
13. Carnevale, Cheah, and Strohl (2012); Han, Tumin, and Qian (2016); Kim, Tamborini, and Sakamoto (2015); Roksa (2005); Roksa and Levey (2010).
14. In the conclusion I discuss more fully *when* class inequality manifests for the two sets of majors vis-à-vis labor market outcomes (i.e., after graduation for the liberal arts majors but likely before admittance into the major for the practical arts).
15. Carnevale, Cheah, and Strohl (2012); Gerber and Cheung (2008); Han, Tumin, and Qian (2016); Kim, Tamborini, and Sakamoto (2015); Roksa and Levey (2010).
16. See Roksa and Levey (2010) on degree-specificity and occupation-to-degree matching measures.
17. Robst (2007); Roksa and Levey (2010).
18. Arnett (2014); Furstenberg, Rumbaut, and Settersten (2005).

19. Carnevale, Cheah, and Strohl (2012); Gerber and Cheung (2008); Han, Tumin, and Qian (2016); Kim, Tamborini, and Sakamoto (2015); Roksa and Levey (2010).

Chapter Six

1. Of course, as chap. 2 shows and as Cech (2021) investigates, students may not fully differentiate between "passion" and "practical" majors. However, thinking of the majors in dichotomous terms is a key component of media narratives and other public narratives about degree fields.
2. See appendix A for more detail on how I gathered information on entry-level job tasks using in-depth interviews.
3. Substantive tasks are defined as any work that is not clerical.
4. Brooks (2011); Gordon (1996); Kalleberg (2007; 2011).
5. In this chapter and in chap. 7, I present the results in a gender balanced way to show the lack of differences within each major by gender or other demographic characteristics. However, given the distribution of people across majors, communications and English majors are more likely to be either women or to be men who are not White and middle class.
6. Clarke (2013).
7. In some ways, the graduates' employment outcomes reflect what sociologist Jessi Streib (2023) argues in her study of a mid-tier business school, that working-class and middle-class students from this school end up in jobs with similar pay because of a lack of transparency in what their entry-level jobs will entail.
8. See Bowen (2003) on "glamorous" perceptions of public relations.
9. Grenada is a pseudonym for the city where Marty works and lives.
10. Streib et al. (2019).
11. For more on occupation-to-degree matching see Roksa and Levey (2010).
12. Although a library sciences degree might better match her occupation, English as a discipline matches closely to the occupation of librarian.
13. See Callaghan and Thompson (2001). Also see Kaplan (2015) on workplace monitoring in general.
14. Bills (2003); Di Stasio and van de Werfhorst (2016); Humburg and van der Velden (2015).
15. Brint et al. (2005); Roksa and Levey (2010).
16. See table 5.1 for employment outcomes by major.
17. See Ridgeway (2011).
18. Gordon (1996).

Chapter Seven

1. Mullen (2014, 290).
2. Goyette and Mullen (2006, 498).
3. Here I refer to "liberal arts skills" as general skills most college graduates should learn regardless of major. This contrasts with occupation- or major-specific skills

covered in particular liberal arts majors (e.g., English majors learning to write in different voices).

4.   See Indeed Editorial Team (2023).

5.   Goyette and Mullen (2006, 498).

6.   This triangulation process is important because students may not be fully aware if they are using their coursework, but of course their subjective understanding of how their degrees translate into entry-level work are still valuable for understanding their experiences.

7.   See Bills (2003) on the theories for how increased schooling leads to labor market outcomes.

8.   See Brint et al. (2005) on the differences between the practical and liberal arts.

9.   Roksa and Levey (2010).

10. Roksa and Levey (2010, 395–96).

11. Di Stasio and van de Werfhorst (2016); Humburg and van der Velden (2015); Nunley et al. (2016).

12. Becker (1964); Humburg and van der Velden (2015); Nunley et al. (2016).

13. Graeber (2018).

14. Brint et al. (2005).

15. Deming (2019).

16. See Collins (1979) on credentialism.

17. If a student's degree represents human capital acquired elsewhere, this is in line with signaling theory (see Spence 1974) rather than human capital theory, which is explicitly about schools building students' human capital.

18. Northern State and Rolling State are pseudonyms for other public research universities in the same region as CSU. Northern State is less than 250 miles from CSU, and Rolling State is less than 125 miles from CSU.

19. Cech (2013).

20. Bills (2003); Di Stasio and van de Werfhorst (2016); Humburg and van der Velden (2015).

21. Brint et al. (2005); Roksa and Levey (2010).

22. Recall that, within practical arts majors, access to career conveyor-belt internships did not vary along race, class, or gendered lines.

23. See Frenette (2013) and Taylor and de Laat (2013) on negative internship experiences.

24. See Bills (2003) on the theories for how increased schooling leads to labor market outcomes.

25. See Brint et al. (2005) on the differences between the practical and liberal arts.

26. Streib et al. (2019).

27. For example, see Heller's (2023) *New Yorker* article ominously titled "The End of the English Major."

28. In fact, prior research has demonstrated that salaries are often opaque to job applicants and not tied to traditional economic factors such as human capital or profitability (Rosenfeld 2021; Streib 2023).

29. Arum and Roksa (2011).

30. Becker (1964); Grayson (2004).
31. See Arum and Roksa (2011) on college student learning.
32. Becker (1964); Bills (2003).
33. Collins (1979); Rivera (2012).
34. See Berg (1970) for an early statement on credential inflation and Moss-Pech, Lopez, and Michaels (2021) for a recent discussion.
35. Finamore et al. (2013).

Chapter Eight

1. Burning Glass Institute (2018); Thompson (2016); Van Dam (2022).
2. Deming (2019); Townsend (2012).
3. Anders (2017); Levenson (2013); Schmidt (2018).
4. Pearson (n.d.).
5. Burning Glass Institute (2018).
6. Bessner (2023); Feder (2012).
7. Quadlin (2018); Ridgeway (2011).
8. Armstrong and Hamilton (2013); Hamilton and Armstrong (2021).
9. Hamilton and Nielsen (2021); Jack (2019).
10. Mellon Foundation (2019).
11. Blackwood (2023).
12. Stevens, Armstrong, and Arum (2008).
13. By "interinstitutional approach" I mean substantively studying both higher education and labor market institutions.
14. Kalleberg (2007).
15. See Bills, Di Stasio, and Gërxhani (2017); Di Stasio and van de Werfhorst (2016); Nunley et al. (2016); Rivera (2020).
16. Di Stasio and van de Werfhorst (2016); Humburg and van der Velden (2015); Nunley et al. (2016).
17. Binder, Davis, and Bloom (2016); Rivera (2015).
18. See Gerber and Cheung (2008).
19. Brooks (2011); Christin (2018); Graeber (2018); Kalleberg (2011); Lebovitz, Lifshitz-Assaf, and Levina (2022); Sitkin, Long, and Cardinal (2020).
20. Brooks (2011).
21. Frenette (2013); Perlin (2012).
22. Of course, even internships that give students substantive tasks may be unpaid or dead-end internships. These types of internships have significant downsides, especially for students who are not from privileged backgrounds.
23. Kalleberg (2011); Leicht and Fennell (2023).
24. Kalleberg (2007).
25. The Associated Press (2012).
26. Beaudry, Green, and Sand (2015).
27. Brooks (2011); Kalleberg (2011); Lane (2011); Leicht and Fennell (2023); Pech (2017).

28. See Binder, Davis, and Bloom (2016); Rivera (2015).
29. Mauldin (2019).
30. Gordon (1996).
31. Graeber (2018).
32. Ho (2009).
33. Gershon (2017).
34. Gordon (1996); Graeber (2018).
35. Bourdieu (1997); Ridgeway (2011).
36. For those outside the United States, freshman year is a student's first year at college, sophomore is the second year, and junior is the third. Senior year means a student's final year in college, which is typically their fourth year.
37. See Lichtenstein (2013) for a history of the US labor movement.
38. Ibid.
39. See Kalleberg (2007; 2011).
40. Bogage and Fowers (2021); Cook (2021); Thompson (2021).
41. Brint et al. (2005); Cottom (2017); Moss-Pech, Lopez, and Michaels (2021).

Appendix A

1. Weiss (1994).
2. Hermanowicz (2013).
3. O'Shaughnessy (2011).
4. Roy (1954); Sherman (2007).
5. Some respondents had double majors. For example, one communications major also majored in Japanese. However, (a) this was very few respondents and (b) every double major in this study had their career aspirations more in line with one of the four sampled majors than their second field.
6. Frenette (2013).
7. Carnevale, Cheah, and Strohl (2012); Roksa and Levey (2010).
8. Kim (2015); Shauman (2016).
9. Bernard (2006).
10. Ragin (2000).
11. Heckathorn and Jeffri (2001).
12. See appendix C for the questions and prompts from wave one.
13. Cohen (2006).
14. See appendix C for the questions and prompts from wave two.
15. For a classic and recent example see Roy (1954) and Sherman (2007).
16. This exchange is also briefly recounted in chap. 6 when discussing Mickey's entry-level work tasks.
17. See Vallas (1990) on skills.
18. See chap. 6 for more details on how I define clerical work.
19. See the discussion of scope conditions in chapter 1.
20. See Hamilton et al. (2019) on intersectional feminist analysis and the limitations of a variable-centric approach to social science.

21. For another example of this kind of work see Mullen (2011), where she studies Yale University and Southern Connecticut State University, two schools that vary in fundamental type rather than along one specific variable (i.e., they are not the same *except for* one variable).

22. Nationally, business and engineering are the two most prevalent majors among men in college (Wright, Roscigno, and Quadlin 2023).

REFERENCES

American Academy of Arts and Sciences. 2020. "Humanities Indicators: Gender Distribution of Degrees in English Language and Literature." https://www.amacad.org/humanities-indicators/higher-education/gender-distribution-degrees-english-language-and-literature.

Anders, George. 2017. "The Unexpected Value of the Liberal Arts." *Atlantic*. August 1, 2017. https://www.theatlantic.com/education/archive/2017/08/the-unexpected-value-of-the-liberal-arts/535482/.

Armstrong, Elizabeth A., and Laura T. Hamilton. 2013. *Paying for the Party: How College Maintains Inequality*. Cambridge, MA: Harvard University Press.

Armstrong, Elizabeth A., and Johanna C. Masse. 2014. "The Sociology of Higher Education: Contributions and New Directions." *Contemporary Sociology* 43 (6): 801–11.

Arnett, Jeffrey Jensen. 2014. *Emerging Adulthood: The Winding Road from the Late Teens through the Twenties*. New York: Oxford University Press.

Arum, Richard, and Josipa Roksa. 2011. *Academically Adrift: Limited Learning on College Campuses*. Chicago: University of Chicago Press.

Arum, Richard, and Josipa Roksa. 2014. *Aspiring Adults Adrift: Tentative Transitions of College Graduates*. Chicago: University of Chicago Press.

Ashworth, Jared, and Tyler Ransom. 2019. "Has the College Wage Premium Continued to Rise? Evidence from Multiple US Surveys." *Economics of Education Review* 69 (1): 149–54.

The Associated Press. 2012. "Overqualified, Underutilized: Many College Grads Facing Underemployment, Joblessness." *New Haven Register*. April 28, 2012. https://www.nhregister.com/news/article/Overqualified-underutilized-Many-college-grads-11503675.php.

Beaudry, Paul, David Green, and Benjamin Sand. 2015. "The Great Reversal in the Demand for Skill and Cognitive Tasks." *Journal of Labor Economics* 34:199–247.

Becker, Gary S. 1964. *Human Capital: A Theoretical and Empirical Analysis*. Chicago: University of Chicago Press.

Berg, Ivar. 1970. *Education and Jobs: The Great Training Robbery*. New York: Columbia University Press.

Bernard, H. Russell. 2006. *Research Methods in Anthropology: Qualitative and Quantitative Approaches*. 4th ed. Lanham: AltaMira Press.

Bessner, Daniel. 2023. "The Dangerous Decline of the Historical Profession." *New York Times.* January 14, 2023. https://www.nytimes.com/2023/01/14/opinion/american -history-college-university-academia.html.

Bills, David B. 2003. "Credentials, Signals, and Screens: Explaining the Relationship Between Schooling and Job Assignment." *Review of Educational Research* 73 (4): 441–49.

Bills, David, Valentina Di Stasio, and Klarita Gërxhani. 2017. "The Demand Side of Hiring: Employers in the Labor Market." *Annual Review of Sociology* 43:291–310.

Binder, Amy J., and Andrea R. Abel. 2019. "Symbolically Maintained Inequality: How Harvard and Stanford Students Construct Boundaries among Elite Universities." *Sociology of Education* 92 (1): 41–58.

Binder, Amy J., Daniel B. Davis, and Nick Bloom. 2016. "Career Funneling." *Sociology of Education* 89 (1): 20–39.

Blackwood, Sarah. 2023. "Letter from an English Department on the Brink." *New York Review of Books.* April 2, 2023. https://www.nybooks.com/online/2023/04/02 /letter-from-an-english-department-on-the-brink/.

Bogage, Jacob, and Alyssa Fowers. 2021. "Workplace Strikes are Surging. Here's Why They Won't Stop Anytime Soon." *Washington Post.* October 31, 2021. https://www .washingtonpost.com/business/2021/10/31/faq-striketober/.

Bourdieu, Pierre. 1997. "The Forms of Capital." In *Education: Culture, Economy, and Society,* edited by A. H. Halsey, H. Lauder, P. Brown, and A. Stuart Wells, 46–58. New York: Oxford University Press.

Bourdieu, Pierre, and Jean-Claude Passeron. 1990. *Reproduction in Education, Society and Culture.* New York: Sage.

Bowen, Shannon A. 2003. "'I Thought It Would Be More Glamorous': Preconceptions and Misconceptions among Students in the Public Relations Principles Course." *Public Relations Review* 29 (2): 199–214.

Brighouse, Harry. 2019. "How Can We Understand 'Liberal Arts Education'?" *The Mellon Research Forum on the Value of Liberal Arts Education.* New York: Andrew W. Mellon Foundation.

Brint, Steven. 2002. "The Rise of the 'Practical Arts.'" In *The Future of the City of Intellect: The Changing American University,* edited by S. Brint, 231–59. Palo Alto: Stanford University Press.

Brint, Steven, Mark Riddle, Lori Turk-Bicakci, and Charles S. Levy. 2005. "From Liberal to the Practical Arts in American Colleges and Universities: Organizational Analysis and Curricular Change." *Journal of Higher Education* 76 (2): 151–80.

Brooks, Robert. 2011. *Cheaper by the Hour: Temporary Lawyers and the Deprofessionalization of the Law.* Philadelphia: Temple University Press.

Brown, Wendy. 2015. *Undoing the Demos: Neoliberalism's Stealth Revolution.* Cambridge, MA: MIT Press.

Brunner, Brigitta R., Kim Zarkin, and Bradford L. Yates. 2018. "What Do Employers Want? What Should Faculty Teach? A Content Analysis of Entry-Level Employment Ads in Public Relations." *Journal of Public Relations Education* 4 (2): 21–50.

Burawoy, Michael. 1979. *Manufacturing Consent: Changes in the Labor Process Under Monopoly Capitalism*. Chicago: The University of Chicago Press.

Burning Glass Institute. 2018. *Majors that Matter: Ensuring College Graduates Avoid Underemployment*. https://www.burning-glass.com/wp-content/uploads/under employment_majors_that_matter_final.pdf.

Burning Glass Institute and Strada Institute for the Future of Work. 2024. *Talent Disrupted: College Graduates, Underemployment, and the Way Forward*. https://strada education.org/wp-content/uploads/2024/02/Talent-Disrupted-1.pdf?utm_source =StradaEducation.org&utm_medium=Website&utm_campaign=TalentDisrupted &utm_content=DownloadButton%20.

Callaghan, George, and Paul Thompson. 2001. "Edwards Revisited: Technical Control and Call Centres." *Economic and Industrial Democracy* 22:13–37.

Carnevale, Anthony P., Ban Cheah, and Jeff Strohl. 2012. "Hard Times, College Majors, Unemployment, and Earnings: Not All College Degrees Are Created Equal." Georgetown University Center on Education and the Workforce. https://repository .library.georgetown.edu/handle/10822/559308.

Carnevale, Anthony P., Jeff Strohl, and Michelle Melton. 2014. "What's It Worth? The Economic Value of College Majors." Georgetown University Center on Education and the Workforce. https://cew.georgetown.edu/wp-content/uploads/2014/11 /whatsitworth-complete.pdf.

Cech, Erin A. 2013. "Ideological Wage Inequalities? The Technical/Social Dualism and the Gender Wage Gap in Engineering." *Social Forces* 91 (4): 1147–82.

Cech, Erin A. 2015. "Engineers and Engineeresses? Self-Conceptions and the Development of Gendered Professional Identities." *Sociological Perspective* 58 (1): 56–77.

Cech, Erin A. 2021. *The Trouble with Passion*. Berkeley: University of California Press.

Christin, Angele. 2018. "Counting Clicks: Quantification and Variation in Web Journalism in the United States and France." *American Journal of Sociology* 123 (5): 1382–1415.

Clarke, Marilyn. 2013. "The Organizational Career: Not Dead but in Need of Redefinition." *International Journal of Human Resource Management* 24 (4): 684–703.

Cohen, Laurie. 2006. "Remembrance of Things Past: Cultural Process and Practice in the Analysis of Career Stories." *Journal of Vocational Behavior* 69 (2): 189–201.

Collins, Randall. 1979. *The Credential Society: An Historical Sociology of Education and Stratification*. New York: Academic Press.

Cook, Ian. 2021. "Who is Driving the Great Resignation?" *Harvard Business Review*. September 15, 2021. https://hbr.org/2021/09/who-is-driving-the-great-resignation.

Cottom, Tressie McMillan. 2017. *Lower Ed: The Troubling Rise of For-Profit Colleges in the New Economy*. New York: The New Press.

Crain, Andrew. 2016. *Understanding the Impact of Unpaid Internships on College Student Career Development and Employment Outcomes*. Bethlehem, PA: The NACE Foundation.

Damaske, Sarah. 2009. "Brown Suits Need Not Apply: The Intersection of Race, Gender, and Class in Institutional Network Building." *Sociological Forum* 24 (2): 402–24.

Daneva, Maya, Chong Wang, and Patrick Hoener. 2017. "What the Job Market Wants from Requirements Engineers? An Empirical Analysis of Online Job Ads from the Netherlands." *ACM/IEEE International Symposium on Empirical Software Engineering and Measurement*, 448–53.

Davis, Daniel B., and Amy J. Binder. 2016. "Selling Students: The Rise of Corporate Partnerships Programs in University Career Centers." *Research in the Sociology of Organizations* 46:395–422.

Davis, Daniel, and Amy Binder. 2019. "Industry, Firm, Job Title: The Layered Nature of Early-Career Advantage for Graduates of Elite Private Universities." *Socius* 5:1–23.

Deming, David. 2019. "In the Salary Race, Engineers Sprint but English Majors Endure." *New York Times*. October 1, 2019. https://www.nytimes.com/2019/09/20/business/liberal-arts-stem-salaries.html.

Dickler, Jessica. 2020. "Colleges Cut Academic Programs in the Face of Budget Shortfalls Due to Covid-19." *CNBC Personal Finance*. June 30, 2020. https://www.cnbc.com/2020/06/23/colleges-cut-programs-in-face-of-budget-shortfalls-due-to-covid-19.html.

Di Stasio, Valentina, and Herman G. van de Werfhorst. 2016. "Why Does Education Matter to Employers in Different Institutional Contexts? A Vignette Study in England and the Netherlands." *Social Forces* 95 (1): 77–106.

Feder, Michael. 2012. "One Decade, One Million More STEM Graduates." *Obama White House Blog*. December 12, 2012. https://obamawhitehouse.archives.gov/blog/2012/12/18/one-decade-one-million-more-stem-graduates.

Finamore, John, Daniel J. Foley, Flora Lan, Lynn M. Milan, Steven L. Proudfoot, Emilda B. Rivers, and Lance Selfa. 2013. "Employment and Educational Characteristics of Scientists and Engineers." *NSF* 13–311. National Center for Science and Engineering Statistics.

Fine, Gary A. 1996. "Justifying Work: Occupational Rhetorics as Resources in Restaurant Kitchens." *Administrative Science Quarterly* 41 (1): 90–115.

Frenette, Alexandre. 2013. "Making the Intern Economy: Role and Career Challenges of the Music Industry Intern." *Work and Occupations* 40 (4): 364–97.

Furstenberg, Frank F. Jr., Rubén G. Rumbaut, and Richard A. Settersten Jr. 2005. "On the Frontier of Adulthood: Emerging Themes and New Directions." In *On the Frontier of Adulthood: Theory, Research, and Public Policy*, edited by R. A. Settersten Jr., F. F. Furstenberg Jr., and R. G. Rumbaut, 3–28. Chicago: University of Chicago Press.

Garcia-Navarro, Lulu. 2018. "How Underemployment is Affecting the Job Market." *Weekend Edition Sunday*, July 15, 2018. National Public Radio. https://www.npr.org/2018/07/15/629212924/the-call-in-underemployment#:~:text=Around%2033%20percent%20of%20college,a%20bachelor's%20degree%20and%20beyond.

Gault, Jack, John Redington, and Tammy Schlager. 2000. "Undergraduate Business Internships and Career Success: Are They Related?" *Journal of Marketing Education* 22 (1): 45–53.

Gerber, Theodore P., and Sin Yi Cheung. 2008. "Horizontal Stratification in Postsecondary Education: Forms, Explanations, and Implications." *Annual Review of Sociology* 34 (1): 299–318.

Gershon, Ilana. 2017. *Down and Out in the New Economy: How People Find (or Don't Find) Work Today*. Chicago: University of Chicago Press.

Gordon, David M. 1996. *Fat and Mean: The Corporate Squeeze of Working Americans and the Myth of Managerial "Downsizing."* New York: Basic Books.

Goyette, Kimberly A., and Ann L. Mullen. 2006. "Who Studies the Arts and Sciences? Social Background and the Choice and Consequences of Undergraduate Field of Study." *Journal of Higher Education* 77 (3): 497–538.

Graeber, David. 2018. *Bullshit Jobs: A Theory*. New York: Simon and Schuster.

Grayson, J. Paul. 2004. "Social Dynamics, University Experiences, and Graduates' Job Outcomes." *British Journal of Sociology of Education* 25 (5): 609–27.

Hamilton, Laura T. 2016. *Parenting to a Degree: How Family Matters for College Women's Success*. Chicago: University of Chicago Press.

Hamilton, Laura T., Elizabeth A. Armstrong, J. Lotus Seeley, and Elizabeth M. Armstrong. 2019. "Hegemonic Femininities and Intersectional Domination." *Sociological Theory* 37 (4): 315–41.

Hamilton, Laura T., and Elizabeth A. Armstrong. 2021. "Parents, Partners, and Professions: Reproduction and Mobility in a Cohort of College Women." *American Journal of Sociology* 127 (1): 102–51.

Hamilton, Laura T., and Kelly Nielsen. 2021. *Broke: The Racial Consequences of Underfunding Public Universities*. Chicago: University of Chicago Press.

Han, Siqi, Dmitry Tumin, and Zhenchao Qian. 2016. "Gendered Transitions to Adulthood by College Field of Study in the United States." *Demographic Research* 35 (31): 929–60.

Hanson, Andrew, and Artem Gulish. 2016. "From to College to Career: Making Sense of the Post-Millennial Job Market." *Georgetown Public Policy Review* 21 (1): 1–23.

Hanson, Melanie. 2024. "College Enrollment & Student Demographic Statistics." *Education Data Initiative*. January 10, 2024. https://educationdata.org/college-enrollment-statistics#enrollment-by-degree.

The Hechinger Report. 2018. "Making the Case for Liberal Arts." *U.S. News & World Report*. May 17, 2018. https://www.usnews.com/news/education-news/articles/2018-05-17/liberal-arts-programs-struggle-to-make-a-case-for-themselves.

Heckathorn, Douglas D., and Joan Jeffri. 2001. "Finding the Beat: Using Respondent-Driven Sampling to Study Jazz Musicians." *Poetics* 28 (4):307-329.

Heller, Nathan. 2023. "The End of the English Major." *New Yorker*. February 27, 2023. https://www.newyorker.com/magazine/2023/03/06/the-end-of-the-english-major.

Hermanowicz, Joseph C. 2013. "The Longitudinal Qualitative Interview." *Qualitative Sociology* 36 (2): 189–208.

Herrity, Jennifer. 2023. "What Are Soft Skills? (Definition, Examples and Resume Tips)." Indeed.com. July 5, 2023. https://www.indeed.com/career-advice/resumes-cover-letters/soft-skills.

Hill, Catherine B., and Elizabeth Davidson Pisacreta. 2019. "The Economic Benefits and Costs of a Liberal Arts Education." *The Mellon Research Forum on the Value of Liberal Arts Education*. New York: Andrew W. Mellon Foundation.

Hill Collins, Patricia. 1990. *Black Feminist Thought*. New York: Routledge.

Ho, Karen. 2009. *Liquidated: An Ethnography of Wall Street*. Durham, NC: Duke University Press.

Hodson, Randy. 2001. *Dignity At Work*. New York: Cambridge University Press.

Hubler, Shawn. 2020. "Colleges Slash Budgets in the Pandemic, With 'Nothing Off Limits,'" *New York Times*. November 2, 2020. https://www.nytimes.com/2020/10/26/us/colleges-coronavirus-budget-cuts.html.

Humburg, Martin, and Rolf van der Velden. 2015. "Skills and the Graduate Recruitment Process: Evidence from Two Discrete Choice Experiments." *Economics of Education Review* 49:24–41.

Ikeler, Peter. 2016. "Deskilling Emotional Labour: Evidence from Department Store Retail." *Work, Employment, and Society* 30 (6): 966–83.

Indeed.com. n.d. "What Is the Definition of Clerical Work?" https://www.indeed.com/hire/c/info/what-is-the-definition-of-clerical-work.

Indeed Editorial Team. 2023. "Top 11 Skills Employers Look for in Candidates." Indeed.com. February 3, 2023. https://www.indeed.com/career-advice/resumes-cover-letters/skills-employers-look-for.

Jack, Anthony Abraham. 2016. "(No) Harm in Asking: Class, Acquired Cultural Capital, and Academic Engagement in an Elite University." *Sociology of Education* 89 (1): 1–19.

Jack, Anthony Abraham. 2019. *The Privileged Poor: How Elite Colleges are Failing Disadvantaged Students*. Cambridge, MA: Harvard University Press.

Kalleberg, Arne. 2007. *The Mismatched Worker*. New York: W. W. Norton.

Kalleberg, Arne L. 2011. *Good Jobs, Bad Jobs: The Rise of Polarized and Precarious Employment Systems in the United States, 1970s–2000s*. New York: Russell Sage Foundation.

Kalleberg, Arne, and Steven Vallas. 2018. "Probing Precarious Work: Theory, Research, and Politics." *Research in the Sociology of Work* 31:1–30.

Kaplan, Esther. 2015. "The Spy Who Fired Me: The Human Cost of Workplace Monitoring." *Harper's Magazine*. March 2015, 31–40.

Kilbourne, Barbara Stanek, Paula England, George Farkas, Kurt Beron, and Dorothea Weir. 1994. "Returns to Skill, Compensating Differentials, and Gender Bias: Effects of Occupational Characteristics on the Wages of White Women and Men." *American Journal of Sociology* 100 (3): 689–719.

Kim, ChangHwan. 2015. "New Color Lines: Racial/Ethnic Inequality in Earnings among College-Educated Men." *Sociological Quarterly* 56 (1): 152–84.

Kim, ChangHwan, Christopher R. Tamborini, and Arthur Sakamoto. 2015. "Field of Study in College and Lifetime Earnings in the United States." *Sociology of Education* 88 (4): 320–39.

Lane, Carrie M. 2011. *A Company of One: Insecurity, Independence, and the New World of White-Collar Unemployment*. Ithaca: Cornell University Press.

Learn.org. n.d. "What is Clerical Work?" https://learn.org/articles/What_is_Clerical_Work.html.

Lebovitz, Sarah, Hila Lifshitz-Assaf, and Natalia Levina. 2022. "To Engage or Not to

Engage with AI for Critical Judgments: How Professionals Deal with Opacity when Using AI for Medical Diagnosis." *Organization Science* 33 (1): 126–48.

Leicht, Kevin T., and Mary Fennell. 2023. *Crisis in the Professions: The New Dark Age.* New York: Routledge.

Leonard, Pauline, Susan Halford, and Katie Bruce. 2015. "'The New Degree?' Constructing Internships in the Third Sector." *Sociology* 50 (2): 383–99.

Levenson, Eric. 2013. "Graduating with a Liberal Arts Degree Won't Ruin Your Job Hopes." *Atlantic.* October 31, 2013. https://www.theatlantic.com/national/archive/2013/10/graduating-non-stem-major-wont-ruin-your-job-hopes/354650/.

Lichtenstein, Nelson. 2013. *State of the Union: A Century of American Labor.* Princeton: Princeton University Press.

Matthew, Susan M., Rosanne M. Taylor, and Robert A. Ellis. 2012. "Relationships Between Students' Experiences of Learning in an Undergraduate Internship Program and New Graduates' Experiences of Professional Practice." *Higher Education* 64 (4): 529–42.

Mauldin, John. 2019. "America Has a Monopoly Problem." *Forbes.* April 11, 2019. https://www.forbes.com/sites/johnmauldin/2019/04/11/america-has-a-monopoly-problem/?sh=364c670d2972.

McCaughey, Robert A. 2019. "Still Here: Change and Persistence in the Place of the Liberal Arts in American Higher Education." *The Mellon Research Forum on the Value of Liberal Arts Education.* New York: Andrew W. Mellon Foundation.

Mellon Foundation. 2019. *The Mellon Research Forum on the Value of Liberal Arts Education.* New York: Andrew W. Mellon Foundation.

Meyer, John W. 1977. "The Effects of Education as an Institution." *American Journal of Sociology* 83 (1): 55–77.

Monaghan, David, and Sou Hyun Jang. 2017. "Major Payoffs: Postcollege Income, Graduate School, and the Choice of "Risky" Undergraduate Majors." *Sociological Perspectives* 60 (4): 722–46.

Moss-Pech, Corey. 2021. "The Career Conveyor Belt: How Internships Lead to Unequal Labor Market Outcomes among College Graduates." *Qualitative Sociology* 44:77-102.

Moss-Pech, Corey, Steven H. Lopez, and Laurie Michaels. 2021. "Educational Downgrading: Adult Education and Downward Mobility." *Sociology of Education* 94 (2): 143–58.

Mullen, Ann L. 2011. *Degrees of Inequality: Culture, Class, and Gender in American Higher Education.* Baltimore: Johns Hopkins University Press.

Mullen, Ann L. 2014. "Gender, Social Background, and the Choice of College Major in a Liberal Arts Context." *Gender & Society* 28 (2): 289–312.

Narayanan, V. K., Paul M. Olk, and Cynthia V. Fukami. 2010. "Determinants of Internship Effectiveness: An Exploratory Model." *Academy of Management Learning & Education* 9 (1): 61–80.

National Association of Colleges and Employers. n.d. "What Is Career Readiness?" *NACE Center for Career Development and Talent Acquisition.* https://www.naceweb.org/career-readiness/competencies/career-readiness-defined/.

National Center for Education Statistics. 2020. "National Center for Education Statistics (NCES) Home Page, a Part of the US Department of Education." https://nces.ed.gov/.

Nunley, John, Adam Pugh, Nicholas Romero, and R. Ala. Seals Jr. 2016. "College Major, Internship Experience, and Employment Opportunities: Estimates from a Résumé Audit." *Labour Economics* 38:37–46.

O'Connor, Liam. 2020. "The Great Recession Strangled the Humanities. Will Coronavirus Deal the Last Blow?" *Daily Princetonian.* May 29, 2020. https://www.daily princetonian.com/article/2020/05/the-great-recession-strangled-the-human ities-will-coronavirus-deal-the-last-blow.

O'Shaughnessy, Lynn. 2011. "20 Surprising Higher Education Facts." *U.S. News & World Report.* September 6, 2011. https://www.usnews.com/education/blogs/the -college-solution/2011/09/06/20-surprising-higher-education-facts.

Parker, Eugene T., Cindy A. Kilgo, Jessica K. Ezell Sheets, and Ernest T. Pascarella. 2016. "The Differential Effects of Internship Participation on End-of-Fourth-Year GPA by Demographic and Institutional Characteristics." *Journal of College Student Development* 57 (1): 104–9.

Pearson, Amy. n.d. "Majoring in Something You Love vs. Something Practical." *Seattle Post-Intelligencer.* https://education.seattlepi.com/majoring-something-love-vs -something-practical-1292.html.

Pech, Corey. 2017. "Dealing with Downsizing: New Organizational Careers in Financial Services After the Great Recession." *Research in the Sociology of Work* 30:33–57.

Pech, Corey, Elizabeth Klainot-Hess, and Davon Norris. 2020. "Part-Time by Gender, Not Choice: The Gender Gap in Involuntary Part-Time Work." *Sociological Perspectives* 64 (2): 280–300.

Perlin, Ross. 2012. *Intern Nation: How to Earn Nothing and Learn Litte in the Brave New Economy.* New York: Verso Press.

Pitt, Richard N., and Lin Zhu. 2019. "The Relationship Between College Major Prestige/ Status and Post-baccalaureate Outcomes." *Sociological Perspectives* 62 (3): 325–45.

Pugh, Allison J. 2014. *The Tumbleweed Society: Working and Caring in an Age of Insecurity.* New York: Oxford University Press.

Quadlin, Natasha. 2018. "The Mark of a Woman's Record: Gender and Academic Performance in Hiring." *American Sociological Review* 83 (2): 331–60.

Quadlin, Natasha. 2020. "From Major Preferences to Major Choices: Gender and Logics of Major Choice." *Sociology of Education* 93 (2): 91–109.

Ragin, Charles. 2000. *Fuzzy-set Social Science.* Chicago: University of Chicago Press.

Redden, Elizabeth. 2020. "41% of Recent Grads Work in Jobs Not Requiring a Degree." *Inside Higher Ed.* February 17, 2020. https://www.insidehighered.com/quicktakes /2020/02/18/41-recent-grads-work-jobs-not-requiring-degree.

Ridgeway, Cecilia. 2011. *Framed by Gender: How Gender Inequality Persists in the Modern World.* New York: Oxford University Press.

Rivera, Lauren A. 2012. "Hiring as Cultural Matching: The Case of Elite Professional Service Firms." *American Sociological Review* 77 (6): 999–1022.

Rivera, Lauren A. 2015. *Pedigree: How Elite Students Get Elite Jobs*. Princeton: Princeton University Press.

Rivera, Lauren A. 2020. "Employer Decision Making." *Annual Review of Sociology* 46:215–32.

Robst, John. 2007. "Education and Job Match: The Relatedness of College Major and Work." *Economics of Education Review* 26 (4):397–407.

Roksa, Josipa. 2005. "Double Disadvantage or Blessing in Disguise? Understanding the Relationship Between College Major and Employment Sector." *Sociology of Education* 78 (3): 207–32.

Roksa, Josipa, and Tania Levey. 2010. "What Can You Do with That Degree? College Major and Occupational Status of College Graduates over Time." *Social Forces* 89 (2): 389–415.

Rosenbaum, James E., and Amy Binder. 1997. "Do Employers Really Need More Educated Youth?" *Sociology of Education* 70 (1): 68–85.

Rosenfeld, Jake. 2021. *You're Paid What You're Worth: And Other Myths of the Modern Economy*. Cambridge, MA: The Belknap Press of Harvard University Press.

Roy, Donald. 1954. "Efficiency and 'The Fix': Informal Intergroup Relations in a Piecework Machine Shop." *American Journal of Sociology* 60 (3): 255–66.

Ryff, Carol D. 2019. "Linking Education in the Arts and Humanities to Life-Long Well-Being and Health." *The Mellon Research Forum on the Value of Liberal Arts Education*. New York: Andrew W. Mellon Foundation.

Schmidt, Benjamin. 2018. "The Humanities Are in Crisis." *Atlantic*. August 23, 2018. https://www.theatlantic.com/ideas/archive/2018/08/the-humanities-face-a -crisisof-confidence/567565/.

Selingo, Jeffrey J. 2017. "Six Myths About Choosing a College Major." *New York Times*. November 3, 2017. https://www.nytimes.com/2017/11/03/education/edlife/choos ing-a-college-major.html.

Shade, Leslie Regan, and Jenna Jacobson. 2015. "Hungry for the Job: Gender, Unpaid Internships, and the Creative Industries." *Sociological Review* 63 (suppl. 1): 188–205.

Shandra, Carrie L. 2022. "Internship Participation in the United States by Student and School Characteristics, 1994–2017." *Socius* 8:1–4.

Shauman, Kimberlee A. 2016. "Gender Differences in the Early Career Outcomes of College Graduates: The Influence of Sex-Type of Degree Field Across Four Cohorts." *RSF: The Russell Sage Foundation Journal of the Social Sciences* 2 (4): 152–93.

Sherman, Rachel. 2007. *Class Acts: Service and Inequality in Luxury Hotels*. Berkeley: University of California Press.

Sitkin, Sim B., Chris P. Long, and Laura B. Cardinal. 2020. "Assessing the Control Literature: Looking Back and Looing Forward." *Annual Review of Organizational Psychology and Organizational Behavior* 7:339–68.

Smith, Vicki. 2010. "Review Article: Enhancing Employability: Human, Cultural, and Social Capital in an Era of Turbulent Unpredictability." *Human Relations* 63 (2): 1–22.

Sodhi, M. S., and B-G Son. 2010. "Content Analysis of OR Job Advertisements to Infer Required Skills." *Journal of the Operational Research Society* 61 (9): 1315–27.

Spence, Michael. 1974. *Market Signaling: Informational Transfer in Hiring and Related Processes.* Cambridge, MA: Harvard University Press.

Stevens, Mitchell, Elizabeth Armstrong, and Richard Arum. 2008. "Sieve, Incubator, Temple, Hub: Empirical and Theoretical Advances in the Sociology of Higher Education." *Annual Review of Sociology* 34:127–51.

Streib, Jessi. 2023. *The Accidental Equalizer: How Luck Determines Pay After College.* Chicago: The University of Chicago Press.

Streib, Jessi, Jane Rochmes, Felicia Arriaga, Carlos Tavares, and Emi Weed. 2019. "Presenting Their Gendered Selves? How Women and Men Describe Who They Are, What They Have Done, and Why They Want the Job in Their Written Applications." *Sex Roles* 81 (9): 610–26.

Taylor, Judith, and Kim de Laat. 2013. "Feminist Internships and the Depression of Political Imagination: Implications for Women's Studies." *Feminist Formations* 25 (1): 84–110.

Tholen, Gerbrand, Phillip Brown, Sally Power, and Annabelle Allouch. 2013. "The Role of Networks and Connections in Educational Elites' Labour Market Entrance." *Research in Social Stratification and Mobility* 34:142–54.

Thompson, Derek. 2015. "The Economy Is Still Terrible for Young People." *Atlantic.* May 19, 2015. https://www.theatlantic.com/business/archive/2015/05/the-new -normal-for-young-workers/393560/.

Thompson, Derek. 2016. "Fear of a College-Educated Barista." *Atlantic.* September 20, 2016. https://www.theatlantic.com/business/archive/2016/09/fear-of-a-college -educated-barista/500792/.

Thompson, Derek. 2021. "Three Myths of the Great Resignation." *Atlantic.* December 8, 2021. https://www.theatlantic.com/ideas/archive/2021/12/great-resignation-myths -quitting-jobs/620927/.

Toor, Rachel. 2022. "Teach Your Discipline and Help Students Get Jobs." *Inside Higher Ed.* November 2, 2022. https://www.insidehighered.com/advice/2022/11/03 /humanities-should-help-students-find-enlightenment-and-careers-opinion ?utm_source=Inside+Higher+Ed&utm_campaign=2403e7121a-DNU_2021_COPY _02&utm_medium=email&utm_term=0_1fcbc04421-2403e7121a-198637189 &mc_cid=2403e7121a&mc_eid=56bf5f15bb.

Townsend, Robert B. 2012. "Historians React to Proposal from Florida Task Force on State Higher Education Reform." *Perspectives on History.* November 15, 2012. https:// www.historians.org/research-and-publications/perspectives-on-history/novem ber-2012/historians-react-to-proposal-from-florida-task-force-on-state-higher -education-reform.

US Bureau of Labor Statistics. n.d. "MOG-Level Definitions." *Occupational Classification System Manual.* https://www.bls.gov/ncs/ocs/ocsm/commogadef.htm.

Vallas, Steven. 1990. "The Concept of Skill." *Work and Occupations* 17 (4): 379–98.

Van Dam, Andrew. 2022. "The Most-Regretted (and Lowest-Paying) College Majors." *Washington Post.* September 2, 2022. https://www.washingtonpost.com/business /2022/09/02/college-major-regrets/.

Weiss, Robert S. 1994. *Learning from Strangers: The Art and Method of Qualitative Interview Studies*. New York: Simon and Schuster.

White, James W. C. 2019. "Believe the Liberal Arts are Dead as Doornails? Think Again." *Colorado Arts and Sciences Magazine*. December 28, 2019. https://www.colorado.edu/asmagazine/2019/12/28/believe-liberal-arts-are-dead-doornails-think-again.

Whitford, Josh. 2005. *The New Old Economy: Networks, Institutions, and the Organizational Transformation of American Manufacturing*. New York: Oxford University Press.

Wingfield, Adia Harvey. 2009. "Racializing the Glass Escalator: Reconsidering Men's Experiences with Women's Work." *Gender & Society* 23 (1): 5–26.

Woodhams, Carol, Ben Lupton, and Marc Cowling. 2015. "The Presence of Ethnic Minority and Disabled Men in Feminised Work: Intersectionality, Vertical Segregation, and the Glass Escalator." *Sex Roles* 72 (7–8): 277–93.

Wright, Ashley L., Vincent J. Roscigno, and Natasha Quadlin. 2023. "First-Generation Students, College Majors, and Gendered Pathways." *Sociological Quarterly* 64 (1): 67–90.

Yakubovich, Valery. 2006. "Passive Recruitment in the Russian Urban Labor Market." *Work and Occupations* 33 (3): 307–34.

Yavorsky, Jill, Philip N. Cohen, and Yue Qian. 2016. "Man Up, Man Down: Race–Ethnicity and the Hierarchy of Men in Female-Dominated Work." *Sociological Quarterly* 57 (4): 733–58.

INDEX

Page numbers in italics refer to figures and tables.